Advances in Computing Communications and Informatics

(Volume 1)

Blockchain Applications for Secure IoT Frameworks: Technologies Shaping the Future

Edited by

Sudhir K. Sharma

Institute of Information Technology and Management
D-29, Institutional Area
Janakpuri
New Delhi
India

Bharat Bhushan & Parma N. Astya

School of Engineering Technology
Sharda University
Uttar Pradesh 201310
India

&

Narayan C. Debnath

School of Computing and Information Technology
Eastern International University
Bình Dương
Vietnam

Advances in Computing Communications and Informatics

Volume # 1

Blockchain Applications for Secure IoT Frameworks: Technologies Shaping the Future

Series Editors: Pradeep Kumar Singh, Bharat Bhargava & Wei-Chiang Hong

Volume Editors: Sudhir K. Sharma, Bharat Bhushan, Parma N. Astya and Narayan C. Debnath

ISBN (Online): 978-1-68108-862-4

ISBN (Print): 978-1-68108-863-1

ISBN (Paperback): 978-1-68108-864-8

Bentham Science Publishers Ltd.
Executive Suite Y - 2
PO Box 7917, Saif Zone
Sharjah, U.A.E.
Email: subscriptions@benthamscience.net

BENTHAM
SCIENCE

CONTENTS

PREFACE

The Internet of Things (IoT) is an emerging technology that has enabled connection and communication between both virtual and physical objects, thereby improving our quality of life. The definition of IoT has evolved because of the convergence of numerous technologies such as embedded systems, commodity sensors, machine learning, and real-time analytics. IoT contributes towards the concept of connected vehicles, connected health, wearable technology, home automation, and appliances having remote monitoring capabilities. Even though these systems provide numerous advantages, the current centralized architecture brings forth numerous issues related to privacy, security, transparency, data integrity, and single point of failure. This, in turn, inhibits the future development of these IoT-based applications. Further, the radical digitization of industry coupled with the explosion of the Internet of Things (IoT) has set up a paradigm shift for industrial and manufacturing companies. Owing to these issues, it becomes necessary to integrate IoT with a distributed ledger technology. Blockchain technology, an immutable, shared, distributed ledger, is the most suitable choice for a variety of reasons. It stores the various transaction information in a peer-to-peer (P2P) network and promotes information sharing among the network users. Owing to the fault tolerance capabilities, decentralized architecture and cryptographic security benefits such as authentication, data integrity, pseudonymous identities, security analysts and researchers consider blockchain to resolve privacy and security issues of IoT. The use of hash functions, timestamps, and sophisticated cryptographic algorithms in blockchain technology enables a secure computing environment and provides a tamper-proof ledger that can safeguard against possible attacks. Also, blockchain is used in numerous applications such as healthcare, intelligent transportation, supply chain management, identity management, voting, and maintaining government records. Due to these reasons, blockchain is considered the most disruptive and emerging future technology that will provide numerous opportunities to various industries. The emerging and promising state-of-the-art IoT and blockchain technology motivated us to propose this book, focusing on various aspects of IoT and blockchain systems like trust management, identity management, security threats, and access control and privacy. The book provides a comprehensive discussion on integrating the IoT system with blockchain technology, highlights the benefits of integration, and how blockchain technology resolves the issues of IoT systems.

Sudhir K. Sharma
Institute of Information Technology and Management
D-29, Institutional Area, Janakpuri
New Delhi
India

List of Contributors

Aashna Jha	Department of Electronics and Communication, Netaji Subhas University of Technology, Dwarka, Delhi 110078, India
Ana Carolina Borges Monteiro	School of Electrical Engineering and Computing (FEEC), State University of Campinas (UNICAMP), Campinas, São Paulo , Brazil
Arepalli Peda Gopi	Vignan's Nirula Institute of Technology & Science for Women, Peda Palakaluru, Guntur-522009, Andhra Pradesh, India
Bharat Bhushan	School of Engineering and Technology, Sharda University, Greater Noida, India
C. Priya	Department of Information Technology, Vels Institute of Science, Technology and Advanced Studies (VISTAS), Chennai, India
Deepak Kumar Sharma	Department of Information Technology, Netaji Subhas University of Technology, Dwarka, Delhi 110078, India
Deepti Gupta	Amity School of Engineering and Technology, Amity University, Noida, U.P., India
H Abhijith	Amity School of Engineering and Technology, Amity University, Noida, U.P., India
Ila Kaushik	Krishna Institute of Engineering & Technology, Ghaziabad, U.P, India
Jawed Ahmed	Department of Bioengineering, University of California, Riverside, CA, USA
J. S. Shyam Mohan	Department of Computer Science and Engineering, Sri Chandrasekharendra Saraswathi Viswa Mahavidyalaya (SCSVMV), Tamil Nadu 631561, India
K. Sheela	Department of Information Technology, Vels Institute of Science, Technology and Advanced Studies (VISTAS), Chennai, India
Khwaja M. Rafi	Director, Mewat Engineering College, Palla, Distt. Nuh, HaryanaIndia,
Mohd. M. Haque	School of Computer and Systems Sciences, Jawaharlal Nehru University, New Delhi, India
Mohammad Maksuf Ul Haque	Department of Computer Science, Jamia Millia Islamia, New Delhi, India
Mohammad Sufian Badar	Department of Bioengineering, University of California, Riverside CA, USA
Nagendra Panini Challa	Department of Information Technology, Sri Vishnu Engineering College for Women, Bhimavaram, Andhra Pradesh 534202, India
Nikhil Sharma	HMR Institute of Technology & Management, Delhi, India
Nuggu Kowshiki	Department of Computer Science and Engineering, Sri Chandrasekharendra Saraswathi Viswa Mahavidyalaya (SCSVMV), Tamil Nadu 631561, India
Pasumarthy Swathi	Department of Computer Science and Engineering, Sri Chandrasekharendra Saraswathi Viswa Mahavidyalaya (SCSVMV), Tamil Nadu 631561, India
Rangel Arthur	Faculty of Technology (FT), State University of Campinas (UNICAMP), Limeira, São Paulo, Brazil

Reinaldo Padilha França	School of Electrical Engineering and Computing (FEEC), State University of Campinas (UNICAMP), Campinas, São Paulo , Brazil
R.S.M. Lakshmi Patibandla	Department of IT, Vignan's Foundation for Science, Technology and Research, Andhra Pradesh, India
Saakshi Bhargava	Department of Physical Sciences and Engineering, Banasthali Vidyapith, Tonk, Rajasthan, India
Shazmeen Shamsi	Department of Computer Science, Jamia Millia Islamia, New Delhi, India
Shilpi Sharma	Amity School of Engineering and Technology, Amity University, Noida, U.P., India
Shweta Paliwal	Department of Computer Science and Engineering, Meerut Institute of Engineering and Technology (MIET), Meerut, India
Somya Goyal	Manipal University Jaipur, Jaipur, India Rajasthan and Guru Jambheshwar University of Science and Technology, Hisar, India
Sudhir Kumar Sharma	Institute of Information Technology and Management, Janakpuri, New Delhi, India
Sukriti Goyal	HMR Institute of Technology & Management, Delhi, India
Sushil Kumar	Department of Computer Science, Jamia Hamdard University, New Delhi, India
Vejendla Lakshman Narayana	Vignan's Nirula Institute of Technology & Science for Women, Peda Palakaluru, Guntur-522009, Andhra Pradesh, India
Vishakha	HMR Institute of Technology & Management, Delhi, India
Yuzo Iano	School of Electrical Engineering and Computing (FEEC), State University of Campinas (UNICAMP), Campinas, São Paulo , Brazil

CHAPTER 1

An Overview of Smart Grid in the Current Age

Reinaldo Padilha França[1,*], **Ana Carolina Borges Monteiro**[1,*], **Rangel Arthur**[2] and **Yuzo Iano**[1]

[1] *School of Electrical Engineering and Computing (FEEC), State University of Campinas (UNICAMP), Campinas, São Paulo, Brazil*

[2] *Faculty of Technology (FT), State University of Campinas (UNICAMP), Limeira, São Paulo, Brazil*

Abstract: Smart Grid is defined as an intelligent electrical distribution system that offers bi-directional energy, which flows from producers to consumers, intending to optimize use to reduce costs and improve the performance of the electricity network, which requires a balance between generators, operators, and system distributors, providing benefits , including reduced power losses, lower costs, and better measurement of consumption with better control, enabling a reduction in carbon emissions. With sensors installed in the electrical networks sending data related to energy consumption directly from the consumer unit, they enable more effective and efficient network planning. Besides, the network is designed to reduce the occurrence and duration of power outages as much as possible. In it, electromechanical consumption meters are replaced by digital smart meters, representing a true revolution in energy supply, meaning that the Smart Grid is a system that automates not only the monitoring but the entire management of electricity use. This chapter contributes to the discussion and overview of Smart Grids, their applications in the current era, as well as categorizing and synthesizing the technology's potential.

Keywords: Bi-directional energy, Data analysis, Intelligent electrical, IoT, Sensors, Smart architecture, Smart cities, Smart grid.

1. INTRODUCTION

The search for sustainability-related to digital transformation has created new possibilities for the world, with actions aimed at reducing environmental damage with a greater objective than simply saving, but it is necessary to make intelligent and conscious use of what is at disposal.

* **Corresponding authors Reinaldo Padilha França and Ana Carolina Borges Monteiro:** School of Electrical Engineering and Computing (FEEC), State University of Campinas (UNICAMP), Campinas, São Paulo, Brazil and School of Electrical Engineering and Computing (FEEC), State University of Campinas (UNICAMP), Campinas, São Paulo, Brazil; E-mails: padilha@decom.fee.unicamp.br and monteiro@decom.fee.unicamp.br

Sudhir K. Sharma, Bharat Bhushan, Parma N. Astya and Narayan C. Debnath (Eds.)

Energy management is a prerequisite for a sustainable environment, and Smart Grids are an essential pillar for its achievement. The spread of renewable energy sources has led to a profound modernization of traditional electricity distribution systems and how they are effectively distributed. Smart Grid is defined as an intelligent electrical distribution system that delivers bi-directional energy flows from producers to consumers. Unlike traditional power grids, where power is generated by only one plant and distributed to end customers through the large transformer and substation networks, in Smart Grid, end customers also act as producers [1, 2].

Internet of Things technology is enabling cities around the world to implement a series of digital transformation projects, such as reducing car traffic in major cities and energy consumption. In addition to its use in home life, IoT promises to revolutionize industries, the security market, and even the medical field. Electricity consumption was also largely impacted by technology. Efforts are being made to design and implement energy-efficient networks that use Smart Grid parameters and apply the Internet of Things, making it possible for the network to work in less time and reduce power consumption [3].

A company's entire infrastructure depends on electricity, which requires continuous management of its use. In parallel with the search for sustainability, digital transformation has also added to the creation of new possibilities for managing this resource. The concept of this trend refers to a new power distribution architecture that can automate all management of electricity use. For the Smart Grid to function, it is necessary to switch analog meters to digital meters. These are safer, and especially intelligent, devices that enable the integration of information between other connected users [4].

Smart Grid is generic for applying computational intelligence and networking skills to an electricity distribution system. In recent times, this concept has gained a lot of prominences , especially in Smart Grid projects that seek to improve operations, maintenance, and planning, ensuring that each component of the power grid can "talk" and "listen."It is, therefore, a highly automated, efficient, self-healing, a bi-directional pathway of energy, enabling i nterconnected communications for a highly reliable and efficient utopian world of energy production and distribution [5].

Considering that in many places, a power company will only know that service is disrupted if a customer calls in a Smart Grid scenario, the company will immediately know why certain network components, such as the use of smart meters in the affected area, have stopped to send sensor data. By ensuring that all network components, from transformers and power lines to household, commercial and industrial electrical meters, have IP addresses and are capable of using bidirectional communication, the company can manage distribution more efficiently. Also, it needs to be proactive in maintenance and respond to outages faster. So, another important component of Smart Grid technology is automation [6].

Basically, it must communicate in an integrated automated way between components of the power grid, employ detection and measurement technologies, automated controls for distribution and repairs, better dashboard management, and decision support software. It is correct to say that a Smart Grid is an example of the Internet of Things (IoT), in which almost any object can be equipped with a unique identifier and given the ability to communicate over the web [7].

A Smart Grid is equipped with sensors that collect and transmit data since this information transmission allows to automatically adjust the electricity flows. Remotely located controllers are then informed of the situation in real-time and can act immediately if there is a problem occurring virtually without human intervention. Besides, this type of grid can communicate with any smart meter , for example, turn on consumer appliances automatically when there is too much electricity on the grid, and its prices are therefore lower [8].

One of Smart Grid's biggest advantages is the ability to track energy performance in real-time. Unlike the traditional meter, where consumption data is collected once a month, digital allows constant tracking. In this way, irregularities are quickly identified and predictive, preventive, and corrective actions can be taken to avoid waste and set goals to improve the company's energy consumption. Also, a more sustainable business model is established, as it enables the reduction of carbon dioxide emissions and other pollutant residues [9].

Smart Grid is a promise of a flexible, resilient, performance-safe power grid that allows network resources to be exploited in real-time to optimize productivity. Characterized by the deployment of many thousands of intelligent and interactive control devices, sensors and meters, it ensures the correct interaction between all these elements, as well as significantly improving the network's efficiency, reliability, and freedom for the end customer to control. their consumption conditions [10].

Among leading distribution automation and distributed power resource applications, this model can provide intelligent energy storage and provide real-time response to fluctuating demand. All this plus client-side demand management from a two-way conversation between devices on the network and also intelligent consumer devices on the edge of the user. In addition to placing the customer “in control” of their own energy use, this ploy ensures highly automated flexible distribution, encouraging the release or containment of consumption according to the load's circumstances over the infrastructure [11].

Just as the Internet of Energy (IoE) is a technological term that refers to the upgrading and automation of electricity infrastructures, allowing energy production to advance more efficiently and cleanly with the least amount of waste, being a derivation brought by the increasingly prominent market of IoT technology, which helped develop the distributed energy systems that makeup IoE [12].

The technology surrounding IoE can be quite a complex concept, since it is the use of IoT technology, which refers to the idea of connecting devices to the Internet with a variety of different power systems, including smartphones, tablets, and mobile devices from television to major appliances, headsets, and cars [13].

IoT is reaching a branch of applications by creating a sensor network with multiple possibilities such as power monitoring and demand-side power management, and IoT-enabled consumer appliances could help balance energy demand, who operate in a scenario since a washing machine can be connected to the internet and turned on only when there is sufficient solar power on the grid, even for consumers, the use of off-peak energy can save money [7, 12, 13].

Therefore, this chapter aims to provide an updated overview of Smart Grids, showing and approaching its success relationship, with a concise bibliographic background, categorizing, and synthesizing the potential of technology.

The present chapter is organized as follows: Section 2 argues Smart Cities concepts. Section 3 lectures the Smart Grid concepts. Section 4 speaks about Smart Grid and its infrastructure. Section 5 presents how a current discussion around the technologies covered. In section 6 the conclusions of the research are presented, finally, Section 7, presents future trends for Smart Grid.

2. SMART CITIES CONCEPTS

Cities are achieving rapid evolution along with increasing population levels, while new challenges are appearing in parallel, which leads to the need for public development aiming at continuous improvements that support more quality of life. It is in this sense that smart cities, with the concept that involves the need to build a city adapted to current needs, and, at the same time, prepared for the future, focused on improving the comfort of its inhabitants, allowing more efficient mobility, to have connectivity and to be sustainable, are planned together with digital transformation, creating more opportunities for the population and economic growth [14].

Smart Cities are those that use information and communication technologies to provide more security, socioeconomic stability, sustainability, and reduced cost of living, that is, it is an innovative urban ecosystem characterized by the widespread use of technology in the management of its resources and infrastructure, *i.e.,* in a smart city where everything becomes connected, it is possible to have high-speed public Wi-Fi for everyone and the interconnected functioning of lighting, traffic, public transport systems, among others. Thus, technology and innovation are merged in a coordinated and integrated way with the traditional urban infrastructure [15].

In many cities across the globe, this evolution is still in its early stages and presents several challenges related to the provision of essential services in an intelligent way, such as energy, transport, health, education, among others. Therefore, for a city to be considered intelligent, the environment, the economy, and society must be interconnected and coexist, creating a unified ecosystem, *i.e.,* this process involves several aspects of development, such as efficiency and management of public lighting and telecommunications networks that allow offering services in real-time to connected users, development of mobility solutions to save time and reduce pollution, buildings with positive energy coefficient, optimization of waste management, for example. Infrastructure is essential to define how the main services will be made available, offering several possibilities of support with the promotion of the effectiveness of the processes [16].

Digital Cities are not only synonymous with Smart Cities, since the first focus only on the implementation of free internet signal distribution points throughout the territory, while the second represents all unified technologies, with a connection between the various technological initiatives, resulting in the efficiency in the use of resources, mobility, and services [17].

The resources are used to promote public policy based on some important points in population development, improving the quality of life and the services offered, such as urban and organizational planning; improving transportation services, and developing new models that can be sustainable and affordable for the entire population; better community life; easy mobility; modern architecture and infrastructure; advanced technologies and resources; clean energy; more efficient and organized emergency services, being possible, mainly related to the optimization of response times; implementation of technologies in school environments, with easy access to equalizing the opportunities of all students; as well as the replacement of printed teaching materials with digital versions [18].

Smart Cities is an urban model based on the use of information and communication technologies, approaching the vision of the future built on decisive, independent, and conscious attitudes of the different actors of the urban space, such as government, civil society, and academia in the dimensions of economy, governance, mobility, people, environment and quality of life. Where common aspects are environmental issues (energy production, waste management, and others), communication between different users (companies, collectives, institutions, and individuals), use of information and communication technologies to improve the operational functioning of the network, social aspects (health care, education and cultural services available) and urban efficiency [19].

The phases of building a smart city range from public lighting networks to remote management of urban equipment, electromobility, applications for the operation and maintenance of urban assets and interface with citizens, distributed energy generation, hypervisor, and operation centers. Technological resources allow for a more balanced urban expansion, aiming at sustainability and democracy. Enabling the reduction of the barrier that exists between citizens and the administration, through technological resources that make it possible to obtain information and services [20].

Since one of the main objectives of the smart city is to promote sustainability, that it is necessary to have planned, acting in the whole process of implantation, review, operation, and maintenance of resources, from the most common ones as urban lighting to reach, among others objectives, energy savings with luminous efficiency and high availability rates, aiming at an efficient functioning of the commercial, residential and business areas of the region, making it easier to obtain services and leisure, also counting on the distribution of green areas, encouraging integration between all built environments. In addition to lighting, traffic lights, and equipment for remote management, which help to streamline and optimize traffic control, contributing to improving the environmental quality of emblematic urban buildings and improving the management capacity of cities with intelligent technology applications [21].

The development of transport infrastructures, with intelligent electric trams, recover the energy generated by braking, or even with the installation of charging stations for electric vehicles. Creating an intelligent ecosystem with the principle of respecting and promoting ecological actions, paying attention to sustainable eco-development. Thus, there is a concern to reduce heat islands, making the distribution of green areas more functional, generating well-being for the population, and still considering a view of nature [14, 18, 21].

Smart City is a concept based on recent technological innovations that make municipalities optimized, enabling planned growth for the benefit of human beings, since naturally the concept is also designed to focus on the population and the essential measures for its good functioning, implementation of urban environments based on interaction and social inclusion [15, 20, 21].

Thus, smart cities tend to improve people's lifestyles, helping the environment, management, and the community to get involved with more quality and efficiency, combining fundamental elements such as transformative social project, sustainability, and administrative autonomy, evaluating categories such as mobility, environment, technology and innovation, urbanism, economy, education, health, security, entrepreneurship, governance, and energy. Which generates a transformation of urban infrastructures, integrating the citizen, and adding management and sustainability capacity for the construction of increasingly intelligent cities [16, 21, 22].

3. SMART GRID CONCEPTS

Energy management is a requirement for a sustainable environment and smart grids represent an essential pillar for its achievement since the dissemination of renewable energy sources has led to a profound modernization of traditional electricity distribution systems and in the way of distribution over there. Together with the search for sustainability, the digital transformation has also added to the creation of new possibilities for the management of electric energy, aiming at reducing environmental damage with the objective of more than simply saving, that is, making intelligent and conscious use. Therefore, a way was developed to optimize energy production intelligently using technology such as IoT, giving rise to Smart Grid [1, 2, 20 - 22].

Smart Grid is generic for the application of computational intelligence with Internet of Things (IoT) devices, in which almost any object can be equipped with a unique identifier and receive the ability to communicate through the web, and network resources to one electricity distribution system, provided that the Internet of Things (IoT) technology allows the implementation of a series of digital transformation projects [3, 21, 22].

3.1. Smart Grid and IoT

Considering the concept of IoT where all digital devices can interconnect, using the internet, making it possible to remotely control all connected devices since the technology has known potential for revolution and industrial innovation such as the automobile, security, medical, smart cities, and recently electricity consumption. And so, allowing users to integrate communication systems, control energy and electrical flow, measure consumption, monitor the health of their systems, and automate their energy systems, among other applications [23].

Characterized by the implementation of many thousands of control devices, sensors that allow to automatically adjust the electricity flows, controllers that are located remotely, are informed of the situation in real-time and can act immediately if there is a problem, practically without the need for intervention human, and interactive and intelligent meters, Smart Grid not only guarantees the correct interaction between all these elements, but also provides the expressive improvement of the network in terms of efficiency, reliability, and freedom for the final customer to control their consumption conditions [24].

Smart Grid is not a project to be implemented but an evolution, in this sense it is necessary to plan the implementation of an architecture that, continuously, includes new technologies adopted, always taking into account the importance of integration between them. The implementation of Smart Grid, in practice, means in cutting edge technologies, such as IoT, Artificial Intelligence, and cloud computing, implementing sensors and software to deal with this information, making the devices installed on the network allow the identification of fluctuations or peak consumption at certain points, causing this captured data to be sent to the software, which can generate reports or act according to pre-established measures [2, 6, 24].

3.2. Smart Grid Applications

Besides, this type of network can communicate with any smart meter and, connecting consumers' appliances automatically at specific times to reduce financial expenses with electricity, for example. Thus, the monitoring and exchange of information on energy flows are additional applications of Smart Grids, through this use of smart meters, automatic control devices, smart switches, and appliances, making the Grid able to anticipate demands in advance expected energy consumption and adapt production and consumption, consequently avoiding peak loads, eliminating possible blackouts and acting promptly in case of failures [4, 24].

Among the main automation applications through Smart Grid, distributing and generating distributed energy resources, especially in smart grid projects that seek to improve operations, maintenance, and planning, ensuring that each component of the power grid can “speak” and "listen", are the possibility to provide intelligent energy storage and offer a real-time response to fluctuations and demand management from the client-side, based on "bidirectional conversation" between devices on the network and consumer devices as well on the user's edge [25].

From the customer's point of view, information related to electricity consumption can also be delivered, to raise awareness about consumption habits and encourage more rational use of energy, giving "control" of your own energy use, ensuring flexible distribution highly automated, encouraging the release or containment of consumption according to the circumstances of the load on the infrastructure. Since the distributors can offer incentives to conscious consumption or even flexibility in the tariffs charged according to the consumption profile [26].

From a structural point of view, a distributor will only know that the service is interrupted if a customer complaint, in contrast, in a Smart Grid scenario, the company will know immediately why certain components of the network, considering the smart meters in the affected area have stopped sending sensor data. Therefore, obtaining a vision of an automated, efficient, and self-recovering bidirectional way of energy and interconnected communications, suggesting a highly reliable and efficient energy production and distribution environment [5, 26].

In the context of Smart Grid, it is ensured that all components of the network, from transformers and power lines to domestic, commercial, and industrial electrical meters, have IP addresses and can use bidirectional communication, enabling more distribution management efficiency. Still considering the proactive ability to maintain and respond to interruptions more quickly. However, one of the biggest problems with the deployment of these many thousands of smart devices and characterized by dispersion is exactly how to control them. Related to the dissemination of control points, making a control issue highly critical, that is, there is a great demand for resources to ensure communication with each of these devices and protect them from cyber threats [27].

In this respect, encryptions with a minimum key size of 128 bits are the minimum initial criteria for protecting the data flow and devices in this configuration, since 256-bit keys are indispensable. As well as public-key infrastructure technology (PKI), consisting of a system of resources, policies, and services that support the use of public-key cryptography to authenticate the parties involved in the transaction. There is no single standard that defines the components of public-key infrastructure, but a public-key infrastructure generally includes Certification Authorities (CAs) such as Issuing digital certificates, validating digital certificates, Revoking digital certificates, and public-key distribution and Registration Authorities (RAs). The most suitable technology to ensure that each device has a unique key so that in case an invasion occurs on a device, it does not mean access to the entire system [28].

3.3. Smart Grid Advantages

One of the biggest advantages of Smart Grid is the possibility of monitoring energy performance in real-time, in contrast to the traditional meter, in which consumption data is collected once a month, digital allows constant monitoring. Another important component of Smart Grid is automation since it is present in the integrated automated communication between components of the electrical network; automated controls for distribution and repairs; detection and measurement technologies; better management of dashboards and decision support software, among other aspects. In this way, irregularities are quickly identified, and predictive, preventive, and corrective actions can be adopted avoiding waste and establishing goals that improve energy consumption, whether for the company or the end customer, establishing a more sustainable business model enabling the reduction of emissions carbon dioxide and other polluting waste [4, 28].

Making a contrast analogy between the characteristics that differentiate a traditional electrical network from a Smart Grid are the flexibility, which facilitates the management of variations in generation and consumption; accessibility related to all the different energy sources that can be integrated into the network, and due to the interconnections present, consumers can take advantage of the renewable energy generated in large quantities in distant regions, when there is not enough in the locality; reliability due to information sent in real-time and remote network management, the risk of power outages and incidents is reduced; and from an economic point of view concerning better management results in reduced costs [29].

In this way, Smart Grids is defined as an intelligent electrical distribution system that offers bi-directional energy flows from producers to consumers, which benefit from reduced power losses, lower costs, and better measurement of consumption with better control, enabling a reduction in carbon emissions. Still considering that with Smart Grid, end customers also act as producers, which, unlike traditional energy networks, energy is generated only by a plant and distributed to end customers through large networks of transformers and substations. In the context of energy production in Smart Grid, the energy produced by consumers in "microgrids", which can be through wind turbines, solar panels, among other forms, is sent to the main Grid, which, in turn, performs the management and storage [30].

Thus, a Smart Grid is an intelligent electrical network that reduces costs, optimizes management, and enables better control by electric companies, domestic consumers, and companies. They can also be integrated with Smart Cities for the development of other services, taking energy performance to a new level, ensuring quality, safety, and financial return. As long as there is an efficiently planned system, it allows adaptation, monitoring, and administration in real-time energy consumption, avoiding failures to the multiple energy sources connected to the system. It is a trend that not only solves infrastructure problems but can be considered a first step for cities and companies to take their intelligent path through the digital age [30, 31].

4. SMART GRID INFRASTRUCTURE

Smart meters are devices used to measure electricity consumption regularly and the integration of the electrical network as a whole is facilitated by the large flow of information through them, as long as they allow the bidirectional flow of energy, in addition to performing the collecting a lot of information about consumption. It is also possible to know the offers and demands of energy in each region and their respective variations over time, which through this information makes it possible to achieve a better distribution of energy avoiding that there is little supply for regions that have a lot of demand. In this sense, more detailed energy monitoring and charging can be done, compared to traditional meters [32].

A Smart Grid is composed of a structure composed of basically three networks taking into account that each household has its own network, consisting of a HAN (Home Area Network) which is the smallest of the networks and is present in each residence, and is composed of microgeneration's of each household, such as solar panels on the roof of the houses and smart energy-consuming devices, it connects these smart, energy-consuming devices, and micro-generations if any. Regarding all information and data related to the electrical consumption and energy production of each HAN, the occurrence of blackouts, and the overall quality of energy use are stored in a smart meter [33].

In the same sense that the set of several meters in a neighborhood makes up a NAN (Neighborhood Area Network), since the energy demand of several NANs in a region is sent to a data concentrator, which processes this information and sends it to the concessionaire, considering also that each such NAN network sends the information to a data concentrator, which is connected to the measurement management center *via* a WAN (Wide Area Network) network. Thus, a HAN is the home network, at that same level there is the BAN (Bussiness Area Network), which is a type of commercial network; the NAN would be the neighborhood network comprising multiple HAN; and finally, the WAN encompasses multiple

NANs. In the same way that a type of protocol is necessary for this communication since many of the meters and sensors, smart generators, and other IoT devices have some type of information processing done by microprocessors, it is convenient to use communication protocols similar to those of computer networks [34].

One of these protocols that can be used is DNP3, which has functions equivalent to some layers of the OSI model, having functions for data multiplexing and also division and packaging functions, it is an open-source communication protocol, it defines two types of stations, a master and another slave/outstation, which is useful for using different devices in the same medium, data prioritization, error checking, addressing services (data link layer), transport (transport layer) and functions application (application layer), for an interface between the user and the system because it enables the communication between devices within an automation system such as smart grids [35].

Another example is PROFINET which is an Ethernet-based protocol for connecting process devices such as sensors, actuators, and devices similar to control systems, following the IEEE 802 Ethernet standard in IEC 61784 and IEC 61158, meaning the possibility of connecting an appliance and an electric meter on the same network. Just like PROFIBUS, which is a traditional digital protocol based on serial communication [36, 37].

Furthermore, the TCP/IP (Transmission Control Protocol/Internet Protocol) protocols are the main protocol for sending and receiving data over the internet. And UDP/IP also based on the sending of information packets to speed up the data sending process but removing all the error checking part of TCP/IP, since all the communication steps necessary to verify the integrity of a package and to resend it, if necessary, contribute to slowing it down. The use of these protocols due to the wide use of such protocols on the internet, facilitates, even more, the creation of the internet of things, in which all devices are smart and connected to the internet [38].

However, the implementation of the smart grid is still a slow, costly process, both the installation of its infrastructure and the equipment that the user must have access to obtain the benefits of the smart grid, such as solar panels, for example and is still in progress development around the globe and it is a distant reality for developing countries [39, 40].

Still considering the disadvantage concerning opportunities for fraud and cyber-attacks, it is necessary to invest more in this area, because the number of such devices on the network is large, causing immense growth in the data flow, which is constant. Still reflecting on another point that is the existence of protocols that are proprietary that many energy distribution companies create to make their automation systems [39, 40].

5. DISCUSSION

Many large urban centers around the world, housing millions of inhabitants, still have little planning and unrestrained growth based on car dependence, facing a series of challenges such as lack of mobility, floods, heat islands, polluted rivers, among other aspects. Resolving these bottlenecks is not a simple task, but it is possible. Requiring smaller projects, local actions, with the application of intelligence on urban roads that can be the start for a giant transformation, it is necessary to start small and then scales, that is, start to apply solutions in condominiums, neighborhoods, and finally, have a sustainable city, for example.

Large cities have a challenge ahead of them in terms of infrastructure problems and, at the same time, integrate into the digital age, and in this scenario, Smart Grids for smart cities can enable various utilities, such as remote lighting monitoring, public security, water and gas supply, electricity distribution and traffic control.

The transformations of cities reflect the wishes and new behaviors of society, however, in certain dimensions of the smart city, technology has a more decisive role, such as in energy networks, mobility, and management of natural resources; while, on the other hand, there are dimensions where they do not have as much protagonist, such as education, culture, social and political inclusion. In parallel, governments, companies, and institutions must adhere to the ecosystem of a Smart City and Smart Grid promoting actions for sustainable and technological development, always focusing on people.

Technology is just one of several resources that can result in greater economic, human, and environmental sustainability in smart cities since the effectiveness of these systems concerning the objective of the concept of a smart city will depend on the results they present in a perspective centered on citizens taking into account scalable alternatives that can be adopted to improve the quality of life. For cities to become more and more intelligent, understanding the smart city not only by the use of digital technologies, but by the evaluation of categories such as mobility, urbanism, economy, education, health, environment, technology and innovation, security, entrepreneurship, governance, and energy, to remodel the infrastructure of an urban center, considering the joint efforts of the public and private sectors, in addition to civil society initiatives.

5.1. Infrastructure generated by Smart Grid

Creation of distributed green infrastructure to improve drainage, microclimate, biodiversity, and access to free areas, for example with the construction of bio-valets and rain gardens, which respect the natural course of the land, leading rainwater to spaces with native plants, forming natural gardens rich in biodiversity, removing the overload of the public network and restoring the natural hydrological cycle with the recharge of the water table.

Considering the efficient water management as to the control and treatment of rainwater and sewage, control and restoration of floods, and adopt innovative measures to protect watersheds. In addition to not suffering from polluted rivers and supply crises, its inhabitants find sources of drinking water in different parts of the city. Use of energy-saving systems and generation of energy from renewable sources, encouraging the use of alternative energies such as solar and wind. Data transparency and civil society engagement with the use of Big Data as a powerful tool for the education and engagement of the population in public management, providing data and graphics without any filter, separated by social sector such as Health, Housing, Environment, Transport, among others, transparently and automatically, essential for the cooperative management of the smart, democratic and inclusive city.

In a didactic context what turns the cell phone into a smartphone is the computer that exists within it, in this analogy, Smart Grids through all the technology inserted in it, take the electrical network to the digital age. Since these smart grids need to be composed of smart electronic meters at various stages of the transmission and distribution of electricity.

P eople are consuming more and more electricity every day, in addition to essential equipment for any home, such as an electric shower, refrigerator, television, coffee maker, microwave, cell phones and chargers, computers and notebooks and, a multitude of gadgets, iron ironing, among several other appliances, and to save natural and financial resources, it is necessary to reduce energy consumption or consume it more intelligently. For this purpose, Smart Grid emerges as an efficient system.

5.2. Smart Grid as an Instrument of Innovation

Smart Grid is a system that automates not only the monitoring but the entire management of electricity use. This technology is based on a new, more secure, and intelligent electricity distribution architecture, which promotes integration and enables actions for users connected to it. Due to the high level of added technology, smart grids can respond to various demands of modern society, both in terms of energy needs and concerning sustainable development.

Smart grids are intelligent networks for the transmission and distribution of energy, which control the generation of energy and avoid overloading the network since all the time only as much energy is generated as necessary, based on interactive communication between all parts of the network energy conversion chain, connecting decentralized large and small power generation units with consumers to form a broad structure.

Smart grids have also been identified as a providential tool for countries to adjust to the demands resulting from the Kyoto Protocol, since this has the objective of reducing the emission of greenhouse gases and the consequent global warming, to mitigate the impact of environmental problems caused by the models of industrial development and consumption in force on the planet. What considers the power generation systems of developed countries are based on the consumption of fossil fuels, *i.e.,* the main emitters of gases that cause the greenhouse effect. In these countries, smart grids are identified as the instrument that will allow the dissemination of renewable energy sources, through the concepts of distributed generation and microgeneration. Smart grids allow the connection of small wind generation systems (driven by the force of the wind) and photovoltaics (plates that take advantage of sunlight) and in low voltage consumers (residential and commercial customers), in addition to enabling the operation of these systems in tune with the entire electrical system. In this way, it will be possible to expand power generation in a decentralized way (without the need to build large and expensive generation projects), and in a pulverized way (allowing the final consumer to be a micro-generator of energy).

5.3. Smart Grid Benefits

Smart Grids use the roofs of the houses to generate solar energy since the photovoltaic roof generates a good amount of electricity. Without the smart grid, a house that manages this energy is restricted to charging batteries, like those of the electric vehicle. With it, the house can supply this energy to the grid, in addition to storing it in its batteries. This avoids waste,after all, it is the intelligent use of energy generation that will not be consumed or stored. Still considering that electric cars can help in storage and smart grid, in distribution. What is far beyond electrification of transport, is a form of energy use that does not generate pollution, *i.e.,* electric energy.

Another benefit of smart grids is the possibility of establishing a more accurate control of commercial fraud or operational energy losses, which can be identified through changes in consumption behavior. Smart grids connect decentralized generation units large and small with consumers to form a broad structure. They control the generation of energy and avoid overloading the network since all the time only as much energy is generated as necessary. These characteristics offer smart cities advantages, such as greater security of energy supply and reduction of investments in the expansion of the transmission and distribution system itself, as well as of the generating complex.

Through smart grids, instead of a few power generators, there may be several generators distributed throughout the network, which will reduce losses since the path between suppliers and consumers will be much shorter.

With the advent of smart grids, it is possible that the vehicle not only charges itself in the electrical network but also that returns energy to the electrical system if it is convenient. Since the technology allows not only the car to consume electricity from the grid when charging its batteries, but at peak consumption times, when people normally have returned home, the electric car can supply electricity to the grid. In some countries, electricity supplied at certain times, such as at dawn, is cheaper than that sold at peak times. With this, it is possible to recharge batteries at times when energy is cheaper and sell energy to the system when it is more expensive.

Innovations as a result of research and development of projects aimed at Smart Grids can be seen in electric cars fueled in the garage of the home, online monitoring of energy consumption, energy savings through intelligent systems and devices, residential power grid integrated with alternative energy sources, automatic detection and correction of power outages and cities transformed by automation and energy efficiency, technology and process automation, intelligent sensors capable of measuring energy quality providing the sending and receiving of information in time among many other applications allowing for more efficient energy consumption, for better use of network automation equipment to maximize its potential in the event of power outages.

5.4. Blockchain for Smart Grids

Blockchain technology consists of blocks (including a link with the previous block that links the two) that contain timestamps (time stamps) of batches of valid transactions, so these linked blocks form a chain with only one successor and one predecessor, it is an extraordinary innovation to be used in Smart Grid, offering more security, automation, and efficiency of operation and maintenance, including measurements for billing, expansion of digital security, the communication of IoT devices, which allows the collection of new types of data from sensors installed remotely. This whole process uses strong cryptography requiring a huge computational effort to break it since the blocks are stored on a distributed computer network and every new transaction is authenticated.

Currently, the traditional system used by the electric power system is complex to handle and operate, since everything is practically mechanical, yet pondering that several processes are difficult and even depend on manual operations. On the other hand, Smart Grid generates flexibility to perform several automated operations, even those remote operations. Still pondering that one of the differentials of the technology is the Smart Meters, making it possible to monitor data in real-time and still act in some actions, such as cutting off the power reconnection (acting remotely) and monitoring the load itself to be consumed by a given region. However, through this information technology environment, data traffic is naturally generated on the network, which opens loopholes for this new system to suffer cyber-attacks.

The use of Blockchain technology in Smart Grid offers the advantage of using a single data transport technology, safely, for various applications such as monitoring, control, and measurement. In this way, energy, gas, and water utilities could use a shared computer network infrastructure to transport remote data. Due to the distributed design of blockchain technology, the risks of service paralysis due to failure in a node are minimized, increasing the availability of services.

CONCLUSION

Considering that the obsolescence of the current electric grid in the future will not be able to supply the growing demand from consumers, it stimulates the need for an improvement of the grid and even reflecting on modern renewable sources, such as wind, solar, and wave, depending on external factors to determine its generation, such as the presence of winds and sunny days. The context of a Smart Grid makes it possible to store this energy and future replacement while maintaining the balance of the electrical system.

Since society lives in an era of greater awareness and concern regarding issues of sustainability and better use of natural resources, taking into account the new demands related to the energy sector, it is extremely important to use these resources more efficiently, conscious ly , and intelligent ly . So, intelligent action is to have better use guaranteed by the reduction of waste, making evident that changes are essential for the continuous growth of society.

Besides, investments in energy storage and production solutions accelerate this energy revolution related to the Smart Grid, which is a new architecture of electricity distribution, safer and more intelligent, which integrates and enables actions for all users to be connected, to increase the performance of the electrical network through savings in production and operation, increasing its electrical stability and reducing pollution and showing a system less susceptible to failures.

However, despite the improvements brought about by the modernization of the network, it implies the need for investments in several areas, such as research, infrastructure, and security, composing a complex and not yet fully developed theme, which is based on the automation of new networks with quality meters , which provi de s more efficient energy consumption, allows the sending and receiving of information in real-time, and requires the formulation of well-structured projects for its gradual implementation.

In the Smart Grid concept, the flow of electricity and information takes place in a bidirectional manner, introducing a two-way dialogue, where electricity and information can be exchanged between suppliers and consumers. Thus, the energy traditionally generated, transmitted, and distributed radially from the concessionaires' facilities may be integrated into the electrical networks from consumer units, in addition to monitoring energy consumption, revolutionizing the electrical infrastructure, contributing to the movement of the use of clean energy, meeting expectations related to sustainability. Furthermore, from the digitization of processes , equipment, and protocols, intelligent sensors will be able to measure the quality of the energy.

The logic of Smart Grid is in one word: intelligence, enabling efficient transmission of the generation, distribution, and consumption of electricity, avoiding waste, combating energy inefficiency, that is, the loss of energy along with the transmission, making more use aware and providing real-time information.

However, security and privacy issues are still sensitive points of this concept, and for this reason, it is an area that still needs research and further development to reach a fully functioning stage.

TRENDS

The microgrid is an intelligent, independent, and reliable network that allows the integration, management, and optimization of the use of energy resources, which is defined by the integration of several distributed generation resources, energy storage, and loads in a small system capable of operating connected to the main network and, in cases of emergency or scheduled events, to operate in isolation, controlling the frequency and voltage and providing conditions for recovery actions. This system is completely modular and adaptable to your needs [40, 41].

A microgrid can work either connected to the local distributor's electrical network or in an isolated way, that is, totally independent of the electrical network, integrating and managing all sources of generation, storage, and energy consumption points. Acting autonomously, the system analyzes in detail the way energy is consumed offering the best solution for each moment, *i.e.,* the system can be optimized so that if there is a higher cost-benefit, between a solar generation and a storage system of energy, solar energy will be stored and dispatched at peak times [41].

Smart Grid offers interoperability laying the foundations for expanding the level of applications by providing a platform for advanced metering infrastructure or used for charging electric vehicles, to support functions such as charging, charging, load limitation, storage, and more. Pointing to an increasingly extensive list of technological possibilities for the energy sector, which should evolve within its characteristics, allowing the establishment of an evolutionary vision and to add value with innovative technologies and applications to the electric power network [42].

CONSENT FOR PUBLICATION

Not Applicable.

CONFLICT OF INTEREST

The author declares no conflict of interest, financial or otherwise.

ACKNOWLEDGEMENT

Declared none.

REFERENCES

[1] A. Gupta, G. Verma, and H.K. Maheshwari, *Smart Grid Automation, Techniques and Tools. Advancement of Signal Processing and its Applications,* F. A. Silva, Ed., vol. 12. Smart Grid Handbook [Book News]: IEEE Industrial Electronics Magazineno. 1, pp. 59-60.

[2] J.A. Momoh, *Smart grid: fundamentals of design and analysis.* vol. 63. John Wiley & Sons, 2012. [http://dx.doi.org/10.1002/9781118156117]

[3] K. Siozios, D. Anagnostos, D. Soudris, and E. Kosmatopoulos, *IoT for Smart Grids.* Springer, 2019. [http://dx.doi.org/10.1007/978-3-030-03640-9]

[4] S. M. Muyeen, and S. Rahman, "Communication, Control and Security Challenges for the Smart Grid", *Stevenhage: The Institution of Engineering and Technology,* 2017.

[5] I. Colak, "Introduction to smart grid", In: *2016 International Smart Grid Workshop and Certificate Program (ISGWCP)* IEEE., 2016, pp. 1-5.

[6] W. Tushar, C. Yuen, B. Chai, S. Huang, K.L. Wood, S.G. Kerk, and Z. Yang, "Smart grid testbed for demand focused energy management in end-user environments", *IEEE Wirel. Commun.,* vol. 23, no. 6, pp. 70-80, 2016.

[http://dx.doi.org/10.1109/MWC.2016.1400377RP]

[7] B.L.R. Stojkoska, and K.V. Trivodaliev, "A review of Internet of Things for smart home: Challenges and solutions", *J. Clean. Prod.,* vol. 140, pp. 1454-1464, 2017. [http://dx.doi.org/10.1016/j.jclepro.2016.10.006]

[8] W.J. Miller, Internet of things (IoT) for smart energy systems.*Smart energy grid engineering.* Academic Press, 2017, pp. 237-244. [http://dx.doi.org/10.1016/B978-0-12-805343-0.00011-5]

[9] Z.H. Gontar, Ed., *Smart Grid Analytics for Sustainability and Urbanization.* IGI Global, 2018. [http://dx.doi.org/10.4018/978-1-5225-3996-4]

[10] Y. Kabalci, "A survey on smart metering and smart grid communication", *Renew. Sustain. Energy Rev.,* vol. 57, pp. 302-318, 2016. [http://dx.doi.org/10.1016/j.rser.2015.12.114]

[11] M.S. Hossain, N.A. Madlool, N.A. Rahim, J. Selvaraj, A.K. Pandey, and A.F. Khan, "Role of smart grid in renewable energy: An overview", *Renew. Sustain. Energy Rev.,* vol. 60, pp. 1168-1184, 2016. [http://dx.doi.org/10.1016/j.rser.2015.09.098]

[12] E. Kabalci, and Y. Kabalci, *From Smart Grid to Internet of Energy.* Academic Press, 2019.

[13] G. Liu, L. Qu, R. Zeng, and F. Gao, *Energy Internet in China. The Energy Internet.* Woodhead Publishing, 2019, pp. 265-282. [http://dx.doi.org/10.1016/B978-0-08-102207-8.00012-6]

[14] H. Song, R. Srinivasan, T. Sookoor, and S. Jeschke, *Smart cities: foundations, principles, and applications.* John Wiley & Sons, 2017. [http://dx.doi.org/10.1002/9781119226444]

[15] S. McClellan, J.A. Jimenez, G. Koutitas, Ed., *Smart Cities: applications, technologies, standards, and driving factors.* Springer, 2017.

[16] O. Gassmann, J. Böhm, M. Palmié, O. Gassmann, J. Böhm, and M. Palmié, *The Future of Cities and the Concept of Smart Cities.* Smart Cities, 2019. [http://dx.doi.org/10.1108/978-1-78769-613-620191007]

[17] K.S. Willis, and A. Aurigi, *Digital and smart cities.* Routledge, 2017. [http://dx.doi.org/10.4324/9781315712451]

[18] R.P. Dameri, *Smart city implementation. Progress in IS.* Springer: Genoa, Italy, 2017. [http://dx.doi.org/10.1007/978-3-319-45766-6]

[19] V. Ratten, *Entrepreneurship, innovation and smart cities.* vol. 11. Taylor & Francis, 2017. [http://dx.doi.org/10.4324/9781315407463]

[20] C. Coletta, L. Evans, L. Heaphy, R. Kitchin, Ed., *Creating smart cities.* Routledge: London, 2019.

[21] O. Gassmann, J. Böhm, M. Palmié, O. Gassmann, J. Böhm, and M. Palmié, *The Future of Cities and the Concept of Smart Cities.* Smart Cities, 2019. [http://dx.doi.org/10.1108/978-1-78769-613-620191007]

[22] N. Balani, and R. Hathi, *Enterprise IoT: A Definitive Handbook.* CreateSpace Independent Publishing Platform, 2016.

[23] R.P. França, Y. Iano, A.C.B. Monteiro, and R. Arthur, Intelligent Applications of WSN in the World: A Technological and Literary Background.*Handbook of Wireless Sensor Networks: Issues and Challenges in Current Scenario's.* Springer: Cham, 2020, pp. 13-34. [http://dx.doi.org/10.1007/978-3-030-40305-8_2]

[24] M. Mittal, S. Tanwar, B. Agarwal, L.M. Goyal, Ed., *Energy Conservation for IoT Devices: Concepts, Paradigms and Solutions.* vol. 206. Springer, 2019. [http://dx.doi.org/10.1007/978-981-13-7399-2_1]

[25] A. Gupta, G. Verma, and H. K. Maheshwari, "Smart grid automation, techniques and tools", *Advancement of Signal Processing and its Applications,* vol. 1, no. 3, pp. 11-15, 2018.

[26] W. Chen, K. Zhou, S. Yang, and C. Wu, "Data quality of electricity consumption data in a smart grid environment", *Renew. Sustain. Energy Rev.,* vol. 75, pp. 98-105, 2017. [http://dx.doi.org/10.1016/j.rser.2016.10.054]

[27] A. Sanjab, W. Saad, I. Guvenc, A. Sarwat, and S. Biswas, "Smart grid security: Threats, challenges, and solutions", *arXiv preprint arXiv:1606.06992.,* 2016.

[28] J. Mendel, "Smart grid cybersecurity challenges: Overview and classification", *e-mentor,* vol. 68, no. 1, pp. 55-66, 2017.

[29] C. Tu, X. He, Z. Shuai, and F. Jiang, "Big data issues in smart grid–A review", *Renew. Sustain. Energy Rev.,* vol. 79, pp. 1099-1107, 2017. [http://dx.doi.org/10.1016/j.rser.2017.05.134]

[30] H. F. Usman, S. Hamid, W. A. Khan, and M. Ali, "Smart Grid Intelligent Energy Management System with Cost Optimization in Power System", In: *Advances in Science and Engineering Technology International Conferences (ASET)* IEEE, 2019, pp. 1-6.

[31] R.K. Pandey, and M. Misra, "Cybersecurity threats—Smart grid infrastructure", In: *National Power Systems Conference (NPSC)* IEEE, 2016, pp. 1-6.

[32] M. Jin, R. Jia, and C.J. Spanos, "Virtual occupancy sensing: using smart meters to indicate your presence", *IEEE Trans. Mobile Comput.,* vol. 16, no. 11, pp. 3264-3277, 2017. [http://dx.doi.org/10.1109/TMC.2017.2684806]

[33] Y. Huo, G. Prasad, L. Lampe, and V.C. Leung, "Efficient access control for broadband power line communications in home area networks", *IEEE Trans. Commun.,* vol. 66, no. 4, pp. 1649-1660, 2017. [http://dx.doi.org/10.1109/TCOMM.2017.2749398]

[34] N.S. Nafi, K. Ahmed, M.A. Gregory, and M. Datta, "Software-defined neighborhood area network for smart grid applications", *Future Gener. Comput. Syst.,* vol. 79, pp. 500-513, 2018. [http://dx.doi.org/10.1016/j.future.2017.09.064]

[35] I. Darwish, O. Igbe, and T. Saadawi, "Vulnerability Assessment and Experimentation of Smart Grid DNP3", *Journal of Cyber Security and Mobility,* vol. 5, no. 1, pp. 23-54, 2016. [http://dx.doi.org/10.13052/jcsm2245-1439.513]

[36] A.L. Dias, G.S. Sestito, A.C. Turcato, and D. Brandão, "Panorama, challenges and opportunities in PROFINET protocol research", *13th IEEE International Conference on Industry Applications (INDUSCON),* IEEE, pp. 186-193. [http://dx.doi.org/10.1109/INDUSCON.2018.8627173]

[37] V. Watson, X. Lou, and Y. Gao, *A Review of PROFIBUS Protocol Vulnerabilities,* 2017.

[38] J.W. Jorgensen, *U.S. Patent No. 9,712,289.,* Washington, DC U.S. Patent and Trademark Office, .

[39] Y. Zhukovskiy, and D. Malov, "Concept of smart cyberspace for smart grid implementation", *J. Phys. Conf. Ser.,* vol. 1015, no. 4, 2018.042067 [). IOP Publishing.]. [http://dx.doi.org/10.1088/1742-6596/1015/4/042067]

[40] M.L. Tuballa, and M.L. Abundo, "A review of the development of Smart Grid technologies", *Renew. Sustain. Energy Rev.,* vol. 59, pp. 710-725, 2016. [http://dx.doi.org/10.1016/j.rser.2016.01.011]

[41] Z. Shuai, Y. Sun, Z.J. Shen, W. Tian, C. Tu, Y. Li, and X. Yin, "Microgrid stability: Classification and a review", *Renew. Sustain. Energy Rev.,* vol. 58, pp. 167-179, 2016. [http://dx.doi.org/10.1016/j.rser.2015.12.201]

[42] S. Bahrami, and A. Mohammadi, *Smart Microgrids.* Springer International Publishing, 2019. [http://dx.doi.org/10.1007/978-3-030-02656-1]

CHAPTER 2

Dynamic Strategies of Machine Learning for Extenuation of Security Breaches in Wireless Sensor Networks

Shweta Paliwal[1,*]

[1] *Department of Computer Science and Engineering, Meerut Institute of Engineering and Technology (MIET), Meerut, India*

Abstract: Wireless sensor networks (WSNs) have turned up as a promising technology due to their deployment nature and the knock-off feature of cost-effectiveness. The rapid increase in the demand for wireless applications has opened up new security vulnerabilities which are related to their infrastructure-less nature and their nature of transmission and hence made WSNs the centre point of attraction for attackers and intruders. Machine Learning has embedded comprehensive solutions to accord with modern security breaches. It has gained a mark of deterrent technology by shoring up the infrastructure of security through mapping security breaches and performing the identification of unknown patterns. This chapter focuses on the illustration of security breaches in wireless sensor networks along with the glimpse of reduction in attacks through dynamic algorithms and strategies of Machine Learning. We have proposed some feature selection methodologies in order to identify the best features out of the available network dataset. These feature selection methods are evaluated against the existing machine learning classifiers in order to identify the best feature selection strategy and the best classifier.

Keywords: Cyber security, Feature selection, Machine learning, Wireless Sensor Networks (WSNs).

1. INTRODUCTION

The tremendous growth in the field of Information Technology and Communication has paved the way for the evolution of Wireless Sensor Networks (WSNs). Today wireless sensor networks have marked their presence in various application areas of medicine, military, smart spaces, and many others. A wireless sensor network (WSN) is defined as a collection of spatially dispersed network devices along with dedicated sensors to monitor and record the physical condition

* **Corresponding author Shweta Paliwal:** Department of Computer Science and Engineering, Meerut Institute of Engineering and Technology (MIET), Meerut, India; E-mail: shwtplwl23@gmail.com

Sudhir K. Sharma, Bharat Bhushan, Parma N. Astya and Narayan C. Debnath (Eds.)

of the environment. Wireless sensor networks can either be demand-driven or event-driven. In event-driven sensor networks, the network triggers as soon as it senses changes in the monitored area, whereas, in demand-driven, the network serves as an updated database for a client. Wireless sensor networks are comprised of several tiny sensor nodes that are deployed either randomly or deterministically [1]. These nodes gather the data from the environment and transmit the sensed data to the base stations for further processing. WSNs provide cross-layer design and scalability along with the capacity to handle the failure of nodes. Different types of sensors such as seismic, magnetic, visual, *etc.* are embedded within the WSNs, thereby monitoring ambient situations.

The characterization of sensor nodes depends on their storage capacity, limited processing power, and limited energy. Based on the nature of nodes, wireless sensor networks are classified into two types of networks, namely homogeneous and heterogeneous sensor networks. A network where all sensor nodes have a similar property for communication, memory, energy, and reliability is termed a homogeneous network [2]. Due to the nature of transmission of wireless networks, security has become a critical issue. Not only security but the designers of wireless sensor networks must also focus on the issues related to the reliability of data, aggregation of data, and fault detection. Since the sensor nodes are capable of operating both in ad hoc networks as well as the normal networks, security goals could be categorized into two types; Primary Security Goals and Secondary Security Goals.

Machine learning provides low complexity estimation for the model of the system, thereby being deployed in a complex environment of the wireless sensor networks. Designers of wireless sensor networks are focusing on machine learning algorithms to gain new insights and knowledge about the unreachable location. It can be seen that wireless sensor networks are adopting machine learning to increase the security of the communication channel as machine learning is capable of dealing with the dynamic behavior of the wireless sensor networks.

The paper has identified different feature selection methodologies from the network dataset. Feature selection methodologies are important as they fasten up the training of the ML model and at the same time reduce the complexity of the model, thus providing easier interpretation. We have identified the best feature selection strategy and then evaluated it against several machine learning classifiers to identify the algorithm with optimized performance in the detection of security breaches.

Section 2 describes the security concerns in WSNS followed by a description of Machine learning in Section 3. Section 4 describes how ML addressed different security issues, and Section 5 describes the approaches that have been developed to combat these issues. The proposed methodology has been described in Section 6. Section 7 describes the conclusion of the entire work.

2. SECURITY CONCERNS IN WIRELESS SENSOR NETWORKS

Evolution in the field of manufacturing industries and wireless communication networks has contributed to the growth of WSNs. They are made up of cost-effective sensor nodes that release a high amount of energy. Several characteristics make WSNs prone to security attack which includes resource-constrained nature of sensor nodes and ad hoc deployment of nodes. The basic requirement for WSNs to survive includes reliability, availability, and energy efficiency. Denial of service attacks and eavesdropping attacks targets the confidentiality and integrity of the data being transmitted over the network, and Flooding and Jamming attacks are related to the power consumption of the network [3-4]. Hence it can be stated that there are several security attacks that target the sensitive points of WSNs, such as Bandwidth, Power, and Routing Mechanism of WSNs, thus opening up new gateways for intruders. WSNs are more vulnerable to Man in the Middle-Security Attack as they provide complete control over information that is transmitted over the network. The attackers target the confidentiality and integrity of data.

2.1. Eavesdropping Attack

Eavesdropping attack forms the base for other attacks and is a serious security threat to wireless sensor networks. There are two sorts of eavesdropping attacks in wireless sensor networks; passive eavesdropping, where the information is detected by malicious nodes through the listening of message transmission in a wireless broadcasting medium. Active eavesdropping, where information is captured by malicious nodes disguising themselves to be authorized nodes through queries sent to the transmitter.

2.2. Jamming Attack

Jamming is considered as a special class of DOS (Denial of service) attack. In a Jamming attack, high-frequency radio signals are emitted that disrupt the operations of the transmitter. A jammer could either be a simple transmitter or an entire jamming station equipped with special equipment.

2.3. Tampering

In this attack, the original node is replaced by a fake node, and the intruder gets access to sensitive information like cryptographic keys. The attack usually occurs at the physical layer.

2.4. Exhaustion and Collision Attack

In this attack, MAC (Media Access Control) protocol is hampered by a malicious node through transmission over the channel making other nodes deprived of access to the channel. Time-division multiplexing is used as a countermeasure for this attack [5]. A collision attack occurs when an attempt is made to transmit a packet at the same frequency by two nodes.

2.5. Sybil Attack

WSNs are vulnerable to Sybil attacks. Here multiple identical nodes are created by a malicious node. Based upon the fabrication of identities, a Sybil attack can be launched in various ways in WSNs. An identical node could easily get access from the normal node and achieve the information during one-hop communication. This communication to unauthorized nodes results in the loss of data. Sybil attacks lead to the degradation of the integrity of data, security, and utilization of resources. Sybil attacks are classified into two categories:

Stolen Identity Attack and Fabricated Attack: New malicious nodes are created from the legal node. For example; the ID of 16 bits of an authorized sensor node can be used to create a fabricated node with the same ID of 16 bits.

Direct and Indirect Attack: Communication between Sybil nodes and real nodes is carried out directly, whereas, in indirect attack, it is carried out through a malicious node [6].

2.6. Blackhole Attack

In this attack, the data traffic is attracted to a malicious node. This malicious node disguised itself as the shortest route for absorption of packets. Once the nodes are captured, they are programmed again so that they can not transmit the data packets to the destination. Re programmed nodes are called “black-hole nodes”.

2.7. Wormhole Attack

The intruder tunnels the message received from one part of the network and transmits them to another part of the network through replaying at a low latency link. Hidden and exposed are the two modes in which the wormhole attack exists. A wormhole attack is a type of denial of service attack that can affect the network without considering the techniques of cryptography that have been implemented, thus making detection of an attack difficult [7].

2.8. Grayhole Attack

In this attack, the malicious node acts as a normal node in the network to drop the packets that are being transmitted over the network, thus hiding the information that needs to be sent out to the destiny node [8]. Gray holes in wireless sensor networks can be classified into two categories using the number of nodes in WSNs and the drop of packets.

2.9. Sinkhole Attack

It is a type of insider attack, where the intruder first converts a normal node to a compromised node, and then all the traffic is attracted towards the compromised node based on the routing metric of the routing protocol that is being used [9-10]. Communication pattern in wireless sensor networks makes the detection of sinkhole attack a great challenge.

2.10. Hello Flood Attack

A few nodes in wireless sensor networks broadcast a "hello" message to mark their presence to all the neighboring nodes. Hello flood attack can be caused out by such nodes so that it can be chosen as a parent node by a large number of nodes present in a network. In this attack, the intruder gets hold of a node and declares itself to be the neighbor of other nodes by sending out Hello messages. When a node receives this message it assumes that the node is in communication range and thus starts transmission with the captured node.

3. MACHINE LEARNING EMERGING AS A SAFEGUARD TO WSNS

The term Machine Learning (ML) came into existence when the first-ever neural network was designed. Machine learning can be described as "designing the system with a capability to automatically learn and keeps on improving with experience without the need of being programmed explicitly". In wireless sensor networks, machine learning will not only improve the performance but will also help in accessing the large amount of data that have been captured by the sensors. The sensor nodes required to cover a target area could be easily predicted using ML techniques. The categorization of existing machine learning techniques is based on the structure of the model and the ability to learn. Fig. (**1**) describes the basic process behind the working of the ML model.

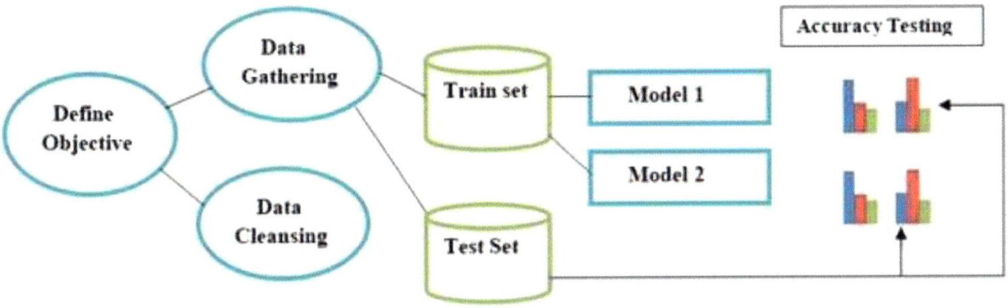

Fig. (1). Design of machine learning model.

In the domain of cybersecurity, machine learning is depicting progressive results by performing the analysis of previous scenarios and predicting the compelling measures for defense. There are certain scenarios where the technology is surpassing traditional security measures.

a. Machine Learning is offering the identification of critical real-time incidents.
b. Algorithms are capable of revealing advanced defense mechanisms by analyzing the network traffic and patterns of security breaches held out in past.
c. Machine Learning can detect insider threats and violations in policy for the network Infrastructure.
d. Advanced IDS have been designed through approaches of machine learning.
e. Machine learning provides synchronization and congestion control for wireless sensor networks.

For wireless sensor networks, there are certain points where machine learning is offering advanced analytical solutions.

Localization: Sometimes, identification of sensor nodes in the infrastructure of WSN after its deployment becomes a critical task, for which reconfiguration is required. Algorithms of machine learning provide ease of classification for unknown and anchor nodes of the network. Moreover, cluster nodes are trained to find the specific node in a sensor network.

Coverage in WSN: Sensor nodes are responsible for covering the field of interest in a network. Machine Learning will let you know the minimum number of sensor nodes required to provide complete coverage for the network.

Detection of Anomaly: Data is accumulated continuously from the environment and thus transmitted to base stations at a continuous pace. Hence protection of this sensing data is a concern point; machine learning is implementing hybrid detection strategies for the identification of malicious data traffic over the network.

Data Aggregation and Clustering: It poses a challenge to transmit the data efficiently in a distributed large-scale sensor network. Machine learning performs compression of data at cluster heads through the extraction of similar and dissimilar functions.

Query processing and Event detection: Machine Learning algorithms help in the development of advanced detection strategies with limited system requirements.

Machine Learning has witnessed improvements in the learning process of the sensor network and a reduction in end-to-end delay transmission. It is also providing a significant decrease in the communication overhead through the application of dimensionality reduction algorithms at the sensor node. Algorithms are continuously advancing the synchronization of nodes and moderating themselves to adapt to the dynamic changing environment of the wireless network so that reconfiguration can be achieved easily.

4. SUPERVISED LEARNING

These are the systems where the labeled input and output data are classified to form a basis of learning. Models based on supervised learning are used to represent learned relations between system parameters along with input and output. For wireless sensor networks, problems of routing, localization, fault detection, and synchronization are solved using machine learning techniques.

4.1. Linear Regression and Logistic Regression

It is a simple supervised learning method where a dependent value (y) is predicted based upon the independent variable (x). Regression can either be linear regression or logistic regression and could have continuous or quantitative variables. The mathematical notation of linear regression is represented below as equation 1.

$$Y = a + bx \tag{1}$$

Logistic Regression states that there exist only two possible classes which describe the nature of dependent or target variable. The dependent variable is defined in the form of 0 and 1.

Apart from these two, another regression is Bayesian Regression that uses probability estimates for the formulation of linear regression. The resultant variable is defined as y, which is generated from Gaussian distribution. Bayesian Regression helps in the determination of posterior probabilities and is not focused on finding the best solution.

Support Vector Regression is used for real value estimation and comes under the supervised learning approach. It is based on the usage of kernels and is used for the training of symmetrical functions. SVMs solve binary classification problems by formulating them as convex optimization problems.

4.2. Artificial Neural Networks (ANN)

It is a supervised-based learning model that functions on biological neural networks. ANN consists of a large number of processing units called neurons and operates on 3 layers, namely an input layer, a hidden layer, and an output layer. In wireless sensor networks, ANN is used to improve the efficiency of routing, congestion control, and aggregation of data. Artificial neural networks can memorize multiple outputs and boundaries of a decision in one go, hence are considered appropriate for resolving the challenges of a network, and they also come up with cost-effective solutions.

4.3. Decision Tree

Decision trees are based on if-then rules and consist of two nodes, namely decision nodes and leaf nodes. It is a supervised learning algorithm that splits the data set on the basis of different conditions. The leaf nodes of the decision tree represent class labels and the attributes are represented by the internal nodes of the tree. The attributes of the root node are selected through either using the process of the Gini Index or the Information Gain method. In wireless sensor networks, decision trees are used to deal with issues such as detection of anomalies, selection of mobile sink paths, *etc*. They also help in the identification of features such as corruption rate and loss rate.

4.4. Random Forest

Random forest algorithm is based on ensemble and comprised of a large number of decision trees. Random forest algorithm performs its operation in two stages; First the creation of a random forest classifier and second the prediction of results. The Random forest can be used for problems based on either classification or regression. In a random forest algorithm, it is considered that "higher the number of trees, higher the accuracy in predicted results," thus reducing the level of sensitivity when compared with other machine learning techniques. With this algorithm, there will be no problem of overfitting, and it also helps in feature engineering. The issues related to Media Access Control (MAC) have been resolved using the random forest algorithm.

4.5. Bayesian Learning

Bayesian learning is supervised learning based on statistical model parameters being considered as random variables and the results are drawn using posterior distribution. A Bayesian inference usually considers a small number of training samples and follows the Bayes rule given by equation 2.

$$P(A|B) = \frac{P(B|A).P(A)}{P(B)} \quad \mathbf{(2)}$$

4.6. Support Vector Machine (SVM)

SVM is a supervised learning approach where each data item is plotted as a point in n-dimensional space with the value of each feature being the value of a particular coordinate. Thus we can say that SVM is a classifier that suggests the optimal hyperplane for the categorization of data, and in two-dimensional spaces, this hyperplane is considered as the line. In wireless sensor networks, SVM can be used to detect the malicious behavior of the node and the connectivity problem. SVM works well when the data is either in unstructured form or in semi-structured form. The complexity of the SVM model is not affected by the number of features encountered in the training data.

4.7. K- Nearest Neighbor (K-NN)

K-NN is a supervised learning instance-based learning method used to deal with the problems of classification and regression. Euclidean distance, Manhattan distance, and Minkowski distance are the functions of distance used in the KNN method. The size of the input dataset is one of the parameters on which the complexity of KNN depends.

5. UNSUPERVISED LEARNING

It is a learning method where the algorithms are trained using information that is neither trained nor classified. The information is categorized into groups by the system on the basis of similarities and differences between them. The systems based on unsupervised learning are capable of performing more complex tasks as compared to supervised learning methods. In wireless sensor networks, unsupervised learning is used for the clustering of nodes and tackling the issues of connectivity and routing.

5.1. K- Means Clustering

K means clustering partitions the n objects into k clusters where the objects belong to the cluster that has the nearest mean value. The main objective of K means clustering is to minimize the intracluster variance. The algorithm firstly considers the random locations of the K number and forms the clusters with the data points. Once the cluster has been formed, a new centroid is recalculated from each cluster. The process continues until there are no more changes in the value of centroid of all the clusters. This clustering method helps in the selection of optimal cluster heads for routing in wireless sensor networks.

5.2. Fuzzy C- Means Clustering

Fuzzy C means clustering was first developed by Dunn in 1973, and was later improved in 1981 by Bezdek, and is used in pattern recognition. Here each data point is assigned a membership function corresponding to each cluster center. The membership is assigned on the basis of the distance between the cluster of the center and the data point. In the case of overlapped datasets, optimal clustering is offered by Fuzzy c means clustering as compared to K means clustering.

6. SEMI-SUPERVISED LEARNING

Algorithms based on semi-supervised learning are comprised of both labeled and unlabeled data set, thus it can be said that semi-supervised learning is a combination of supervised and unsupervised learning. The ultimate goal of semi-supervised learning is to classify the unlabelled data using some labeled set of information. Application areas of semi-supervised learning include speech analysis, protein sequence classification, classification of web content, and spam filtering. Semi-supervised learning has been used in wireless sensor networks for addressing the issue of localization.

7. REINFORCEMENT LEARNING

Reinforcement learning is described as the capability of taking suitable action for maximization of reward in a particular environment. It is a learning methodology that enables an agent (can be a sensor node for WSNs) to learn by interacting with its environment. Q learning is one of the popular techniques of reinforcement learning. Q learning lets an agent know what actions need to be performed in a particular situation and could handle the problems with stochastic transitions. The routing problem in the wireless sensor networks has been reduced to an extent using the Q learning technique.

8. MACHINE LEARNING ADDRESSING ISSUES IN WSNS

8.1. Machine Learning Addressing Issue of Security

Securing the wireless sensor networks against different attacks (discussed in the above section) is a challenging issue. However machine learning has emerged as a safeguard against these attacks, researchers have proposed several techniques that use algorithms of machine learning for the detection and prevention of attacks on WSNs. An intrusion detection system (IDS) plays an important part in the detection of malicious nodes in wireless sensor networks. Parras *et al.* [11] designed a Markov decision process-based framework to deal with the problem of ad-hoc defense and optimality using reinforcement learning. The approach is tested against spectrum sensing attack in a wireless sensor network

In order to improve the fusion classification, four classification techniques namely Enhanced K – nearest Neighbor (EKNN), Enhanced Extreme Learning Machine (EELM), Enhanced Support Vector Machine (ESVM), and Enhanced Recurrent Extreme Learning Machine (ERELM) were proposed by Javaid *et al.* [12]. A total of twenty datasets were prepared and simulated using MATLAB. These proposed techniques give better accuracy and detection than the existing techniques.

These researchers have designed the approaches and then tested them against several subdivisions of the datasets. They have shown significant improvements in an overall analysis of performance measures that include the accuracy of the detection rate and other standard performance measures. A synthetic minority oversampling technique (SMOTE) for the balancing of datasets and Random Forest algorithm is applied for detection of intrusion in the wireless sensor networks by Tan *et al.* [13]. SMOTE is a technique proposed to resolve the problem of class imbalance and overfitting which is caused by non-heuristic oversampling. KDD-99 data set has been used which comprises forty-one attributes that were later divided into five categories of attacks. This research work concluded that a combination of random forest along with SMOTE has resulted in an accuracy of 92.57%. The protocols were verified using the AVISPA tool and HLPSL language. AVISPA stands for automated validation of Internet security Protocols and applications and has been used for the verification of protocols concerning authentication and Denial of service attacks by Chandre *et al.* [14].

A hybrid framework for the detection of a black hole and sinkhole attack in WSN was designed. The framework is based on the Proportional Overlapping Score (POS), and Minkowski K means to reduce the complexity and increase the detection accuracy. Features in the dataset are reduced and the data is converted into a preprocessed form using POS. Minkowski K means algorithm is used for the training and classification. The framework has achieved a high detection rate and low packet loss rate. It has also minimized the communication overhead in the network and the results are simulated using network simulator 2. The detection accuracy was 85.93% for Minkowski K means. Kumar *et al.* [15] proposed a detection framework that captures the sinkhole and black hole attacks and thus activates the normal sensor nodes through alert messages.

Intrusion detection systems are used for the detection of malicious behavior of nodes in a network. IDS for the detection uses a statistical tool based on binary logistic regression. This system takes node parameters for malicious behavior as input. This m- ID was deployed in real-time using various network topologies. Ioannou *et al.* [16] proposed twenty-four malicious scenarios for each network topology and attack. Later a machine learning technique for the detection of spoofing attacks in wireless sensor networks was developed. Two machine learning classifiers were hybridized to process and analyze the samples of signals for the detection of attacks. The K means algorithm and K-NN algorithm were the machine learning algorithms used in this technique. De *et al.* [17] proposed an algorithm for optimization of scenarios where the attacking and legitimate nodes are either at the same distance or placed at a very close distance from one another. This approach resulted in a 10% increase in the accuracy as compared to one of the existing technique

Qu *et al.* [18] designed a knowledge-based intrusion detection strategy (KBIDS) to bridge out the gap between detection rate and false alarm rate. Mean Shift Clustering Algorithm has been used for differentiating the abnormal patterns from the network traffic and support vector machine to minimize the classification error. The QUAL Net was used as a network simulator where 100 sensor nodes were randomly deployed in each region. KBIDS has provided the highest detection rate when compared with the existing six different models.

Outlier detection forms an important part of security concerns in wireless sensor networks. A survey on the outlier detection using machine learning techniques is conducted and it has been observed that Bayesian classification has emerged as the best approach for the detection by Dwivedi *et al.* [19]. A novel detection approach for the detection of intrusion based on a support vector machine is designed. Here genetic algorithm has been used for feature selection. The wireless network is simulated using a network simulator and parameters such as packet delivery were taken into consideration. Vijayanand *et al.* [20] proposed a feature selection technique and observed that the proposed genetic algorithm-based feature selection technique provides higher accuracy, less overhead, and computational complexity.

Random Forest algorithm has been used for the detection of DOS attacks in wireless sensor networks. Park *et al.* [21] proposed algorithm is compared against Artificial Neural Network based model and it has been observed that the proposed random forest algorithm has shown 99% accuracy for black hole attack, 96% for flooding attack, and 96% for normal and scheduling attacks. Later on, an algorithm was proposed for the detection of wormhole attacks in wireless sensor networks that reduced the rate of drop-in packets. A dynamic threshold value is considered for the detection of wormhole attacker nodes followed by the clustering technique for the selection of optimistic communication paths. Simulation of WSNs coding organization is performed using MATLAB, thus reducing the overall packet dropping and improving the performance of WSNs by Harpal *et al.* [22].

There exists one more category of denial of service attacks known as Vampire attacks. These attacks are designed to drain the power of the battery from the nodes and are difficult to detect as they are protocol compliant. Afterward, a neural network-based detection algorithm for the detection of compromised nodes in Vampire attack is proposed by Tanguturi *et al.* [23]. The data is divided into three categories training, validation, and testing. Performance metric mean square node was used for the performance evaluation of the designed detection node. The approach provided low errors and a high detection rate.

Researchers designed a classification and prediction model using Logistic Regression, Naïve Bayes, Support Vector Machine, and Random forest. These machine learning algorithms were tested against the KDD data set. It has been observed that Random forest has achieved the highest true positive rate (TPR) and provided an accuracy of 99% compared with other algorithms [24].

The research work is focused on a specialized dataset that provides detection and classification of four types of attacks on wireless sensor networks named as a black hole, gray whole, flooding, and scheduling attacks. LEACH hierarchical protocol has been used for routing. Twenty-three features were processed and simulated using network simulator 2. Artificial Neural Network is used for training the datasets, detection, and classification of DOS attacks. It has been concluded by Almomani *et al.* [25] that detection is 92.8% accurate for black hole attack, 99.4% for flooding attack, 92.2% for scheduling attack, and 99.8% for gray hole attack.

A hybrid anomaly detection scheme for the detection of the wormhole and black hole attacks using K-Means Clustering has been proposed. Wazid *et al.* [26] have used OPNET modeler for the creation of a WSN dataset and divided the sensor networks into clusters. The wireless sensor network is simulated under the normal traffic and attack scenarios using the OPNET simulator. They concluded that this hybridized approach provides a 98.6% detection rate with a false positive rate of 1.2%

8.2. Machine Learning Addressing Issue of Routing in Wireless Sensor Network

Expansion in need of massive video streaming creates an environment for effective routing transmission for maintenance of load balancing. A routing-based load balancing framework using Principal Component Analysis was designed and then the network has been trained on Neural Network. The framework proposed by Yao *et al.* [27] provided better throughput and delay.

Researchers stated that intelligent routing is needed for the internet of things WSNs therefore they developed an approach using the neuro-fuzzy rule cluster approach. This routing algorithm provided better network performance in accordance with energy utilization and packet utilization by Thangamarya *et al.* [28]. Later a reinforcement learning-based routing algorithm was proposed for the optimization. It uses a fuzzy link for cost estimation. The algorithm proposed provided significant improvements for the dynamic environment by Singh *et al.* [29]. Harmony routing-based energy-efficient algorithm is designed for addressing the issue of energy consumption in sensor nodes. The local strategy has been developed for improving the performance measure of the accuracy of the algorithm by Zeng *et al.* [30].

8.3. Data Aggregation in WSNs with Machine Learning

Apart from these, there are several other issues in a wireless sensor network that has been addressed through approaches of machine learning. Table **1** presents a few more work done in the field of wireless sensor networks through strategies of machine learning.

Table 1. Applications of ML in WSNs.

Algorithm	Applications in WSN
Random Forest	• Intrusion Detection • Detection of Security Attacks • Fault Detection
Support Vector Machines	• Fault Detection • Energy Efficiency • Routing
K- Nearest Neighbor	• Localization • Node Estimation
Bayesian Networks	• Energy Management • Sensor Management • Mobility Management

Hence so far it has been observed that Machine Learning is successfully dealing with and mitigating the threats related to wireless sensor networks. The scope of the algorithms is not only limited to mitigation of security breaches but they are also dealing with issues of node localizations, routing, sensor management, and various others. If we talk on the point related to the security of networks there are several publicly available datasets such as KDD99, NSL- KDD, DARPA, and UNSWNB15 dataset. These datasets describe the behavior of networks through several identified network attributes known as features. The selection strategy for an optimal feature set improves the performance measures of the classifier and helps in the identification of the best features from the complete given dataset.

Hence we have identified three methods of Feature Selection on a publicly available dataset and observed the performance of ML classifiers on each of the feature set in order to predict the best set of features from the dataset.

9. PROPOSED FEATURE SELECTION METHOD AND COMPARATIVE ANALYSIS OF MACHINE LEARNING ALGORITHMS

After discussing the point of security concerns and the applied methodologies that are mitigating these effects in wireless sensor networks, we describe the Feature Selection strategy and perform an evaluative analysis of machine learning algorithms on a publicly available dataset. The working of the proposed model has been depicted in Fig. (**2**).

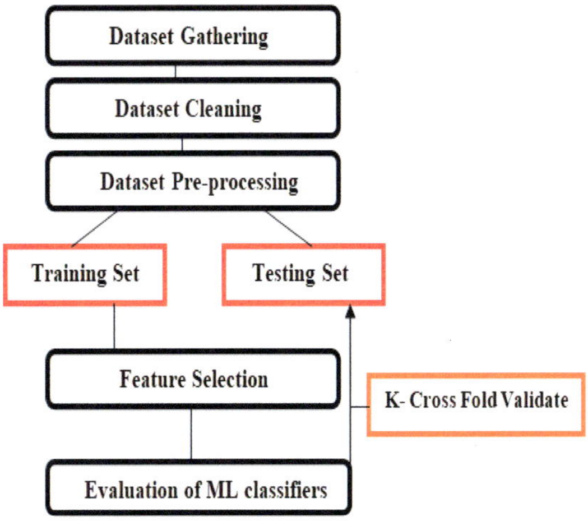

Fig. (2). Flow diagram of methodology.

Overview of the Adopted Method

a. A suitable dataset has been collected, and the stages of data cleaning and data preprocessing have been performed. Thus, a final clean dataset has been prepared for processing.
b. Several feature selection strategies have been applied and the best feature set has been identified.
c. Evaluative Analysis of the ML algorithms on each of the feature sets has been performed and a comparison has been drawn in terms of performance measures for the identification of the best feature set and algorithm.

9.1. Dataset Gathering

KDD99 dataset has been used for the evaluation procedure. The dataset comprises instances of several security attacks that have been grouped into four basic categories of security attacks. The KDD 99 dataset consists of twenty-two different attacks known as denial of service attack, User to root, remote to local and probing attacks.

9.2. Feature Selection Methodology

The feature selection is an important step of the data preprocessing stage, as it helps in the reduction of dimensionality as well as removes irrelevant features.

9.2.1. Correlation-based Feature

The strategy comprises of two methods; firstly selection of compatible features from class and performing recognition and secondly elimination of redundant features from the dataset.

The correlation coefficient takes values +- 1 for the linearly dependent features and marks the value 0 if they are not related to each other.

9.2.2. Info Gain Method

This is an evaluation method based upon the entropy and amount of information given by features for text. Entropy is important in decision tress as it decides the spitting of data and it affects how boundaries of decision trees are drawn using equation 3.

$$\text{Entropy}=\sum p(x)logp(x) \tag{3}$$

Consider a dataset (D) and a variable (v), the information gain is calculated as follows shown by equation 4;

$$\mathrm{IG(D,v) = H(D) - \frac{H(D)}{V}} \tag{4}$$

Where IG (D, v) denotes information for dataset (D) for a variable (v), H(S) denotes entropy of the dataset before the change and H (D/V) denotes the conditional entropy for a dataset with a given variable (v).

9.2.3. CFS Subset Evaluation

The worth of attributes is evaluated using each feature's predictive ability and the degree of redundancy. Feature subsets that have interred correlation are preferred and these features are highly correlated.

10. EXPERIMENTAL RESULTS AND ANALYSIS

After performing the data cleaning and removing duplicates from the dataset, the above feature selection strategies are applied. Machine Learning classifiers are then evaluated on all the three derived subsets, and performance measure for each classifier on each subset has been recorded.

Algorithm 1: Random Tree

Input: Dataset (D) with 41 attributes
Reduce features to 14 through Info Gain attribute selection
Procedure
Step 1: Initialise classification scheme
Step 2: Select base classifier
Step 3: If
(Base classifier = Random Tree)
Step 4: Declare max depth as m
Step 5: For (m=0; m<=5; m++)
Step 6: Initialise batch size
Step 7: Code the model for each feature vector
Output: Final Model E

Algorithm 2: Naive Bayes

Input: Dataset (D) with 41 attributes
Reduction of 41 features to 14 features through attribute selection
Procedure
Step1: Read the dataset (D)
Step2: Initialize the predictor variable as v
Step3: Calculate the mean and standard deviation for each class using v predictor variable
Step4: Estimate the probability function pi for each class
Step5: Calculate the likelihood function for class and estimate greatest likelihood

Algorithm 3: ADA BOOST

Input: Dataset (D) with 41 attributes
Reduce features through feature selection
Procedure
Step1: Initialize weights to instances
Step2: Set a FOR loop for calling of weak learn
Step3: Return the weak classifiers
Step4: Set a normalization factor
Step5: Update weights and produce a strong classifier

In order to avoid the biases and overfitting of the model, each classifier is evaluated using 10- cross-fold validation technique. It helps in the reduction of bias and provides a modest variance. Table **2** describes the detection accuracy measure of each classifier when evaluated against a derived subset of features.

Table 2. Performance measures of classifier.

Algorithm	CFS Feature Selection	Info Gain Feature Selection	Co- Relation Feature Selection
Random Tree	94.55	99.81	90.57
Naive Bayes	92.03	94.87	90.13
ADAboost	93.17	95.84	93.32
Lib SVM	89.02	91.14	89.02
MLP	90.09	91.23	91.23

After recording the performance measures, the training and testing time for each classifier on the subset is recorded and plotted. It has been observed that the Random tree has exhibited higher accuracy measures when evaluated against feature subset achieved by the Info gain method. Figs. (**3-5**) describe the performance of classifiers on each feature selection methodology.

The performance measure such as receiver operating characteristic curve along with precision and recall has also been observed for each algorithm on all the subsets of features. Thus, we have plotted the ROC area, and the values for precision and recall are given in Fig. (**6**). Precision describes the measure of results that are relevant whereas recall describes the total relevant results exhibited by the classifiers. Here, TP and FP describe True Positive and False Positive Instances, whereas, FN and FP describe False Negative and False Positive instances.

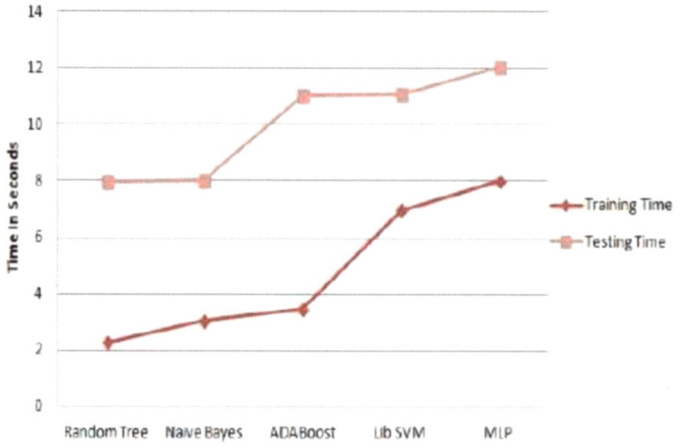

Fig. (3). Graphical representation for Co-relation set.

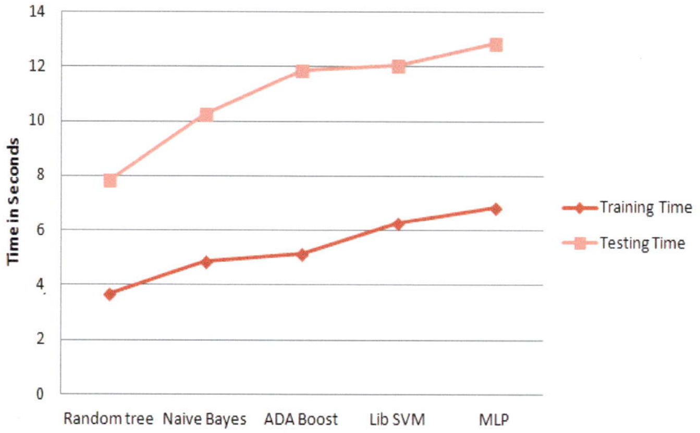

Fig. (4). Graphical representation for info-gain method.

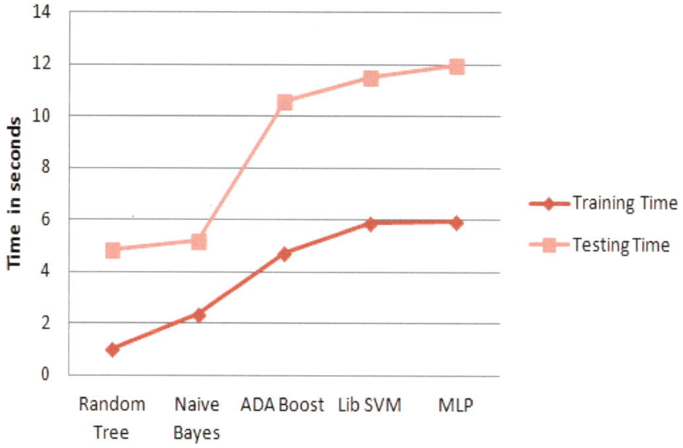

Fig. (5). Graphical representation for CFS subset method.

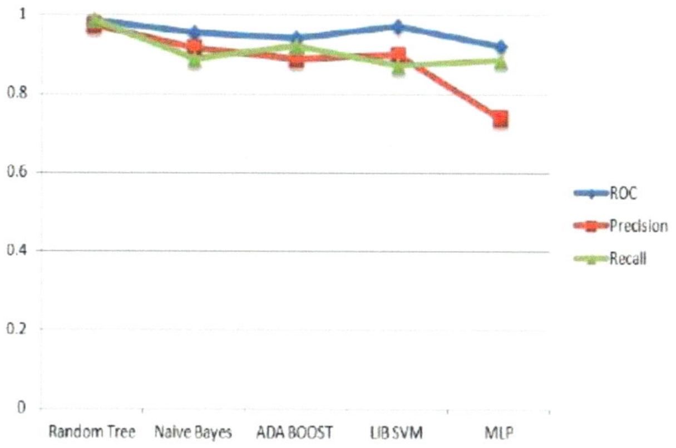

Fig. (6). Graphical representation for other performance measures.

CONCLUSION AND FUTURE WORK

Hence we have evaluated three methodologies of feature selection on a publicly available dataset and observed that the feature set identified through Info Gain Method has provided better accuracy measures for the classifiers. The selection of features depends upon the type of dataset used, and the Random tree is the best machine algorithm for this method on the used dataset. The training and testing time for the feature set using Info gain has also been reduced.

Machine learning is safeguarding the wireless sensor networks against several sorts of denial of service security attacks. Researchers have mentioned that there is a need to develop a proactive resistance system for the detection of intrusions in wireless sensor networks. Wireless sensor networks are protected against these security breaches using frameworks based on machine learning that has provided efficient detection and accuracy. Machine learning designs a framework that provides a high level of security with reduced computational complexity. Future researchers can focus on designing optimal solutions against security attacks in wireless sensor networks and reducing the memory overheads.

Machine Learning is emerging as a promising technology for the future of wireless sensor networks as they are capable of handling issues related to capacity and design-related issues in sensor networks. The strategy adopted by ML algorithms, which train the model from previous experiences, made the sensor networks more optimized. ML algorithm's ability to work in a dynamic environment has made the wireless sensor networks more sophisticated. Future works should be focused on designing optimal solutions using machine learning algorithms for increasing the network's lifetime, and models must also focus on clustering of nodes and mobility of sink nodes.

CONSENT FOR PUBLICATION

Not Applicable.

CONFLICT OF INTEREST

The author declares no conflict of interest, financial or otherwise.

ACKNOWLEDGEMENT

Declared none.

REFERENCES

[1] Victor Garcia-Font, Carles Garrigues, and Helena Rifà-Pous, "A comparative study of anomaly detection techniques for smart city wireless sensor networks", *Sensors (Basel),* vol. 16, no. 6, p. 868,

2016.
[http://dx.doi.org/10.3390/s16060868]

[2] D.R. Kumar, and A. John Clement Sunder, "Minkowski K-Means Intrusion Detection for Mitigating Sinkhole And Blackhole Attack In Healthcare Wireless Sensor Network", *Tagajournal,* vol. 46, p. 500, 2018.

[3] R. Vijayanand, and D. Devaraj, "A novel feature selection method using whale optimization algorithm and genetic operators for intrusion detection system in wireless mesh network", *IEEE Access,* vol. 8, pp. 56847-56854, 2020.
[http://dx.doi.org/10.1109/ACCESS.2020.2978035]

[4] S. Jaitly, H. Malhotra, and B. Bhushan, "Security vulnerabilities and countermeasures against jamming attacks in Wireless Sensor Networks: A survey", *International Conference on Computer, Communications and Electronics (Comptelix),* 2017.
[http://dx.doi.org/10.1109/COMPTELIX.2017.8004033]

[5] P.R. Pereira, A. Grilo, F. Rocha, M.S. Nunes, A. Casaca, C. Chaudet, P. Almström, and M. Johansson, "End-to-end reliability in wireless sensor networks: Survey and research challenges", *In EuroFGI Workshop on IP QoS and Traffic Control,* vol. 54, Paris, pp. 67-74, 2007.

[6] B. Bhushan, and G. Sahoo, "Recent advances in attacks, technical challenges, vulnerabilities and their countermeasures in wireless sensor networks", *Wirel. Pers. Commun.,* vol. 98, no. 2, pp. 2037-2077, 2018.
[http://dx.doi.org/10.1007/s11277-017-4962-0]

[7] S. Otoum, B. Kantarci, and H. Mouftah, Adaptively supervised and intrusion-aware data aggregation for wireless sensor clusters in critical infrastructures.*IEEE international conference on communications.* ICC, 2020, pp. 1-6.

[8] U.S.R.K. Dhamodharan, and R. Vayanaperumal, "Detecting and preventing sybil attacks in wireless sensor networks using message authentication and passing method", *The Scientific World Journal,* vol. 1, 2015.
[http://dx.doi.org/10.1155/2015/841267]

[9] B. Bhushan, and G. Sahoo, "Requirements, Protocols, and Security Challenges in Wireless Sensor Networks: An Industrial Perspective", *Handbook of Computer Networks and Cyber Security,* pp. 683-713, 2020.

[10] J. Parras, and S. Zazo, *Learning attack mechanisms in wireless sensor networks using Markov decision processes.* vol. 122. Expert Systems with Applications, 2019, pp. 376-387.

[11] A. Javaid, N. Javaid, Z. Wadud, T. Saba, O.E. Sheta, M.Q. Saleem, and M.E Alzahrani, *Machine Learning Algorithms and Fault Detection for Improved Belief Function Based Decision Fusion in Wireless Sensor Networks,* 2019.
[http://dx.doi.org/10.3390/s19061334]

[12] A. Mpitziopoulos, D. Gavalas, C. Konstantopoulos, and G. Pantziou, *A survey on jamming attacks and countermeasures in WSNs*, 2009.
[http://dx.doi.org/10.1109/SURV.2009.090404]

[13] X. Tan, S. Su, Z. Huang, X. Guo, Z. Zuo, X. Sun, and L. Li, *Wireless Sensor Networks Intrusion Detection Based on SMOTE and the Random Forest Algorithm,* 2019.
[http://dx.doi.org/10.3390/s19010203]

[14] P.R. Chandre, P.N. Mahalle, and G.R. Shinde, "November. Machine Learning Based Novel Approach for Intrusion Detection and Prevention System: A Tool Based Verification", *IEEE Global Conference on Wireless Computing and Networking (GCWCN),* pp. 135-140, 2018.
[http://dx.doi.org/10.1109/GCWCN.2018.8668618]

[15] M.A. Alsheikh, S. Lin, D. Niyato, and H-P. Tan, *Machine learning in wireless sensor networks: Algorithms, strategies, and applications*, 2014.

[16] C. Ioannou, and V. Vassiliou, *An Intrusion Detection System for Constrained WSN and IoT Nodes Based on Binary Logistic Regression.* Modeling, Analysis and Simulation of Wireless and Mobile Systems, 2018, pp. 259-263.
[http://dx.doi.org/10.1145/3242102.3242145]

[17] E.M. De Lima Pinto, R. Lachowski, M.E. Pellenz, M.C. Penna, and R.D. Souza, *A machine learning approach for detecting spoofing attacks in wireless sensor networks, IEEE.* AINA, 2018, pp. 752-758.

[18] H. Qu, Z. Qiu, X. Tang, M. Xiang, and P. Wang, "Incorporating unsupervised learning into intrusion detection for wireless sensor networks with structural co-evolvability", *Appl. Soft Comput.,* vol. 71, pp. 939-951, 2018.
[http://dx.doi.org/10.1016/j.asoc.2018.07.044]

[19] R.K. Dwivedi, S. Pandey, and R. Kumar, *"A Study on Machine Learning Approaches for Outlier Detection in Wireless Sensor Network", Cloud Computing, Data Science & Engineering.* Confluence, 2018, pp. 189-192.

[20] R. Vijayanand, D. Devaraj, and B. Kannapiran, "Intrusion detection system for wireless mesh network using multiple support vector machine classifiers with genetic-algorithm-based feature selection", *Comput. Secur.,* vol. 77, pp. 304-314, 2018.
[http://dx.doi.org/10.1016/j.cose.2018.04.010]

[21] T. Park, D. Cho, and H. Kim, *"An Effective Classification for DoS Attacks in Wireless Sensor Networks", Ubiquitous and Future Networks.* ICUFN, 2018, pp. 689-692.

[22] E. Harpal, G. Tejpal, and S. Sharma, Machine Learning Techniques For Wormhole Attack Detection Techniques.*Wireless Sensor Networks.* IJMET, 2017.

[23] R.C. Tanguturi, and C. Jayakumar, *VND-NN: Neural Network Based Vampire Node Detection in Wireless Sensor Networks,* 2016.

[24] M.C. Belavagi, and B. Muniyal, "Performance evaluation of supervised machine learning algorithms for intrusion detection", *Procedia Comput. Sci.,* vol. 89, pp. 117-123, 2016.
[http://dx.doi.org/10.1016/j.procs.2016.06.016]

[25] I. Almomani, B. Al-Kasasbeh, and M. Al-Akhras, "WSN-DS: a dataset for intrusion detection systems in wireless sensor networks", *J. Sens.,* 2016.
[http://dx.doi.org/10.1155/2016/4731953]

[26] M. Wazid, and A.K. Das, "An efficient hybrid anomaly detection scheme using K-means clustering for wireless sensor networks", *Wireless Personal Communications, 90,* vol. , no. 4, pp. 1971-2000, 2016.
[http://dx.doi.org/10.1007/s11277-016-3433-3]

[27] H. Yao, X. Yuan, P. Zhang, J. Wang, C. Jiang, and M. Guizani, *"A Machine Learning Approach of Load Balance Routing to Support Next-Generation Wireless Networks", 15th International Wireless Communications & Mobile Computing Conference.* IWCMC, 2019, pp. 1317-1322.

[28] K Thangaramya, K Kulothungan, R Logambigai, M Selvi, S Ganapathy, and A. Kannan, "Energy aware cluster and neuro-fuzzy based routing algorithm for wireless sensor networks in IoT", *Computer Networks,* pp. 151:211-23, 2019.
[http://dx.doi.org/10.1016/j.comnet.2019.01.024]

[29] K. Singh, and J. Malhotra, "Reinforcement learning-based real time search algorithm for routing optimisation in wireless sensor networks using fuzzy link cost estimation", *Int. J. Commun. Netw. Distrib. Syst.,* vol. 22, pp. 363-384, 2019.
[http://dx.doi.org/10.1504/IJCNDS.2019.099967]

[30] B. Zeng, and Y. Dong, "An improved harmony search based energy-efficient routing algorithm for wireless sensor networks", *Appl. Soft Comput.,* pp. 135-147, 2016.
[http://dx.doi.org/10.1016/j.asoc.2015.12.028]

CHAPTER 3

IoT- Fundamentals and Challenges

Mohammad Maksuf Ul Haque[1], **Shazmeen Shamsi**[1], **Khwaja M. Rafi**[2] and **Mohammad Sufian Badar**[3,4,*]

[1] *Department of Computer Science, Jamia Millia Islamia, New Delhi, India*

[2] *Director, Mewat Engineering College, Palla, Distt. Nuh, Haryana, India*

[3] *Department of Bioengineering, University of California, Riverside, CA, USA*

[4] *Salfia Paramedical Institute Darbhanga, SPI Darbhanga, Bihar 846001, India*

Abstract: The Internet of Things (IoT) is a revolutionary technology that aims at embedding everything we interact with or use with the capability to share and receive information over the internet. By everything, we mean all plausible things, from the refrigerator in your kitchen and washing machine to a soil moisture sensor on a farm and sprinklers in a stadium field. It has limitless applications in every field, including medical, industrial/manufacturing, security, *etc.*, to name a few. This myriad of applications makes IoT a difficult concept to comprehend. To tackle this issue, we present this work which aims at defining the loosely bounded concept of IoT comprehensively with related examples and lesser technical jargon than usual. Slowly, we will dwell into technical aspects and real-life applications by talking about Wireless Sensory Networks (WSNs, a subset of IoT), Distributed Ledger Technology (or Blockchain), another revolutionary technology that is merging with IoT to give rise to an even more secure and robust range of applications. Then, we will discuss the third pillar, Artificial Intelligence (AI), that, when paired with the aforementioned systems, breathes life into the devices we interact with daily. Finally, we will weigh the challenges and prospects of the field.

Keywords: AI, Artificial Intelligence, Blockchain, Distributed Ledger Technology, IoT architecture, Internet of Things, IoT, IoT security, Machine Learning, ML.

1. INTRODUCTION

The chapter aims at explaining the fundamental concepts of the "Internet of Things" abbreviated as **IoT**. We humans, as intelligent beings, have always strived to make our lives easier, from the simplest things like a pressure cooker to state of the art self driving cars [1] and UAVs used by the military for

* **Corresponding author Mohammad Sufian Badar:** Department of Bioengineering, University of California, Riverside, CA, USA; Tel: +1318 2783 121; E-mails: msbadar@engr.ucr.edu, director_academic@salfiainstitute.edu.in

Sudhir K. Sharma, Bharat Bhushan, Parma N. Astya and Narayan C. Debnath (Eds.)

surveillance [2], *etc.* IoT is yet another technological paradigm that is working towards making our lives easier and enriching our experiences and interactions with the things around us. The concept of IoT is a little difficult to grasp because of the diversity of things involved and the plethora of current and possible applications. Wikipedia defines IoT as *"The Internet of things (IoT) is a system of interrelated computing devices, mechanical and digital machines provided with unique identifiers (UIDs) and the ability to transfer data over a network without requiring human-to-human or human-to-computer interaction."* [3]. While one can make some sense out of what it means, it is somewhat technical. The definition given by McKinsey, though small, seems more logical and makes the concept a little more understandable, "*Sensors and actuators embedded in physical objects are linked through wired and wireless networks, often using the same Internet Protocol (IP) that connects the Internet"* [4].

As mentioned earlier, the definitions in and of themselves are acceptable, yet they fall short of encompassing the depth and breadth of the concept. In this chapter, we will learn the fundamentals through various examples of what IoT is, but for now, let us talk about the other revolutionary technologies that go hand in hand with IoT to give us that enhanced interaction with devices around us. Artificial intelligence, abbreviated as "AI", is a field of computer science and engineering that makes machines intelligent or, to be more precise, intelligent computer programs [5]. AI-enabled devices can by themselves automatically perform tasks that generally require human assistance or intervention. The definition given by Andrew Moore defines AI simply and concisely as, "*Artificial intelligence is the science and engineering of making computers behave in ways that, until recently, we thought required human intelligence*."

This intelligence is achieved mostly through Machine Learning or ML and enables programs and software to learn and attain or mimic human-like intelligence, *i.e.*, become Artificially Intelligent. One can say that ML is how computers learn to become intelligent or as Tom M. Mitchell said, "*Machine learning is the study of computer algorithms that allow computer programs to automatically improve through experience*."

Next is another Technology whose popularity has erupted in recent years, the Distributed Ledger Technology, more popularly known as Blockchain, which is a way of maintaining records. Technically, Blockchain is a distributed, decentralized, public ledger [6]. At its most basic level, blockchain is just a chain of blocks, but not in the traditional sense of those words. When we say the words "block" and "chain" in this context, we are talking about digital information (the "block") stored in public databases linked together (the "chain"). Both of these technologies, *i.e.*, AI and Blockchain are paving the way for more powerful, beneficial, and secure IoTsystems [7, 8].

The chapter discusses the history of IoT and then goes on to describe what IoT means through various examples and scenarios. After clearing the vast and vague concept of IoT, it talks about the fundamental principles, architecture, and frameworks of the technology. From there, it explores the current challenges in this field like scalability and security [9] and what can be done about it. In the end, this chapter leaves the reader with hints of what and where the future of IoT might be.

The chapter aims at developing a clear understanding of IoT. It provides the reader with a perspective regarding the emergence of IoT, how it came to be what it is now, and then it talks about IoT as in the real world around us, so that the omnipresence of these devices embedded with the internet can be understood more clearly. By discussing the fundamentals, architecture, *etc.*, it familiarizes the reader with the technicalities involved in IoT and the requirements and considerations to be paid attention to while developing an IoT solution. It then enriches the reader with the current challenges of the field to give an understanding of what we lack in. At last, with prospects about the expansion of IoT, we have to give the reader something to think about and work on if they want to pursue a career in the field of IoT.

2. HISTORY OF IOT

In the world of technology, one would consider the IoT as something old. The thought or vision of machines communicating with one another can be found in the works of people like Nikola Tesla's interview with Colliers in 1926 [10] and literature from the early 1800s. In a way, machines can be said to be in contact since the first Telegraph in the mid-1800s. In 1900, the first Voice over Radio transmission (Wireless telegraphy), and many more inventions and innovations in the field of communication and electronics followed, laying the foundation for IoT. Amidst all the rapid advancements, the development of computers began in the 1950s.

The Internet, a significant component of the IoT, started as part of a military defense project called DARPA in 1962 and evolved into the ARPANET in 1969. Commercial service providers started supporting the public use of ARPANET around the 1980s, which allowed the modern Internet to come into existence. Internet and communication technologies were quintessential for IoT's development. IPV6's decision to increase address space was another important component in developing a functional IoT.

2.1. Realizing the Concept

The term IoT was coined in 1999 by **Kevin Ashton**, but the technology came into existence even before that. One of the first examples was a Coca-Cola machine from the early 1980s [11], located at the Carnegie Mellon University. Programmers there connected a refrigerator to sensors and connected it to the internet, so they could keep tabs on the drinks in it, preventing them from futile trips to the vending machine. Then came the toaster presented by John Romkey at Interop in 1990 [12]. It was a toaster connected to the internet that could be turned on and off from a computer. There are some pieces of evidence of the existence of elevators that could be wirelessly controlled in 1979 [13], but it isn't very clear, so the Cola vending machine is considered the first IoT implementation.

The first corporate attention to IoT was from LG when they announced the first internet refrigerator back in 2000. From there, IoT advanced rapidly and started appearing in mainstream media like The Guardian [14], Scientific American, *etc.* around 2003. UN's International Telecommunications Union, ITU, published its first report on the topic *"A new dimension has been added to the world of information and communication technologies (ICTs): from any time, any place connectivity for anyone, we will now have connectivity for anything. Connections will multiply and create an entirely new dynamic network of networks – an Internet of Things"* in the year 2005. IoT rose in recognition and potential from their onwards.

By 2013, IoT evolved into a system engaging many different technologies, like wireless communication, micro-electromechanical systems (MEMS), and embedded systems. The support of IoT nowadays is present in nearly all automation fields from home to industry, present-day sensor networks, control systems, *etc.*

3. INTERNET OF THINGS

3.1. Meaning of IoT

Let's think about our phones today. What can they do? They can call, text, play songs, movies, books, *etc.* How do they carry out these tasks? By using the internet, of course. With no internet, they have limited capabilities. Equipping devices with internet capabilities comes with many benefits. This can be clearly seen in our own devices like smartphones, laptops, and tablets. The same increment in potential upon connection to the internet is also applicable to everything else, from the appliances you own to electrical devices around you, or some other asset of yours, literally everything. The central idea or concept of the

IoT is simple *i.e.* to take everything and connect it to the internet [15]. All the muddle about IoT is basically due to the fact that its definition and idea are so broad and loosely bound, that it gives rise to multitudes of possibilities and examples, making the concept of the IoT difficult to grasp. To understand this further, we will see why connecting things to the Internet matters.

3.2. Importance of IoT

Devices or things connected to the internet gain the ability to receive or send information, and in some cases, do both. With this comes the title of being smart, for example, smartphones, smart TVs, smart homes, *etc.* By connecting them to the internet, these devices exceed their limitations in terms of capabilities, functionalities, and experience. Let's consider our smartphones again. Nowadays, we can listen to any song of our choice on our phones, not because we have them all stored in our phones, as we cannot possibly store all the songs available on our phones. This is the part where the internet plays a crucial role. How does it work? Every song in the world is stored somewhere on some device that can send information (in this case a song) when asked for by another device like our own phones. It uses the information that the internet provides, and hence we can listen to the song of our choice. This exchange of information is the ability that the internet provides us with. This enables even small devices like our phones to have access and utility of high storage capacity devices or even a supercomputer with just a touch. That is the power that comes with connecting our devices to the Internet. All the devices being connected to the internet can be broadly classified into three categories, and they work together to deliver potential beyond the scope of one single device. The categories are:

- Things that Collect and Send Information
- Things that Receive Information and then Act on it
- Things that can do both

3.2.1. Things that Collect and Send Information

Just like we have sensory organs that can sense heat, touch, motion, smell, sound, light, *etc.*, and send this information to our brain for processing, there are devices that can collect information from our surroundings called sensors. They collect data from our surroundings like light, wind, speed, temperature, *etc.* If they are connected to some processing unit, they can send it there for utilization. Providing the sensors with the capability to exchange information over the internet makes them more powerful tools, as the data that was earlier available to the locality of the device can now be accessed from anywhere in real-time and can be processed by powerful computing devices to draw out useful conclusions.

3.2.2. Things that Receive Information and then Act on it

We all have used devices or appliances that start to work or perform a given task when we give them a signal. For example, to change the temperature in refrigerators we usually turn the knob or press the buttons to do so. The commands can be as simple as an on and off button, or as complex as Mozart's melody playing through a speaker. Now, what happens when you connect these things to the internet? The accessibility of the functions or actions of the device skyrockets. You can now change the temperature in your refrigerator while watching TV and sitting on your couch in the living room, you can turn off the lights of another room from a different room or even outside your home. This expansion of accessibility and experience is another powerful tool that comes with connecting things to the Internet.

3.2.3. Things that Can Do Both

These devices are the most powerful ones amongst all IoT devices, as they offer you both utility and accessibility. They can collect information, send it to devices that need it, and receive information and act on it. This is where the real potential of IoT can be seen blooming. Let us now consider through an example the first two points individually and then, later on, we can merge them to understand how the things with the capabilities of both sending and receiving information can enrich our lives and make it easier.

For this example, let's say IoT-enabled sensors that can detect moisture percentage in the soil are installed by a farmer on his farm, which sends data directly to his home computer or mobile informing him about the moisture percentage in the soil. Now the farmer can irrigate his fields on time. This also prevents him from over and under irrigation, therefore saving him money as well. Next, he installed an automatic irrigation system on his farm. If he connects it to the internet, then he can irrigate his crops at any time. The first one was an example of things that collect data and send it, while the second one was an example of things that receive input data and act on it. Now, moving further, he can connect both the moisture sensors and the irrigation system to the internet, and enable them to communicate with each other. To do that he just needs to set the threshold of moisture percentage. If the moisture level of the soil falls below that given threshold, the sensor automatically sends him the data and at the same time signals the automatic irrigation system to start irrigation. This way even at night time or when the farmer is busy, he doesn't have to worry about irrigating the fields if the moisture percentage falls below a certain level because the system will do it by itself as and when necessary. The farmer can also take it a step further by making use of the weather reports. He just needs to check the weather reports about the rain. As soon as the sensor detects a low moisture percentage, it will first look up the weather report. If there is a probability of rain in the next few hours, then it will just wait for the rain. If the prediction fails, then the irrigation system will start after a few hours. This way, the farmer will save on irrigation costs, electricity, and effort. Here, the whole system of moisture sensors, auto-irrigation system, and connection to weather prediction algorithms form this network of devices that can both send and receive information, collect data, and act upon it, thereby making our work easier than before [16].

3.3. Scope of IoT: Applications and Examples

The Internet of Things has the capability to aid every organization, of whatever line of work they may be in. It has the ability and tools to add value to the work of the organization and expand it in a previously unthinkable manner. If we keep on connecting previously existing devices and things to the internet and add new devices with capabilities tailored for IoT, some of the results or outputs will seem like magic. We can see IoT in action around us in our daily lives too. For example, we have all used or know someone who uses smartwatches or smart home devices like smart bulbs or fans. These smartwatches give us insights into our daily activities and health, and they do so by collecting physical data about how much we walk, our heart rate, our body temperature, *etc.* We can also control our smart appliances even when we are away from home, as long as they are connected to the internet. This enhances the experience and drastically increases the accessibility of the devices. For example, a little prior to arriving at our homes we can turn on the air conditioner from our smartphones, or switch on the geyser from our couches before taking a bath, so we don't have to wait for the water to heat up when we get in. Over time, learning from experiences (through ML), these devices can start doing some of these tasks by themselves so you won't have to. While talking about the benefits of IoT systems, we should keep in mind that they do one or more of the following things: increasing efficiency, improving health and public safety, and enhancing user experience.

3.3.1. Increasing Efficiency

An increase in efficiency means that we get the same results with less work or better results with the same amount of work. Even though inefficiency on an individual level can be overlooked at times, it is quintessential for organizations or industries to increase efficiency. Because it directly affects investment and revenue, increasing efficiency becomes very important [17]. For example,

- In factories, bottlenecks in the workflow can be identified by embedding sensors in the equipment. Addressing those bottlenecks can help increase the output, therefore increasing efficiency.
- Instead of scheduled maintenance, industries can embed equipment with sensors or sensing machinery and analytics which can predict the exact maintenance period [18]. In this way, the equipment's life is increased. Unnecessary servicing is avoided, therefore lowering expenditure. Real-time monitoring reduces the chances of accidents by preventing malfunctions.

3.3.2. Improved Health and Safety

This aspect influences all levels of human society, from individuals to organizations and even Governments [19]. Advanced sensory devices and real-time monitoring play an important role here. For example,

- Minute changes in the physiological conditions of patients can be monitored continuously, notifying doctors in real-time of any concerning anomalies. Detection of a heart attack prior to any discernible symptom or pain is possible through well-trained algorithms [20].
- Natural disasters like cyclones or tsunamis can be predicted by using IoT sensors and connected analytical devices that can monitor and decipher the minute changes in the environment(pressure, humidity, wind speed, *etc.*) before these cataclysmic events [21]. This ensures a considerable reduction in damage to life and property as warnings can then be issued well in time for evacuation and rescue.

3.3.3. Enhancing Experience

Until now, most of our devices, if not all, work on the basis of passive input. With the advent of the IoT, along with Machine Learning, this status quo is changing. We are using our devices more than ever before, and our devices are not just responding, but rather, interacting with us and sometimes even further suggesting things or performing tasks on their own. This enhances the user experience and makes us feel more comfortable while interacting with other devices. It might make us feel a bit uneasy knowing that our devices can act without permission, but the reality is that they learn from our habits over time by observing our activities, what are our preferences, or time of usage, *etc* [22, 23]. For example, a smart home equipped with smart air conditioners or thermostats can change the temperature of the room based on how we usually keep it at night or day or at a specific time. Further, it can adjust the temperature depending upon the weather outside. This helps reduce energy consumption as well.

Looking at all of this, we can say that ML and IoT are both on their own powerful technologies, and their coalition opens to us an array of new opportunities to grow and enhance our lives and our interaction with technology.

4. FUNDAMENTALS OF IOT

Now that we've understood what IoT does, let's see how it works.

4.1. IoT Device Architecture

There are four layers in the device architecture [24].

- The base layer consists of IoT devices and includes all the components like sensors with the ability to sense, compute, and connect other devices.
- The second layer, which is the IoT gateway or aggregation layer, significantly aggregates data from various sensors.
- The third layer is based on the cloud. It is called the processing engine or event processing layer. It has numerous algorithms and data processing elements that are ultimately displayed on a dashboard, this layer processes the data obtained from the sensor layer [25].
- The last layer is called the application layer or the API management layer. It acts as an interface between a third-party application and the infrastructure.

The entire landscape is supported by device managers and identity and access managers, which are useful for the security of the architecture.

4.2. IoT Reference Architecture

There are various layers in IoT reference architecture [26]:

- **Device layer:** The device layer is the main component, where there are various devices like sensors that are interconnected. Examples include Bluetooth connected *via* mobile phone and Zigbee *via* Zigbee gateway. The other devices include the Raspberry pi that is connected to the ethernet *via* wi-fi. This is directly connected to the communication layers which are a part of the second layer.

- **Communication layer:** The communication layer or gateway layer has rest protocols and other application-level protocols. Both layers are tightly coupled and generate an enormous amount of data.
- **The bus layer:** Also known as the aggregation layer, it forms a bridge between the data and the communication layer for the sensors. It is an important layer for three reasons
- It supports an HTTP server hand or an MQTT broker
- It aggregates and combines communications *via* a gateway
- It bridges and transforms data between different protocols
- **The event processing and analytics layer:** It drives data and provides the transformation of the data generated. It provides the ability to do event processing. The data is stored in the database.
- **The client layer:** This layer is used to create a web-based engine to interact with external APIs. This can be fed into the API management systems. This layer helps create a dashboard and provides a view of the analytics event processing. This layer helps communicate with systems outside the network using the machine-to-machine communication.

So far, we have seen the comprehensive IoT architecture with various components, rule engines, interfaces, and security systems embedded in it.

Now, Cross-functional architecture is possible using the device manager. It provides a single platform for remote management [27, 28]. The device manager communicates with devices through set protocols, device management uses device management agents, and is responsible for the remote management of software. The identity layer has cybersecurity capabilities, including policy control and OAuth2 token insurance. Other capabilities include Identity services XACML/PDP and directory of users *e.g.*. LDAP.

There are many frameworks for IoT setup, but the most common is ISO 30141. It provides commonly used vocabulary, reusable designs, and best practices for any developer to design an application. It also has many secure application standards that derive maximum benefit for the organization and reduces risks.

4.3. IoT Standardization and Design Considerations

There are several IoT standards that are evolving. Some of the key ones are [29].

- M2M is a machine-to-machine service layer that can be embedded in hardware and software to connect devices.

- Contiki is an open-source operating system for low-cost low-power IoT microcontrollers.
- Light OS, a UNIX-like operating system, for wireless sensor networks.
- Random phase multiple access is a proprietary standard for connecting IoT objects.
- Sig Fox, a proprietary low power, low throughput technology for IoT and M2M communications.

4.4. IoT Interoperability Challenges

IoT maturity comes with several challenges, specifically about interoperability and interfacing [30]. Some of the prominent reasons are:

- Coexistence of multifarious systems, devices, sensors, equipment, *etc.* that interchange location-time dependent information in varied data formats, languages, data models, constructs, data quality, and complex interrelationships.
- Multivision systems are designed by manufacturers over time for varied application domains, making formulations of global agreements and commonly accepted specifications difficult.
- New things are introduced that support new unanticipated structures and protocols.
- Existence of low-power devices that need to exchange data over lousy networks and may have minimal likelihood or accessibility for a power recharge in months or years.

When choosing an IoT solution, several factors are considered, like its wireless capability, functionality, interoperability, secure storage, immediate boot capacity, device categorization, bandwidth, cryptographic control, and power management. The design considerations should be a mix of the estimated average of all these components and index to balance the user requirements. A dispute-resolution mechanism is also needed in case of failure in the long run.

4.5. IoT Device Architecture Network and Cloud

The IoT architecture is a combination of things, device platforms, and sensors with data. There are four stages of integrating the different IoTprocesses [31],

- Stage one: networked things like wireless sensors and actuators.
- Stage two: sensor data aggregation systems and analog to digital data conversion.

- Stage three: the appearance of edge IT systems.
- Stage four: analysis management and storage of data.

As these stages are evolving, the devices, the network, and the cloud application must be leveled equally in the ecosystem for better stability and security.

Stage 1 of an IoT architecture consists of networked things, usually wireless sensors and actuators. Stage 2 has internet gateways and data acquisition. That includes sensor data aggregation systems and analog to digital conversion. Stage 3 edge IT systems pre-process the data before it moves to the data center or cloud. Stage 4 data center and cloud is where the data is analyzed, managed, and stored on traditional back-end data center systems. Fundamentally, we need to have a functional, scalable, and maintainable architecture. If these are not supported then architecture is not useful.

Now, let's look at the three architecture areas of IoT:

- One, the client-side IoT device layer
- Two, operators on the server-side IoT gateway layer
- Three, a pathway for connecting clients and operators, IoT platform layer.

These three layers interact with each other on a data synchronization front. The path would generate more data from various applications. The feasibility of the layers depends on their application.

4.6. Centralized and Decentralized IoT Architectures

The centralized architecture is a hub and is managed from one point, whereas the decentralized one is based on the use case; they do not help in industrial IoT solutions. The centralized architecture is associated with cloud architectures, in which a central hub provides a series of back-end services to smart devices. In the decentralized architecture, many scenarios require continuous communication between smart devices in an IoT topology without the need for an essential hub. The centralized systems help with event processing and decentralized systems operate more peer-to-peer messaging. Decentralized auditing is one of the essential features of decentralized architecture [32].

5. CHALLENGES

5.1. Security

The issue of security has been an obstacle in the large-scale deployment of IoT systems. Generally, IoT devices are more prone to Distributed Denial of Service (DDoS) attacks because of security vulnerabilities. In these attacks, the central server is bombarded with a huge volume of data requests simultaneously through multiple compromised computers, which causes the service to fail. Several DDoS attacks in recent years have disrupted organizations and individuals. Unsecured IoT devices provide an easy target for cyber-criminals to exploit the weak security protection to hack them into launching DDoS attacks. An overview of some of the attacks on different levels as described by Arora *et al.* is given in (Fig. **1**).

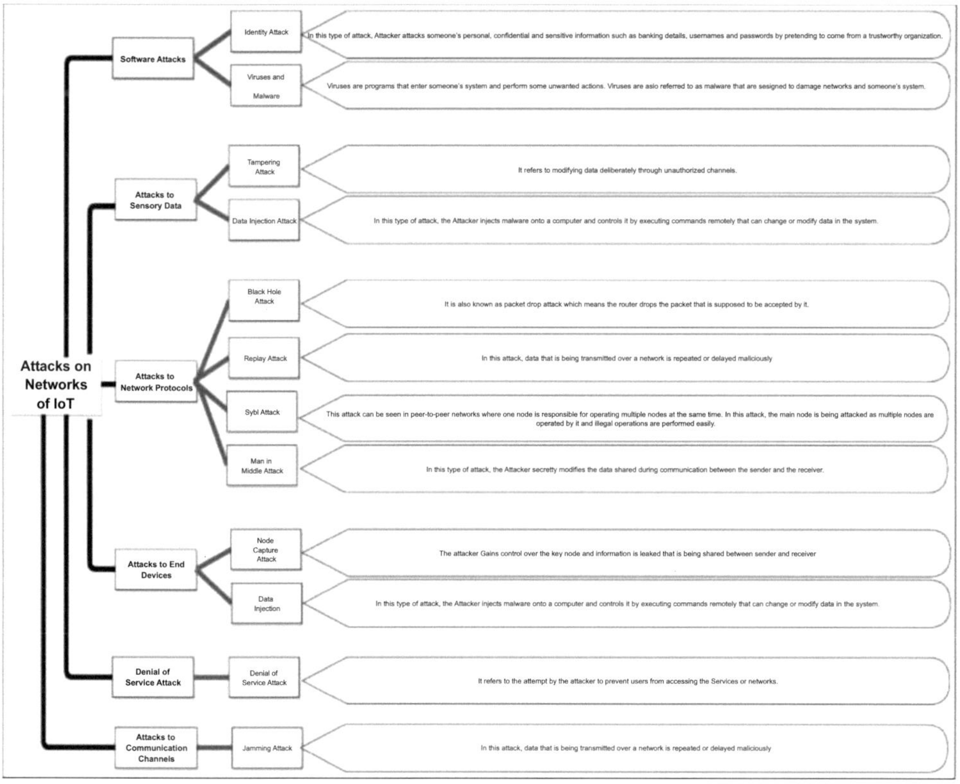

Fig. (1). Types of attacks on networks of Iot.

5.2. Customer Privacy

Sensors and cameras are becoming more and more commonplace these days, from our homes to public spaces. Adding to that we, the consumers, have less and less knowledge of the information being collected, and there is no way to avoid it.

The corporate use of personal data has become an everyday thing, and to some people's displeasure, companies are making millions of dollars from selling our data. From habits to likings to whereabouts, there is a record of almost everything we do these days. According to a survey by CISCO in 2019, 84% of the people said they care about their privacy and the privacy of other members of society and 80% are willing to act to protect it [33].

There are mainly three privacy concerns in IoT:

- Privacy in the device: It means that on the user end, the devices that record information like sensors or cameras are a threat to user privacy because the information they record can be leaked and misused. One way to tackle this is to have these devices made from reliable sources that follow strict standards of security and privacy.
- Privacy during communication: Again, the confidentiality of data is a concern while transferring or transmitting data over the network. There are many ways through which people can tap into these communication channels and extract the information without authorization. Protocols that are designed for secure communications would help tackle this issue.
- Privacy in storage: As it is evident that all the data collected through sensors for cameras or other devices is stored on a central storage server or cloud, it is an easy target to steal massive amounts of private user data. One way to resolve this would be the use of highly secure encryption algorithms while storing the data.

As of now, privacy has been a very black and white issue. The companies put up a front that users agreed to their privacy policy. In reality, very few of us ever read those privacy policies we click yes to, and even if someone does it is usually written in such convoluted fashion that it is hard to understand that we are being exploited. These things have fueled the discussion about privacy quite a bit.

5.3. Scalability

The growing number of devices creates a bottleneck, as the IoT of the present-day is a centralized system, and processes like authentication, authorization, and connection with different nodes with a large number of devices are bound to cause problems. One way out of this would be to make bigger investments to set up more powerful servers with higher computing capabilities. However, if that server faces some issue, the whole system crashes.

The number of IoT devices is steadily growing. A new forecast from the International Data Corporation (IDC) estimates that there will be **41.6 billion** IoT devices, or "things," generating **79.4 zettabytes (ZB)** of data in 2025 [34]. CISCO estimates that **5 quintillion bytes** of data will be produced every day from IoTdevices [35]. With such staggering numbers, one can easily say that IoT will be an integral part of our coming lives and that makes the above concerns even graver.

Cybersecurity researchers and experts have written reports showing their concerns about security loopholes in IoT systems, bringing to light the vulnerabilities of interconnected devices that can be exploited by hackers to wreak havoc. The Federal Trade Commission is also taking it seriously, trying to understand the ways to safeguard privacy in these new interconnected devices and to ensure that proper new regulations and protocols are derived and followed in the devices of the coming age. For example, with the advent of driverless vehicles or self-driving cars, *etc*., the threat of them being hijacked or tapping in their wi-fi or other connection services is a real problem the automotive industry has to tackle. Security risks cannot be overlooked while creating new ways to connect things to IoT, as every new method comes with its own risks and loopholes.

6. FUTURE

IoT can be visualized as a technology that is potentially limitless and can be merged with every possible technology in almost all sectors one can think of. Today, investments in AI-based IoT companies and devices are constantly on the rise owing to the fact that many sectors want to benefit from it. Innumerous companies now want to explore AI and IoT, starting from drafting a strategy to evaluating new projects or impr oving existing ones.

There have been several indicators of this major shift in the market:

- The capital funding of AI-based IoT start-ups is rapidly growing. This can be understood from the statistical data as per which in the first eight months of 2017, the start-ups raised $705 million [36].
- Acquisitions of AI-focused IoT start-ups are on the rise. This can be seen in the data, according to which it was 11 in 2015, 24 in 2016, and 21 in only the first 8 months of 2017 [37].

- The established vendors of IoT platforms like Amazon [38], GE [39], IBM [40], Microsoft [41], *etc.* are integrating AI capabilities.
- Large organizations have already started to leverage the potency of AI with IoT to operate more efficiently, thereby delivering better offerings [42, 43].
- Gartner, a global research and advisory firm predicts that by 2022, more than 80 percent of IoT projects will include an AI component [44].

IoT paired with AI, ML, and Blockchain helps us understand the trends in the market and where all the big companies like SHELL [45], WALMART [46], *etc.* are going. What we see today is just a sliver of the full scope. The potential will only be realized with time. Talking about security, in organizations consisting of thousands of employees, AI is used to determine the regular access patterns and the roles of different employees, providing insights for future job layouts, and potentially detecting suspicious activities. Facial recognition technology has made massive leaps and bounds in the last few years alone. It has probably never been easier, with a camera on nearly every computer and the smartphones present today, to glean information from consumer reactions to products and marketing. We could use the example of Facebook's auto-tagging here, which most people are familiar with.

In the future, it will be nearly impossible to find IoT systems that don't utilize AI services. AI will support an "all effective" IoT effort, and without AI, data from the deployments will have "limited value". We can see that it has nearly come to that as of today. Many IoT vendors are offering at least basic AI support. Companies across the globe in all major industries are already benefiting from AI in their IoT deployments. It is expected that in the future these AI-enabled IoT devices will make lives convenient for us to such an extent that automation will become a reality and technologies like automated house cleaning, AI-enabled smart locks, self-driving cars, augmented and virtual reality, smart cities, Blockchain generated cryptocurrencies, and all other beneficial practical examples of present-day sci-fi technology will become the new normal.

7. CONCLUSION

As is clear from the above discussion, the Internet of Things is an omnipresent technology even in the current scenario and will keep growing exponentially. The advantages by far outnumber the cons of the technology, but the infrastructure to integrate it into our daily life to make IoT a daily commodity and an essential service is yet to be completely manifested. There are several limits currently holding back the best of these devices. Though IoT devices are pretty common these days, as we have seen, the full utilization of the potential of this technology has not yet been realized. There are many reasons for it, from security concerns like attacks from adversaries to privacy concerns of data theft or misuse of data, even by the companies that are collecting them, and the issue of scalability as the larger-scale implementation of IoT will be needed to make industry and businesses profitable. However, there are several restrictions with the current technologies. Several technologies like Artificial Intelligence and Distributed Ledger *etc.*, are being used to tackle these issues. Every day, we see new developments being made and milestones being reached to further enhance the usage and utilization of IoT. There is a lot to be done and a lot of investment and efforts are required to overcome these hurdles. However, it is all worth it if we consider the enormous benefits IoT brings to the table, from improving livelihoods to enriching interactive experiences with devices and surroundings. It even plays a role in sustainable development through smart cities, smart farming, and other services. Hopefully, by reading the above chapter and discussions, the reader now has a clear understanding of the emergence of IoT and its fundamentals like its architecture, frameworks, *etc.*, and also the overview of the challenges faced by the technology and possible solutions and prospects of it. This leaves the reader with the potential to expand their knowledge on the aspects of IoT that interests them and work their way forward for improvement in technology and the society we live in.

CONSENT FOR PUBLICATION

Not Applicable.

CONFLICT OF INTEREST

The author declares no conflict of interest, financial or otherwise.

ACKNOWLEDGEMENT

We would like to acknowledge Director (Admin), Mr. Syed Sharique Hussain, Salfia Paramedical Institute Darbhanga, (SPI) Darbhanga, (director_admin@ salfiainstitute.edu.in), Director, Mr. Asim Raza Ghazali, Madhbuani Medical College, Madhubani, Bihar, Managing Director, Engr Ismail Khurram, Hospital Incharge, Dr. Yusuf Faisal, Faridiya Hospital, Salfia Complex, Darbhanga, GAMS & CO, CA Ms. Ishrat Raza, Nirman Vihar, Delhi-110092, Director, Dr. Mohamamad Rehan Badar (MD Physician), Badar Medical Centre, Shaheen Bagh, New Delhi, India, working at Apollo, Delhi).

REFERENCES

[1] C. Badueet, "Self-driving cars: A survey", *Expert Syst. Appl.,* vol. 165, p. 113816, 2021. [http://dx.doi.org/10.1016/j.eswa.2020.113816]

[2] Y. Han, T. Liu, and Y. Li, *Typical Representative and Trend of Military UAV,* vol. 6, no. 5, p. 5, 2020.

[3] "Internet of things", *Wikipedia,* 2020. Accessed: Sep. 08, 2020. [Online]. Available:

https://en.wikipedia.org/w/index.php?title=Internet_of_things&oldid=975970678

[4] "The Internet of Things | McKinsey", https://www.mckinsey.com/industries/technology-media-a-d-telecommunications/our-insights/the-int ernet-of-things (accessed Sep. 08, 2020).

[5] X. Wang, Y. Han, V.C.M. Leung, D. Niyato, X. Yan, and X. Chen, Fundamentals of Artificial Intelligence.*Edge AI: Convergence of Edge Computing and Artificial Intelligence.,* X. Wang, Y. Han, V.C.M. Leung, D. Niyato, X. Yan, X. Chen, Eds., Springer: Singapore, 2020, pp. 33-47. [http://dx.doi.org/10.1007/978-981-15-6186-3_3]

[6] M. Lacity, "Crypto and blockchain fundamentals", *Ark. Law Rev.,* vol. 73, p. 363, 2020.

[7] T. Sharma, S. Satija, and B. Bhushan, "Unifying blockchian and iot:security requirements, challenges, applications and future trends", *2019 International Conference on Computing, Communication, and Intelligent Systems (ICCCIS),* pp. 341-346, 2019. [http://dx.doi.org/10.1109/ICCCIS48478.2019.8974552]

[8] S.B. Calo, M. Touna, D.C. Verma, and A. Cullen, "Edge computing architecture for applying AI to IoT", *2017 IEEE International Conference on Big Data (Big Data),* pp. 3012-3016, 2017. [http://dx.doi.org/10.1109/BigData.2017.8258272]

[9] A. Arora, A. Kaur, B. Bhushan, and H. Saini, "Security concerns and future trends of internet of things", *2019 2nd International Conference on Intelligent Computing, Instrumentation and Control Technologies (ICICICT),* vol. 1, pp. 891-896, 2019. [http://dx.doi.org/10.1109/ICICICT46008.2019.8993222]

[10] "When Woman is Boss", (accessed Sep. 10, 2020) http://www.tfcbooks.com/tesla/1926-01-30.htm

[11] "The little-known story of the first IoT device", *Industrious,* 2018. https://www.ibm.com/blogs/industries/little-known-story-first-iot-device/ (accessed Sep. 08, 2020)

[12] J. Romkey, "Toast of the IoT: The 1990 Interop Internet Toaster", *IEEE Consum. Electron. Mag.,* vol. 6, no. 1, pp. 116-119, 2017. [http://dx.doi.org/10.1109/MCE.2016.2614740]

[13] "Elevator control system", *Elevator Wiki.* https://elevation.fandom.com/wiki/Elevator_control_system (accessed Sep. 08, 2020).

[14] S. Dodson, "The internet of things", *The Guardian.* Oct. 09, 2003

[15] K. L. Lueth, "IoT basics: Getting started with the Internet of Things", p. 10.

[16] N. Ahmed, D. De, and I. Hussain, "Internet of things (IoT) for smart precision agriculture and farming in rural areas", *IEEE Internet Things J.,* vol. 5, no. 6, pp. 4890-4899, 2018. [http://dx.doi.org/10.1109/JIOT.2018.2879579]

[17] S. Sen, J. Koo, and S. Bagchi, "TRIFECTA: security, energy efficiency, and communication capacity comparison for wireless iot devices", *IEEE Internet Comput.,* vol. 22, no. 1, pp. 74-81, 2018. [http://dx.doi.org/10.1109/MIC.2018.011581520]

[18] F. Civerchia, S. Bocchino, C. Salvadori, E. Rossi, L. Maggiani, and M. Petracca, "Industrial internet of things monitoring solution for advanced predictive maintenance applications", *J. Ind. Inf. Integr.,* vol. 7, pp. 4-12, 2017. [http://dx.doi.org/10.1016/j.jii.2017.02.003]

[19] A.S. Yeole, and D.R. Kalbande, "Use of internet of things (IoT) in healthcare: A survey", *Proceedings of the ACM Symposium on Women in Research 2016,* 2016pp. 71-76 New York, NY, USA [http://dx.doi.org/10.1145/2909067.2909079]

[20] A. Ukil, S. Bandyoapdhyay, C. Puri, and A. Pal, "IoT healthcare analytics: The importance of anomaly detection", *2016 IEEE 30th International Conference on Advanced Information Networking and Applications (AINA),* pp. 994-997, 2016. [http://dx.doi.org/10.1109/AINA.2016.158]

[21] A. Adeel, A Survey on the Role of Wireless Sensor Networks and IoT in Disaster Management.*Geological Disaster Monitoring Based on Sensor Networks,* T. S. Durrani, W. Wang, S. M. Forbes, Eds., Singapore: Springer, 2019, pp. 57-66.

[22] A. Chianese, and F. Piccialli, "Improving user experience of cultural environment through Iot: The beauty or the truth case study", *Intelligent Interactive Multimedia Systems and Services, Cham,* pp. 11-20, 2015.
[http://dx.doi.org/10.1007/978-3-319-19830-9_2]

[23] A. Khattab, H.S. Hamza, and S.M. Khattab, "Enhancing user experience in iotmashup using semantic technology", *2018 IEEE Global Conference on Internet of Things (GCIoT),* pp. 1-6, 2018.

[24] R. Khan, S.U. Khan, R. Zaheer, and S. Khan, "Future internet: The internet of things architecture, possible applications and key challenges", *2012 10th International Conference on Frontiers of Information Technology,* pp. 257-260, 2012.
[http://dx.doi.org/10.1109/FIT.2012.53]

[25] A. Khalaf, W. Akeel, and A. Hashim, "A review on internet of things architecture for big data processing", *Iraqi J. Comput. Inform.,* vol. 46, 2020.
[http://dx.doi.org/10.25195/ijci.v46i1.245]

[26] M. Weyrich, and C. Ebert, "Reference architectures for the internet of things", *IEEE Softw.,* vol. 33, no. 1, pp. 112-116, 2016.
[http://dx.doi.org/10.1109/MS.2016.20]

[27] Y. Lu, and J. Cecil, "An internet of things (IoT)-based collaborative framework for advanced manufacturing", *Int. J. Adv. Manuf. Technol.,* vol. 84, no. 5, pp. 1141-1152, 2016.
[http://dx.doi.org/10.1007/s00170-015-7772-0]

[28] A. Krylovskiy, M. Jahn, and E. Patti, "Designing a smart city internet of things platform with microservice architecture", *2015 3rd International Conference on Future Internet of Things and Cloud,* pp. 25-30, 2015.
[http://dx.doi.org/10.1109/FiCloud.2015.55]

[29] B. Javed, M.W. Iqbal, and H. Abbas, "Internet of things (IoT) design considerations for developers and manufacturers", *2017 IEEE International Conference on Communications Workshops (ICC Workshops),* pp. 834-839, 2017.
[http://dx.doi.org/10.1109/ICCW.2017.7962762]

[30] M. Noura, M. Atiquzzaman, and M. Gaedke, "Interoperability in internet of things: Taxonomies and open challenges", *Mob. Netw. Appl.,* vol. 24, no. 3, pp. 796-809, 2019.
[http://dx.doi.org/10.1007/s11036-018-1089-9]

[31] L. Hou, "Internet of things cloud: Architecture and implementation", *IEEE Commun. Mag.,* vol. 54, no. 12, pp. 32-39, 2016.
[http://dx.doi.org/10.1109/MCOM.2016.1600398CM]

[32] I. Yaqoob, "Internet of things architecture: Recent advances, taxonomy, requirements, and open challenges", *IEEE Wirel. Commun.,* vol. 24, no. 3, pp. 10-16, 2017.
[http://dx.doi.org/10.1109/MWC.2017.1600421]

[33] "Why we must get data privacy right", *Cisco Blogs,* 2019. https://blogs.cisco.com/security/why-w--must-get-data-privacy-right (accessed Oct. 21, 2020).

[34] "Worldwide global datasphereiot device and data forecast, 2020–2024", *IDC: The Premier Global Market Intelligence Company.* https://www.idc.com/getdoc.jsp?containerId=US46718220 (accessed Sep. 10, 2020).

[35] I. G. says, "Internet of things (iot) data continues to explode exponentially. who is using that data and how?", *2018.* https://blogs.cisco.com/datacenter/internet-of-things-iot-data-continues-to-explode - exponentially-who-is-using-that-data-and-how (accessed Sep. 10, 2020).

[36] "Investors back IoT startups", *Semiconductor Engineering,* 2018. https://semiengineering.com/investors-back-iot-startups/ (accessed Sep. 09, 2020).

[37] "Artificial intelligence, the next digital frontier, Mckinsey global institute study - odbms.org", http://www.odbms.org/2017/08/artificial-intelligence-the-next-digital-frontier-mckinsey-global-institut e-study/ (accessed Sep. 09, 2020).

[38] "Aws Iot now supports integration with Amazon machine learning and aws cloudtrail", *Amazon Web Services, Inc.* https://aws.amazon.com/about-aws/whats-new/2016/04/aws-iot-now-sup-orts-integration-with-amazon-machine-learning-and-aws-cloudtrail/ (accessed Sep. 09, 2020).

[39] R. Staff, "GE acquires two artificial intelligence startups", *Reuters,* 2016.

[40] "IBM is bringing in watson to conquer the internet of things", *Fortune.* https://fortune.com/2015/12/15/ibm-watson-iot/ (accessed Sep. 09, 2020).

[41] K. McLaughlin, "Microsoft starts selling azure internet-of-things suite, teases new container management tech for enterprises", *CRN,* 2015. https://www.crn.com/news/cloud/300078261/ microsoft-starts-selling-azure-internet-of-things-suite-teases-new-container-management-tech-for - enterprises.htm (accessed Sep. 09, 2020).

[42] "AT&T Labs working to combine drone video footage with artificial intelligence monitoring", *FierceWireless.* https://www.fiercewireless.com/tech/at-t-labs-working-to-combine-dron- -video-footage-artificial-intelligence-monitoring (accessed Sep. 09, 2020).

[43] "DeepMind AI reduces google data centre cooling bill by 40%", *Deepmind.* https:/blog/article/deepmind-ai-reduces-google- data-centre-cooling-bill-40 (accessed Sep. 09, 2020).

[44] " AI on the edge: Fusing artificial intelligence and iot will catalyze new digital value creation", *Gartner.* https://www.gartner.com/en/documents/3738018/ai-on-the-edge-fusing-artificial - intelligence-and-iot-wi (accessed Sep. 09, 2020).

[45] R. Millman, "Shell saves $1 million using IoT", *Internet of Business,* 2016. https://internetofbusiness.com/shell-reportedly-saves-1m-using-iot/ (accessed Sep. 10, 2020).

[46] B. Marr, "How Walmart is using machine learning ai, iot and big data to boost retail performance", *Forbes.* https://www.forbes.com/sites/bernardmarr/2017/08/29/how-walmart-is-using-mac-ine-learning-ai-iot-and-big-data-to-boost-retail-performance/ (accessed Sep. 10, 2020).

CHAPTER 4

IoT Based Energy Conservation of A Smart Home

Somya Goyal[1,*] and **Sudhir K. Sharma**[2]

[1] *Manipal University Jaipur, Jaipur, Rajasthan and Guru Jambheshwar University of Science and Technology, Hisar, India*

[2] *Institute of Information Technology and Management, Janakpuri, New Delhi, India*

Abstract: Smart home is one of the most attractive application of Industry 4.0. This work proposes a smart system to conserve energy in smart home implementation using wireless sensor networks (WSNs). The proposed work is aimed to lessen the immaterial consumption of electricity in a smart home. The home is supplied with Arduino, sensors, and connected WSN. The model observes the movement within the house premises and controls the power cutoff decided by the control center connected *via* WSNs. To detect the motion, passive infrared (PIR) sensors are deployed. As the PIR sensor detects the motion into the room, the lights are automatically turned on and then, if no motion is observed after a threshold time, the lights are automatically switched off. In this manner, the wastage of electricity can be controlled. Experimental results show that the consumption of power can be decreased by at the rate of 40% with the proposed model in comparison to the situation in absence of any such smart control. The validation of proposed model shows that the proposed system is feasible, effective, and not so expensive to implement.

Keywords: Energy conservation, Passive infrared sensor (PIR), Smart homes, Wireless sensor networks (WSNs).

1. INTRODUCTION

A smart home is a term utilized for a home that is outfitted with electrical and electronic gadgets being worked on utilizing distant regulators (smartphones and so on). It utilizes some innovation for checking the atmosphere by means of introducing different sensors in the premises and afterward control the electronic gadgets from the external world. The keen home has additionally alluded as a home robotization framework. It is discovered to be exceptionally successful for rationing energy and can be easily introduced in structures. Considering multifold advantages of remote innovation over wired one, the smart home idea depends on

* **Corresponding author Somya Goyal:** Manipal University Jaipur, Jaipur, Rajasthan and Guru Jambheshwar University of Science and Technology, Hisar, India; Tel: +91-8168361767; E-mail: somyagoyal1988@gmail.com

Sudhir K. Sharma, Bharat Bhushan, Parma N. Astya and Narayan C. Debnath (Eds.)

the WSN. The attraction for home mechanization frameworks in homes and workplaces is consistently expanding. A smart home or computerized home is an extraordinary arrangement in a house in which the electronic gadgets are controlled remotely or automatically with the help of internet connectivity of the gadgets, exceptionally agreeable premise with the arrangement of offices to distantly control the types of gear along with the capacity of gadgets to get balanced without anyone else to explicit circumstances, as appeared in Fig. (**1**).

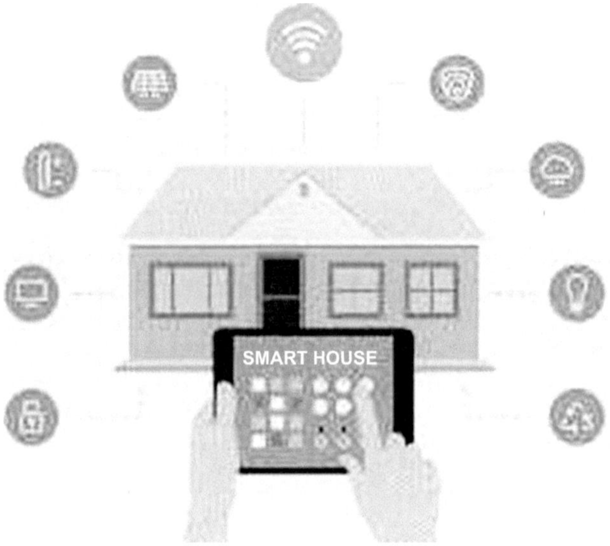

Fig. (1). Smart Home-Controlling all appliances with a single interface.

In 2013, the value of the market business for home automation was approximately US$5.77 billion, and in 2020, it reaches US$12.81 billion [1]. The composition of smart home systems is as follows:

i) Input the readings from the environment *via* sensors – smoke sensors, moisture sensor, temperature sensors, ii) Constant observation and input from the sensor for fire detection, CCTV footage analysis, iii) Automated controlling feature – automated control of lights, fan, A/C, automated water sprinklers in case of fire, fire alarms and iv) AI and Logic – smart security mechanisms.

1.1. Background

IoT is the spine for the home mechanization innovation as these IoT gadgets are basic segments of the smart home idea, which incorporates lighting, heating, and cooling, and security frameworks [2]. One of the significant advantages of such excellent usage of IoT in 'Smart Home' is the energy protection *via* consequently controlling the lights and other electronic apparatuses like turning off the supplies naturally when no one is in the room. Industry 4.0, AI, Cloud computing, and IoT enables the interconnection of devices, vehicles, instruments, allows fabrication of sensors to get readings and the data feed on the sensors is sent *via* a network to the cloud where the AI logic is executed to make smart decisions and automate the control of smart home [3]. IoT enlarged with sensors and actuators, turns into a sort of digital-physical framework, incorporating shrewd homes, keen transportation, and brilliant urban communities.

1.2. Motivation

A home mechanization framework is conveyed to control the lighting, atmosphere, and electrical/electronic machines. It additionally incorporates savvy security like controlling the entrance and disturbing. A smart home associated with the Internet changes the family into IoT gadgets.

1.3. Organization of Chapter

The chapter is composed as follows: Section 2 examines the advantages of Smart Home. Later Section 3 brings a look for energy preservation utilizing Smart Home innovation which is trailed by the conversation of the set of experiences. Section4 depicts the engineering and system for the shrewd home. At that point, Section 5 incorporates the usage with the ZIGBEE standard, and other execution alternatives are likewise talked about here. Segment 6 presents the utilization of IoT for protecting Cultural Heritage (CH). Section 7 finishes up the part with the comments for future investigation.

2. BENEFITS OF SMART HOME

The multi-overlay advantages of Smart Home innovation can be summarized as follows (appeared in Fig. (**2**)):

1. Distantly managing the absolute of your home contraptions from one spot offers comfort and having all the machines related through one interface is an astounding improvement to the degree progression and home affiliation.
2. This creation progress is correspondingly flexible for new contraptions and machines. Sharp home structures are greatly adaptable with the accommodation of new contraptions and other progress.
3. It maximizes home security. when security and surveillance features are laced in your sharp home connection, your home security can take off. Home robotization structures can interface headway finders, surveillance cameras,

modernized passage locks, and other amazing security endeavors all through your home.

4. Smart home increases energy adequacy. Using the skillful home progress astutely, normal parts can be made more energy capable. Like, better controlling over the warming and cooling of your home with a programmable astonishing indoor controllers or lights can change on and off thusly when you go into or leave the room.
5. This movement results in an improved handiness of contraptions as well. Sharp homes can help you with running your devices better. A skilled TV will help you with finding better applications and channels to discover your #1 programming. Everything considered home life ends up being broadly even more fulfilling!

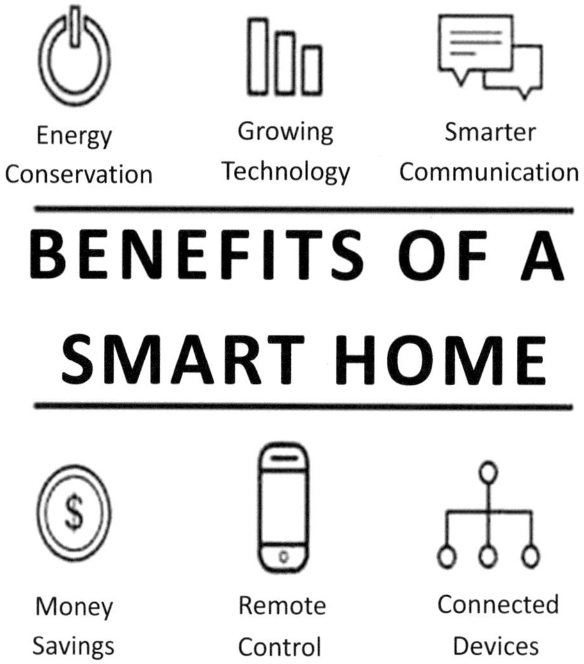

Fig. (2). Benefits of smart home.

3. SMART HOME & ENERGY CONSERVATION

A significant part of savvy home advancements is to decrease the utilization of energy and improve the energy effectiveness in families. A brilliant home gives the adaptability of checking its power utilization and making way of life changes to spare power [5 - 7]. A smart home does not just give advantages of proficient energy to the executives, yet additionally gives advantages, for example, improved way of life, security, and wellbeing. Shrewd metering, machines, and home robotization gadgets are a portion of the numerous advances that can be utilized to change power utilization examples of families.

Shrewd homes and wise structures use energy even more productively in contrast with our customary structure. Conveying brilliant home innovation is proper for decreasing energy utilization. The writing saw the fruitful utilization of remote sensor networks for brilliant home innovation. Truth be told, Wi-Fi is discovered to be more reasonable for distant observing and controlling. The shrewd home executes the knowledge to react to the natural boundaries and human conduct consequently.

The knowledge is to react to the conduct of occupants in the home and make the home agreeable to them. Such mechanization framework is involved sensors thatgather information about the utilization of intensity. These Intelligent Systems are fused with processing offices like by associating with cloud and subsequently, they dissect the gathered information to discover the examples. Based on such examples, the user can be robotized. It straightforwardly adds to diminished expenses and furthermore to the improvement in their expectations for everyday comforts. It covers homegrown applications, yet additionally, open spaces like e-Governance, Health Care, and so on Barely any models incorporate Georgia Tech Aware Home, Place Lab. To date, the brilliant home innovation effectively collected the data and supporting the dynamic to make the way of life more agreeable and more secure for people including the reconnaissance frameworks which catch the climate boundaries and identify the disturbing circumstances (assuming any) and eventually shield the occupants from robberies, burglary and cataclysmic events.

3.1. Glance at the Journey

Significant parts of a brilliant home framework predominantly incorporate (HVAC) warming, ventilation, and cooling, Lighting control, or observation frameworks (including presence reproductions, caution setting off, and clinical alarms). The correspondence norms are X10, Insteon, Zigbee, and Z-Wave. Achievements in till date excursion of 'Savvy Home' are:

- In 1966, the primary 'Home Computer' was planned as an exploratory framework.
- In 1975, X10 was created for the correspondence among viable gadgets distantly utilizing electrical wirings.
- In the 1980's, The Smart House Project was commenced as an undertaking of

the National Research Center of the National Association of Home Builders (NAHB) [8].

- Later, GSM innovation presented which permits remote authority over the home and its apparatuses through PDA or Internet. GSM innovation is valuable for mechanization and security applications.
- Resultantly, three alert frameworks were created utilizing SMS benefits in particular Home Security with Messaging System [9], Security and Control System, and Remote and Security Control by means of SMS [10].
- The framework dependent on GSM innovation [11] is a remote security framework thatcomputerizes family unit machines through SMS.
- nowadays, the structures or homes are intended to be installed with Smart fans which are controlled automatically with the use of sensors, IoT, WSNs, and AI.
- Smart car parking is done with the installed CCTVs. The automated scanning of video footage by AI allows finding the parking space automatically.
- Besides, a smart home system that can control power consumption is capable of distinguishing human traffic and non-living things. It allows reducingconsumption by up to 40%.
- A Smart City is comprised of an interconnected foundation to work in an enhanced way through the correspondence and gathering essential information from the hubs in an association. Adjusted to this idea, the Smart Nation program in Singapore (Spring Singapore, 2015) comprises of different advances to lessen energy utilization all through the country, while observing and gathering information from every single associated buyer, for example, corporate structures and family units (Housing and Development Board, 2014; IDA, 2014).

The plan is to improve the energy effectiveness by proactively and intelligently arranging the 'brilliant urban communities' and coming about into an agreeable and safe climate. Such buildings are given mechanized control to solar energy, water-reusing, LEDs. Information is assembled by utilizing sensors about the trafficbreak down and used to computerize the apparatuses.

3.2. Example: Smart Systems

1. Healthcare - Elderly Alert Systems [11]
2. Home Energy Management System (HEMS) [12]
3. Smart metering system (SESAME) [13]

3.2.1. Healthcare - Elderly Alert Systems

It is a shrewd home well outfitted with a computerized framework, interfacing it to the web and giving medical services offices. The older ready framework causes the family to screen the elderlies by utilizing sensors and movement finders (as in Fig. **3**).

3.2.2. Home Energy Management System (HEMS)

It is a clever framework created (as in Fig. (**4**)) to help mortgage holders to follow the energy utilization and control the apparatuses. EMA Singapore shows that HEMS decreased energy utilization by 20%.

3.2.3. Smart Metering System (SESAME)

The SESAME arrangement is coordinated straightforwardly into the home network and allows the framework to turn on or off apparatuses as appeared in Fig. (**5**). The framework is likewise ready to identify signals from temperature, mugginess, or different sensors, along these lines control apparatuses as indicated by determiningdesign.

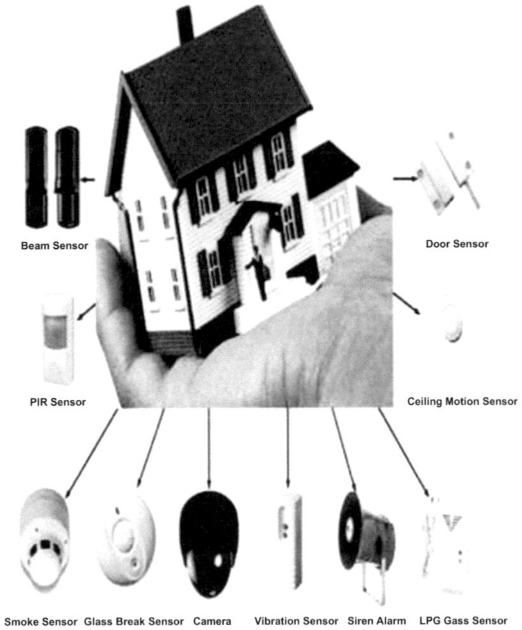

Fig. (3). Elderly alert system.

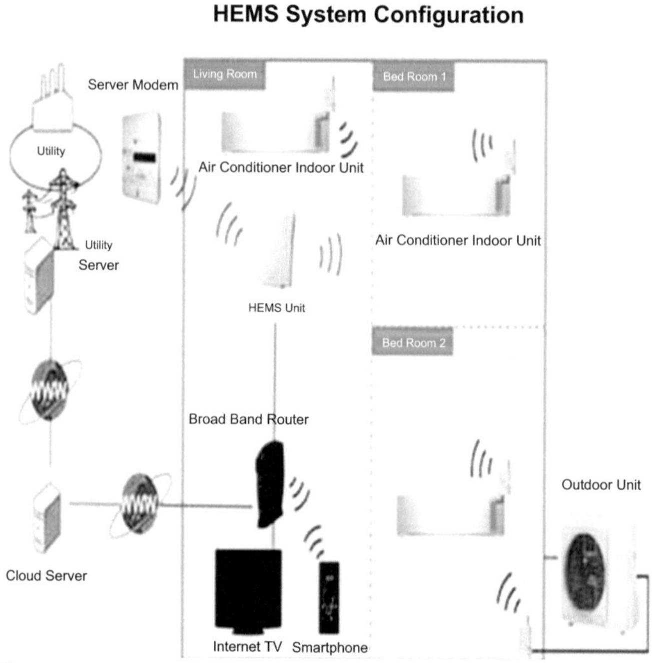

Fig. (4). Sample HEMS system.

The IoT (Internet of Things) concept is the big step towards developing more integrated solutions for smart homes. In nutshell, smart technologies leading to a comfortable and automated environment with afocus on increasing energy efficiency. Smart technologies for reducing energy consumption have an intense effect when integration of Smart Devices, Smart Homes,and Smart Grids takes place [14].

4. ARCHITECTURE & FRAMEWORK FOR SMART HOME ENVIRONMENT

A standard framework is desirable when multiple heterogeneous devices are required to perform jointly in Smart Home Environment (SHE) in a collaborative manner to save energy. Energy-efficient architecture in SHEs is required to analyze the habit patterns and environmental factors to automate smart home appliances. It will bring interoperability among the heterogeneous devices which are developed to work in isolation. This architectural framework is based on the centralized model in Fig. (**6**).

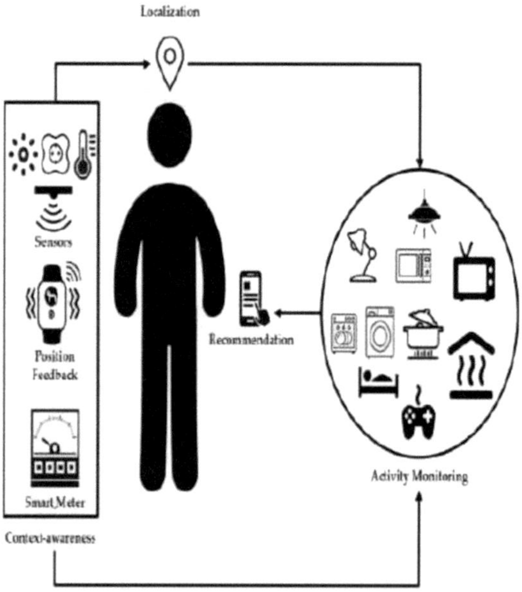

Fig. (5). Sample SESAME system.

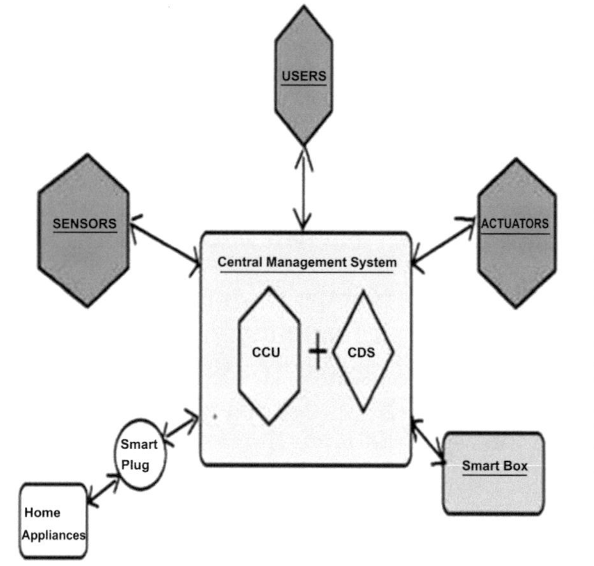

Fig. (6). Smart home environment-architectural framework.

The heart of this centralized framework is the 'Central smart management system'. This Central management system consists of two sub-components - Central Control Unit (CCU) and Central dedicated software (CDS). The CCU is responsible for the data aggregation and decision-making core component. It deals with all entities involved within the system. It is responsible for all real-time information processing and allows decision-making support. It also executes algorithms to forecast energy consumption in SHEs, and also in the reduction of energy consumption, it plays a key role.

The communication among the various components of this architecture is ensured by specific peripheral devices. For example- the communication between CMS and home appliance say refrigerator. Such a specific peripheral is known as a ‘smart plug’. It is so-called as it adds on the intelligence to the ordinary appliance and puts it onto the connected network (Internet). The smart plugs also run energy-controlling tasks on the appliances. It can monitor the energy utilization design alongside the status of the machine. Extra energy-control offices are forced by 'brilliant box'. These are equipped for checking the machines alongside controlling the actuation and de-enactment of the gadgets. This engineering holds a significant component named 'UI' to permit its connection with the clients through committed Web-based applications and additionally versatile applications.

4.1. Data Flow and Management in CMS for SHEs

The engineering incorporates a group of sensors to gather information, shrewd attachments, and keen boxes to run astute rationale. In such a situation, the measure of information and data moving through the framework is colossal and it requires an appropriate information base and the executiveframework to completely misuse the accessible data and interoperability (as in Fig. (7)).

The reason for this information is that the executive framework has to manage the progression of data from the information assortment through information translation to the dynamic. The productive usage of information to help the objective of diminishing the energy utilization and improving the solace level of SHEs is accomplished through data from the board framework. Indeed, from the client's point of view as well, such an administration framework is exceptionally alluring.

The CMS is a Middleware door that gathers the information from Smart Home Environment through association with keen box, brilliant fitting, sensors, actuators, and so on. After the information is gathered, it is kept in the information vault. From this archive, information is brought and handled to decide the enactment/de-initiation of apparatus, evaluate the energy utilization examples of occupants, reconnaissance, and so on.

The information on t he board framework is the cerebrum for the whole design for retaining the data which prompted the general insight of the brilliant homes. The gauging model is likewise imperative to foresee the necessity of energy and consequently naturally booking the energy-productive machines.

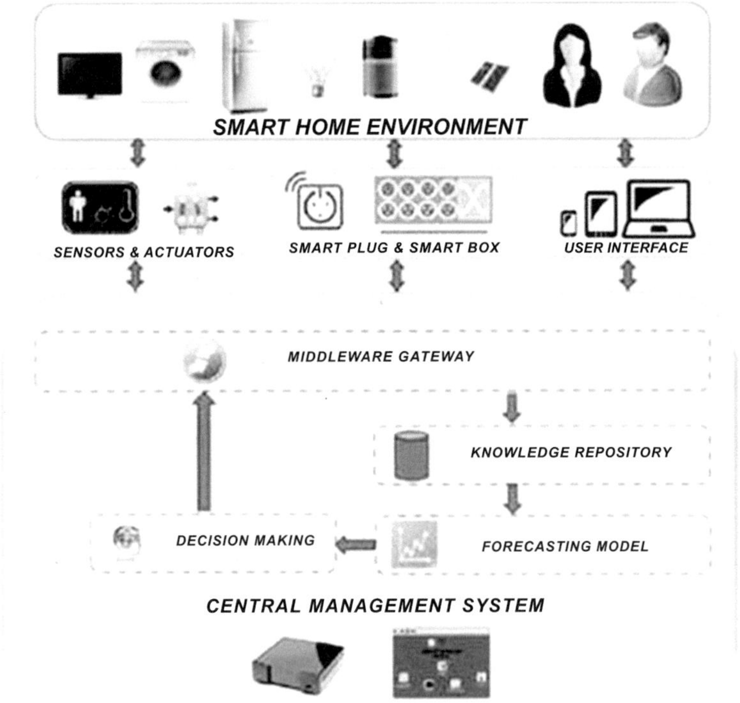

Fig. (7). The flow of information through framework.

The architectural framework and the knowledge management system contribute to energy-efficient smart environment in which heterogeneous multiple devices are interoperated and collaborated to save energy consumption and automate the entire environment to make it automatically customized as per the data collected and interpretations made. This central model is useful and effective in the implementation of SHEs to improve energy efficiency.

5. IMPLEMENTATION OF SMART HOME USING ZIGBEE

This part presents the applications of SHE with Zigbee. The goal is to give energy to the executives in a brilliant home with ease. It gives the far-off administration and control of the family machines. It helps in ceaseless and steady observing of homes from distant areas through IoT to decrease energy utilization. It permits rescheduling the occupant's working time according to the energy request. It includes a PIR sensor to computerize the actuation/de-initiation of lights naturally to moderate the energy.

5.1. Smart Home Control System

The framework includes 3 significant modules: the Data assortment module, the Communication module, and the Device Controlling module, as shown in Fig. (**8**).

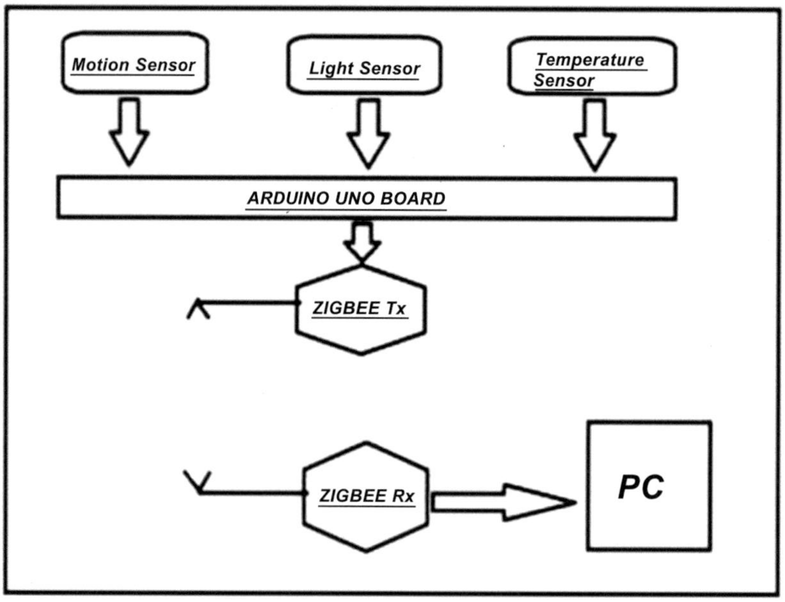

Fig. (8). Implementation for smart home.

Information assortment is executed by means of Wireless Sensor Networks. The collected information acquired with the assistance of Arduino Uno, is shipped off the administration station by means of a Zigbee handset.

The administration module deciphers the assembled information to check the status of home machines, it screens and computerizes them according to prerequisites or the ecological components.

Notwithstanding controlling the machines according to the information accumulated and design watched, this usage introduces a movement sensor, for example, the PIR sensor- Passive Infrared Sensor. It is proficient to detect the presence of humans inside the room and as indicated by that, it naturally turns the light and fan ON. At the point when a human leaves the room, its faculties and turn the light and fan OFF consequently. Further, the Light Sensor, LDR is associated with the sense of sunshine and murkiness to mechanize the brightening. A temperature sensor is used to detect the temperature information, to robotize the turning ON/OFF of the fan. This execution utilizes 3 sensors to detect the presence of any human and the state of need of light and fan. In view of the information gathered, sent by means of Arduino to the focal regulator (PC), initiation/de-actuation is controlled distantly.

5.2. Two Major Functions

5.2.1. Framework Controlling Lights

This framework performs two functions- 1) detection of availability of light in the room and 2) movement of human as some activity in the room. To achieve these functions, light-dependent resistors (LDR) and PIR sensors are embedded in the system respectively (shown in Fig. (**9**)). This control framework automatically turns the lights on depending upon the situation of non-availability of light and movement by humans and vice versa. In this way, as per the need for lights in the room, this control executes automated switching on or off the lights.

5.2.2. Framework Controlling Fan

This framework performs two functions- 1) detection of the temperature of the room and 2) detection of movement in the room by some humans. To perform these two functions, it utilizes a sensor to sense the temperature readings and a PIR sensor to detect movement. It turns the fans on in the situation when the temperature is high and there is some movement in the room and vice-versa. This automated control is capable to handle the over-consumption of energy specifically the wastage of energy.

The entire system is dedicated to automating the switching on the light/fan as per the requirement. It instantly switches off the devices as they are no longer needed. Hence, the wastage of energy meanwhile is minimized.

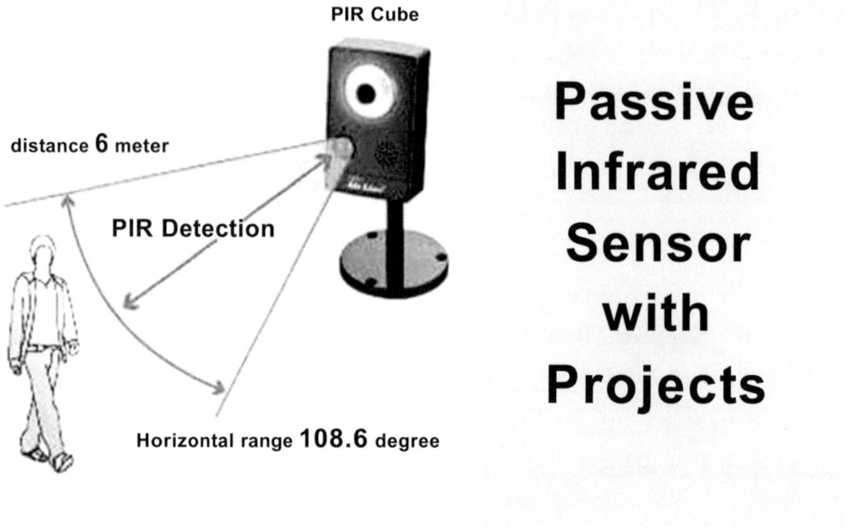

Fig. (9). PIR sensor detection.

This section practically presented the implementation of automated illumination of light for smart homes employing the WSN to sense the data. It exploits the benefits of WSNs and Passive infrared sensors. It reduces energy consumption by cutting out the avoidable wastage of energy. It is a scalable implementation as it can be easily scaled up to and can be applied to intelligent buildings [16].

6. CONSERVATION OF CULTURAL HERITAGE-APPLICATION OF ENERGY CONSERVATION IOT

Cultural Heritage depicts the native cultures of countries and regions which are represented by either the artworks or linguistics or the architectural property. CH is to be preserved for the forthcoming generations because it carries the inherent properties, values, morals, and character from one generation to another. In case, it is damaged, it could cause severe loss which is not repairable. CH is a huge resource as it attracts tourists as per the artefacts and native culture. The motivation for selecting a specific destination for tourism is the inherent property in terms of the artistic and cultural heritage including the monuments, museums, exhibitions, historical villages, and others. The conservation of this artwork is a concern of special attention as time causes the natural deterioration of the heritage, against which CH is needed to be preserved. As time passes, external factors as climate, human, weather conditions, and internal causes like the material affect the heritage adversely and cause damage.

The goal is to implement the IoT concept with the intent of preserving the CH by providing a stable environment under the full control of administrative authorities. The controlled scenario is to be implemented with a smart home concept. It provides constant monitoring and regularization of the environment in which the heritage is preserved.

The stable atmospheres which are under full control are necessary for some buildings or monuments or artefacts that are prone to oxidation or which are light sensitive.

Such a controlled environment is established by appropriate monitoring and control of climate including temperature and moisture. Such a climate control system requires sensors to record the data about the climatic conditions and a microcontroller to control the conditions in the surroundings of the artefacts. This is achieved with the help of IoT architecture that helps to assess the damaging risks of artworks. Such kind of network arrangements are helpful for regular checks and the cumulative data record allows to predict and handle the accidents. The remote monitoring and online control protect and safeguard the artworks. It reduces the risk of vandalism, robbery, or accidental damages.

IoT dealing with CH involves the artwork as the "thing" to be preserved. The very first step is to install the sensor nodes to collect real-time data and gateways to transfer the data to the cloud. The entire setup allows online, real-time, constant monitoring and supervision of the specific CH. Cloud provides easy access to the collected and analyzed data, improving the safety of that artwork.

The collected information *via* sensors is worthy for curators and authorities to find out the most dangerous risk and their factors. After, locating the riskiest deteriorating situation, strategic planning can be made, and follow-up actions are implemented. UPV already launched a multidisciplinary project for preserving CH using IoT. It comprises experts from art restoration, climate monitoring, statistics, wireless communications, cloud engineers, *etc* [17 - 19].

For a specific project, following the requirement statement for conserving a particular CH, the very first step is to design the specific nodes for data transmission that must be capable to monitor the climate with minimum maintenance, as shown in Fig. (**10**). Designing the appropriate nodes in the IoT implementation is the most crucial issue. It covers minimizing the power consumption by considering the communication distances.

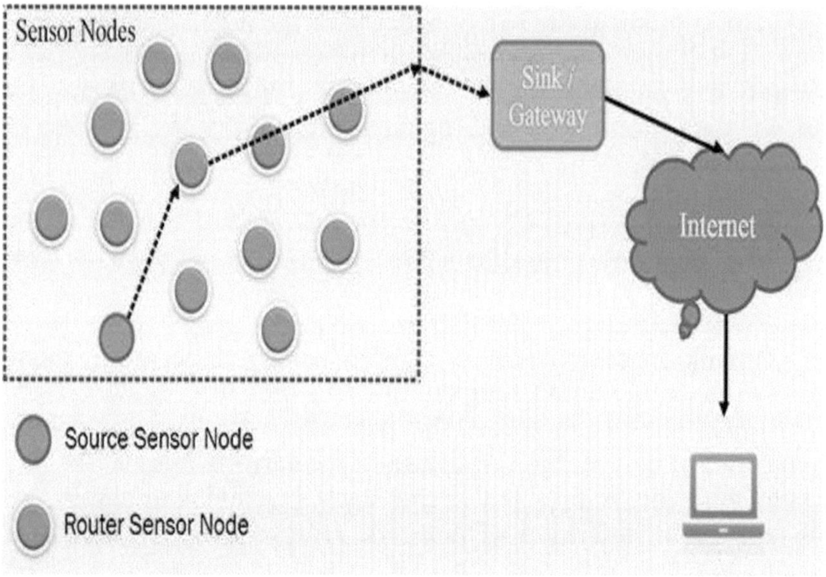

Fig. (10). IoT design with sensors and gateways.

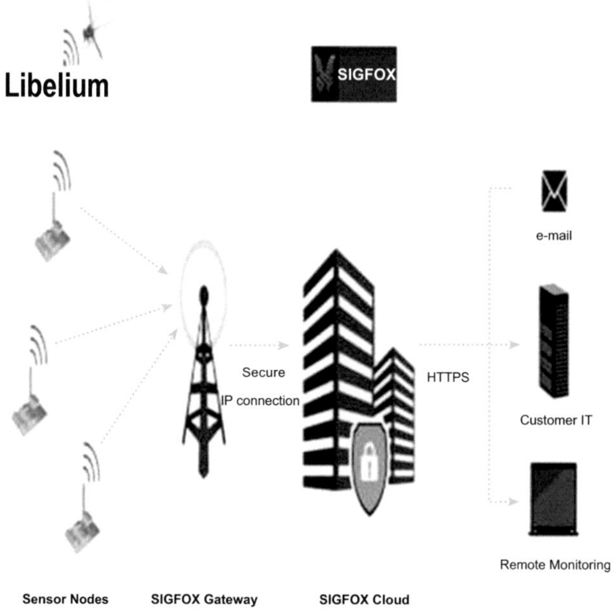

Fig. (11). Sigfox implementation sample.

To date, no ideal usage has been made, yet the correlation with effectively actualized principles can be made. New usage can be improved by making a correlation with previously existing arrangements. Two marked names in these fields are-LoRa [20] and Sigfox [21].

LoRa and Sigfox are business plans for executing WAN [22], as shown in Fig. (**11**), with low force utilization working with sensors. An assortment of hubs is assessed in various conditions for saving the CH. Thinking about the assortment of fine arts, the tricky issues emerging with respect to the force flexibly and Internet associations are various. For instance, the showcase of craftsmanship might be in the gallery or might be in the city. Numerous destinations exist without power flexibly [23] (archeological exhuming, disconnected church, and so on), as shown in Fig. (**12**).

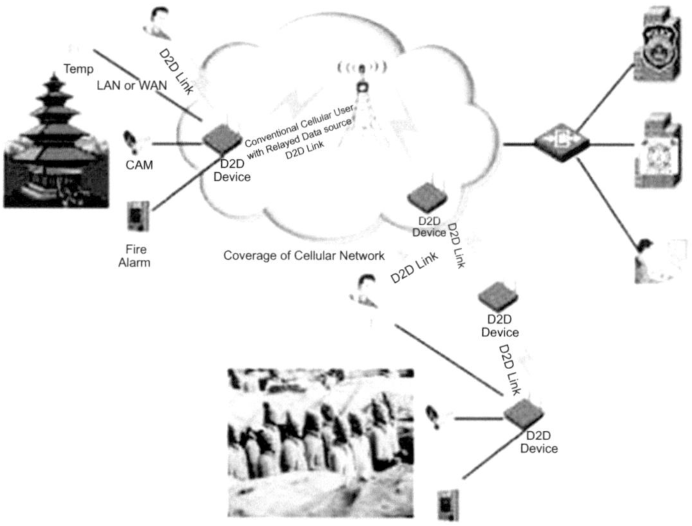

Fig. (12). Preserving CH with different situations.

CONCLUSION AND FUTURE SCOPE

This chapter has assessed the force necessities of the hubs for a standard observing issue of air, temperature, and stickiness. The outcomes recommend that it is conceivable to make a hub with a life expectancy of over 10 years utilizing standard batteries. This work planned a suitable cloud framework to manage CH observing necessities. This work introduced IoT engineering for this reason. The necessities from the craftsmanship stance, information obtaining, Cloud preparing, and information perception to the end client are given. The outcomes introduced in this work centers around the most basic part of the engineering, which are the sensor hubs. An answer dependent on LoRa and Sigfox advances is conceived to create the base effect in the craftsmanship, accomplishing a life expectancy of over 10 years. The arrangement will be fit for scaling the preparing and capacity assets, sent either in a public or on-premise cloud, inserting complex prescient models. This blend of advancements can adapt to various kinds of social legacy conditions in the future. In the future, Machine learning and IoT [24, 25] can be blended to automate decision-making. Classification techniques [26, 27, 28] can be incorporated to extend this current project.

CONSENT FOR PUBLICATION

Not applicable.

CONFLICT OF INTEREST

The author declares no conflict of interest, financial or otherwise.

ACKNOWLEDGEMENTS

Declared none.

REFERENCES

[1] "Research and markets: Global home automation and control market 2014- 2020 - lighting control, security & access control, hvac control analysis of the $5.77 billion Industry", *Reuters,* 2019. Archived from the original on 2016-05-05

[2] O. Hamdan, H. Shanableh, I. Zaki, Al-Ali A. R., and Tamer Shanableh, "IoT-based interactive dual mode smart home automation", *2019 IEEE International Conference on Consumer Electronics (ICCE),* IEEE: Las Vegas, pp. 1-2, 2019.

[3] N. Zhu, A. Anagnostopoulos, and I. Chatzigiannakis, "On mining Iot data for evaluating the operation of public educational buildings", *Pervasive Computing and Communications Workshops (PerCom Workshops) 2018 IEEE International Conference,* pp. 278-283. [http://dx.doi.org/10.1109/PERCOMW.2018.8480226]

[4] M. Prathik, K. Anitha, and V. Anitha, "Smart energy meter surveillance using IoT", *2018 International Conference on Power, Energy, Control and Transmission Systems (ICPECTS),* pp. 186-189, 2018. [http://dx.doi.org/10.1109/ICPECTS.2018.8521650]

[5] S. Karthikeyan, and P.T.V. Bhuvaneswari, *"IoT based real-time residential energy meter monitoring system," 2017 Trends in Industrial Measurement and Automation.* TIMA: Chennai, 2017, pp. 1-5.

[6] E.N. Mustapha Hafiz Bola, "An efficient energy management in buildings using iot – a survey", *Electronics Computer and Computation (ICECCO) 2019 15th International Conference on,* pp. 1-6, 2019.

[7] M.Q. Aldossari, and A. Sidorova, "Consumer acceptance of Internet of Things (IoT): smart home context", *J. Comput. Inf. Syst.,* pp. 1-11, 2018. [http://dx.doi.org/10.1080/08874417.2018.1543000]

[8] C. Sarode, "Intelligent home monitoring system", *International Journal of Engineering Research and Applications (IJERA) ISSN: 2248-9622,* vol. 3, no. 1, pp. 1446-1450, 2013.

[9] A.M. Zungeru, U.V. Edu, and A.J. Garba, "Design and implementation of a short message

servicebased remote controller", *Computer Engineering and Intelligent Systems ISSN 2222-1719 (Paper) ISSN 2222-2863 (Online),* vol. 3, no. 4, 2012.

[10] G. Raghavendran, "Sms based wirelss home appliance control system", In: *2011 International Conference on Life Science and Technology IPCBEE* vol. 3. IACSIT Press: Singapore, 2011.

[11] H.S. Chetana Sarode, "Intelligent home monitoring system", *International Journal of Engineering Research and Applications (IJERA) ISSN: 2248-9622,* vol. 3, no. 1, pp. 1446-1450, 2013.

[12] S. Agarwal, R. Satyanarain, T.F. Sing, and D. Vollmer, "Effects of construction activities on residential electricity consumption: evidence from Singapore's public housing estates", *Energy Econ.,* 2016.
[http://dx.doi.org/10.1016/j.eneco.2016.01.010]

[13] A. Fensel, V. Kumar, and S.D.K. Tomic, "End-user interfaces energy- efficient semantically enabled smart homes", *Energy Effic.,* vol. 7, no. 4, pp. 655-675, 2014.
[http://dx.doi.org/10.1007/s12053-013-9246-2]

[14] P. Hamernik, and P. Tanuska, "Classification of functions in smart home", *Int. J. Inf. Educ. Technol.,* vol. 2, no. 2, pp. 149-155, 2012.
[http://dx.doi.org/10.7763/IJIET.2012.V2.98]

[15] C. Molitor, "—Multiphysics test bed for renewable energy systems in smart homes,‖", *IEEE Trans. Ind. Electron.,* vol. 60, no. 3, pp. 1235-1248, 2013.
[http://dx.doi.org/10.1109/TIE.2012.2190254]

[16] D.M. Han, and J.H. Lim, "—Smart home energy management system using IEEE 802.15.4 and Zigbee,‖", *IEEE Trans. Consum. Electron.,* vol. 56, no. 3, pp. 1403-1410, 2010.
[http://dx.doi.org/10.1109/TCE.2010.5606276]

[17] D. Camuffo, *Microclimate for Cultural Heritage.* Elsevier, 1998.

[18] P. Merello, F-J. García-Diego, and M. Zarzo, "Microclimate monitoring of Ariadne's house (Pompeii, Italy) for preventive conservation of fresco paintings", *Chem. Cent. J.,* vol. 6, no. 1, p. 145, 2012.
[http://dx.doi.org/10.1186/1752-153X-6-145] [PMID: 23190798]

[19] P. Merello, F-J. García-Diego, and M. Zarzo, "Evaluation of corrective measures implemented for the preventive conservation of fresco paintings in Ariadne's house (Pompeii, Italy)", *Chem. Cent. J.,* vol. 7, no. 1, p. 87, 2013.
[http://dx.doi.org/10.1186/1752-153X-7-87] [PMID: 23683173]

[20] LoRa, *Lora Alliance,* 2017. https://www.lora-alliance.org/

[21] S.I.G.F.O.X. Sigfox, *The Global Communications Service Provider For The Internet Of Things (Iot),* 2017. https://www.sigfox.com/en

[22] F-J. García-Diego, E. Verticchio, P. Beltrán, and A.M. Siani, "Assessment of the minimum sampling frequency to avoid measurement redundancy in microclimate field surveys in museum buildings", *Sensors (Basel),* vol. 16, no. 8, p. E1291, 2016.
[http://dx.doi.org/10.3390/s16081291] [PMID: 27537886]

[23] B.L.R. Stojkoska, and K.V. Trivodaliev, "A review of internet of things for smart home: Challenges and solutions", *J. Clean. Prod.,* vol. 140, pp. 1454-1464, 2017.
[http://dx.doi.org/10.1016/j.jclepro.2016.10.006]

[24] S. Goyal, A. Parashar, and A. Shrotriya, *Advances in Parallel Computing Series,* vol. 29, pp. 236-266, 2018.
[http://dx.doi.org/10.3233/978-1-61499-814-3-236]

[25] S. Goyal, P.K. Bhatia, and A. Parashar, *Cloud-Assisted IoT-Enabled Smoke Monitoring System (e-Nose) Using Machine Learning Techniques. Smart Systems and IoT: Innovations in Computing. Smart Innovation, Systems and Technologies.* vol. Vol. 141. Springer: Singapore, 2020, pp. 743-754.

[26] S. Goyal, and P.K. Bhatia, "Comparison of machine learning techniques for software quality

prediction", *International Journal of Knowledge and Systems Science (IJKSS),* vol. 11, IGI Global, no. 2, pp. 21-40, 2020. [http://dx.doi.org/10.4018/IJKSS.2020040102]

[27] S. Goyal, and P.K. Bhatia, *Software Quality Prediction Using Machine Learning Techniques. Innovations in Computational Intelligence and Computer Vision. Advances in Intelligent Systems and Computing.* vol. 1189. Springer: Singapore, 2021, pp. 551-560.

[28] S. Goyal, "Heterogeneous stacked ensemble classifier for software defect prediction", *2020 Sixth International Conference on Parallel, Distributed and Grid Computing (PDGC),* pp. 126-130, 2020. [http://dx.doi.org/10.1109/PDGC50313.2020.9315754]

CHAPTER 5

Blockchain: Concept and Emergence

Shazmeen Shamsi[1], Mohd. M. Haque[2], Sushil Kumar[3], Jawed Ahmed[4] and **Mohammad Sufian Badar[4,5,*]**

[1] *Department of Computer Science, Jamia Millia Islamia, New Delhi, India*

[2] *School of Computer and Systems Sciences, Jawaharlal Nehru University, New Delhi, India*

[3] *Department of Computer Science, Jamia Hamdard University, New Delhi, India*

[4] *Department of Bioengineering, University of California, Riverside, CA, USA*

[5] *Salfia Paramedical Institute Darbhanga, SPI Darbhanga, Bihar 846001, India*

Abstract: Artificial Intelligence (AI), Machine Learning (ML), and Internet of Things (IoT) are incredible instances of the technology paradigm and have brought about revolutionary changes in the communication, internet, and digital sectors coalesced into one and induced a landslide shift in the lifestyle of mankind. But the privacy concerns of the individuals can be trustfully and transparently addressed only by the use of ingenious contemporary technology, the Blockchain. Blockchain is a kind of distributed ledger technology that uses a peer-to-peer, distributed network to make a continuous, growing chain of time-stamped records to form a digital ledger. It is decentralized, which means that it can not be controlled by a central authority. It has numerous advantages like transparency, immutability, decentralization and can be incorporated in almost any sector of the society to increase the security of the transactions being carried out. This chapter predominantly focuses on the concepts of Blockchain and aims to do a comprehensive survey on its advantages and applications and also highlights the future prospects because even though it is so popular today, this technology is still in its infancy.

Keywords: AI, Artificial Intelligence, Blockchain, Decentralization, Distributed Ledger Technology, Immutability, Internet of Things, IoT, ML, Machine learning, Transparency.

1. INTRODUCTION

"The blockchain revolution has a greater potential than anything we've seen in history. It's bigger than the Internet revolution, how it's going to restructure society."

—Patrick Byrne

* **Corresponding author Mohammad Sufian Badar:** Department of Bioengineering, University of California, Riverside, CA, USA; Tel: +13182783121; E-mails: msbadar@engr.ucr.edu, director_academic@salfiainstitute.edu.in

Sudhir K. Sharma, Bharat Bhushan, Parma N. Astya and Narayan C. Debnath (Eds.)

The above remark made by Patrick Byrne, CEO and founder of Overstock.com, is as apt as it can be. Today, Blockchain technology is taking the globe by storm. The enormous amount of buzz and hype that this technology has created is attracting the attention of a massive number of researchers and scientists and will eventually create the dawn of a new revolution. This chapter aims to provide a brief but clear understanding of the important aspects of this technology among the readers.

The ultimate objective of mankind is the absolute modernization of his lifestyle for attaining the highest levels of comfort. This can practically be achieved only with the development and evolution of science and technology, which eventually gives us a plethora of immensely useful applications that make life easy for us. We are currently living in an era where the world is changing at a rapid pace, and there is a constant shift of the common mass towards contemporary technologies. These innovations have affected every industry, be it business, healthcare, energy, financial markets, and so on, to the extent that in recent times, these technologies have reached the comfort of our homes and affected the way we live and socialize [1]. In this world powered by technology, everything comes at a cost We are living in times where we are experiencing a gradual transition from cash to cashless payments. Electronic Cash or E-Cash, the digital form of cash, is allowing easy and hassle-free transactions of money over the internet. This invention is in and of itself a commendable achievement that has caused a stir in the world of trade and commerce, and the immense importance of which can be understood during pandemics like Covid-19. But cybercrooks, with their felonious talents, are ever-ready to make some profit by breaching data of the transactions being carried out. Secure online transactions that involve third parties also cannot always be trusted. Let alone cybercriminals and private third parties, it has often been seen that the economic growth and development of most of the developing countries is often impeded by corrupt government officials who misuse their authority to satisfy their greed for monetary gains. Blockchain technology, which first came into the picture with the advent of Bitcoin in 2008 [2], promises decentralized and secure transactions over the internet and is a successful attempt to solve these problems.

Blockchain is a magical technology that can be clubbed with almost all other technologies available today to add to their benefits and make them safe and secure for use. It is a Distributed Ledger Technology that records and maintains transactions chronologically, occurring on a peer-to-peer scale where every peer essentially maintains a copy of the transactions being carried out. An important point to be noted is that 'no third party is involved' and validation of new blocks to be added to the chain occurs only if at least 51% of the participants vote in favor, otherwise it is rejected. Now you must be wondering, what are blocks?

They can simply be understood as pages of a record book that constantly register the latest transaction being carried out. Once a block runs out of memory (think of it as a page being filled with records), a new block is needed to be generated for which voting is done for its final validation and generation.

Blockchain is a revolutionary technology that came into practical existence with the advent of the cryptocurrency, Bitcoins, which caused a lot of excitement among the people and has intrigued researchers to study it thoroughly. Learning about it would help us remain updated with the most demanding skills of today. The true potential of this revolutionary technology needs to be understood by all so that we can make its best use. It is expected to re-shape the industrial trends and cause a transition from paper-based/non-secure online transactions to secure, privacy-preserving, immutable e-transactions.

This chapter will give you a basic idea of Blockchain Technology. Each topic is explained in a detailed but crisp manner. The authors have tried to make the chapter more interesting by incorporating a hands-on activity about the deployment of smart contracts to attract the interest in this topic of the readers. It is hoped to generate a clear understanding among the readers about this incredible technology which is way ahead of its time.

In the following chapter, we will first study how the need for this technology arose, followed by its history. We will then be introduced to the different elements that are essentially a part of every blockchain network. We will then learn about its features owing to which this technology has become immensely important in today's world. Next, we will study the types, working, applications, advantages, and challenges related to this topic.

2. THE NEED FOR BLOCKCHAIN TECHNOLOGY

The need for this technology arose with the International Banking Crisis which led to the collapse of investment in 2008. Bitcoin cryptocurrency, which was the first practical example of this technology, brings along with it many advantages such as efficiency, cost-effectiveness, reliability, and a privacy-preserving secure system for creating and recording financial transactions. With an ever-increasing human population and urbanization, the number of transactions being carried out is increasing exponentially and is speculated to affect the complexity, efficiency, and cost of the current systems and in turn, increase its vulnerability [3]. The current digital transactions rely on trusted third parties to fulfill their objectives. Whether these parties can be trusted or not is a big question. Though these third parties which can be anyone- a Government Agency or a private owner- claim that the transactions are carried out in a secure environment, is it so? Studies have shown that even though a few central authorities follow strict protocols to preserve the privacy and security of transactions to the extent that they provide certificates of assurance, these technologies are not foolproof. For example, SSL certificates that ensure us that we are on a secure website have also been stolen from few very well-known domains of Microsoft, Twitter, Facebook, and Central Intelligence Agency (CIA), UK.

Also, in today's world where everything is done at the click of a mouse, we need a technology that is efficient, fast, and at the same time affordable. Blockchain is the perfect solution to this. People don't need to pay money to any third party, like a bank or a private organization, to maintain their records as digital ledgers which can be monitored with ease and precision owing to the peer-to-peer, distributed, and decentralized nature of the Blockchain architecture. The world needs a technology like Blockchain which provides a safe and secure platform for carrying out the transactions, complete ownership and authority over one's property, and also transparent transactions to be carried out. The data once stored on the network cannot be changed or deleted because of its immutability. This is an immensely important feature that can be used to store extremely important and private data on the system. This technology also addresses another very important issue- the problem of Double-Spending. Since the records are maintained strictly chronologically, one can easily keep a track of the money spent and avoid the problem and loss caused by double-spending [4]. Having understood its need, let us now learn about this technology in detail.

3. HISTORY AND EVOLUTION

This topic first came into existence on 31st October 2008, when Satoshi Nakamoto's white paper "Bitcoin: A Peer-to-Peer Electronic Cash System" was released [2]. The paper discussed a "peer-to-peer version of electronic cash", which allowed online payments to be sent directly from one party to the other without involving a bank or any other financial institution. This discussion is incomplete without mentioning Bitcoins. Bitcoin is the first practical example of Blockchain technology, that came into existence in 2009 and is the first-ever cryptocurrency to be developed and is the most popular example of this technology. It is an innovative method of payment that has introduced virtual cash and is one of its kind. Considering its design, it only allows the exchange and distribution of digital information and bars its modification. You must remember that Blockchain and Bitcoin are not the same things. Blockchain is the technology used for the creation of the digital currency, Bitcoin. Let us understand this with the help of an example. A mobile phone is just a small metallic object without an Operating System (OS). OS adds life to the phone and is simply software that manages the tasks and its worth can only be understood by the applications it can host. Considering this example, a Blockchain is analogous to the Operating System and Bitcoins to the applications it holds.

To date, three generations of Blockchain have emerged and the fourth one is under evolution. Let's quickly discuss the generations in brief:

3.1. First Generation/ Blockchain 1.0

They were simple ledgers that recorded transactions and were built to improve the existing monetary system. Examples of first-generation cryptocurrencies include Bitcoin, Litecoin, *etc.* All these cryptocurrencies are written using C++ and consider the Bitcoin source code as their basis. Also, they use the Proof-of-Work Mechanism which makes these networks pretty costly because the mining involved here requires a lot of electricity.

3.2. Second Generation/ Blockchain 2.0

It emerged in 2015 with the advent of Ethereum which has much wider functionalities. The most important feature that was added in this generation is the Smart Contracts that make the transactions secure by allowing the automatic execution of all conditions. It is written using Solidity programming language and suffers from the problem of scalability.

3.3. Third Generation/ Blockchain 3.0

It comes with more advantages, like better design and wider functionality, and has tried to address the issue of scalability. Some examples are Cardano, Nano, *etc.* Instead of Proof-of-Work, it incorporates the Proof-Of-Stake consensus mechanism.

3.4. Fourth Generation/ Blockchain 4.0

It has yet to come into existence but it is expected that this generation will evolve when Artificial Intelligence will meet this technology. Keeping in mind the fast pace of research and the growing interest of scientists, it seems that that day is not far when Blockchain 4.0 will become a reality.

4. PREFATORY ELEMENTS

This section introduces you to the generic elements of Blockchain technology.

4.1. Transaction

A transaction can be defined as an agreement between a supplier and a consumer that there will be an exchange of assets either in the present or in the future. It is the fundamental unit of Blockchain and represents exchange by transfer of values from one participant to another [5]. A transaction includes the recipient, signature identifying the sender, amount of cryptocurrency being used for the transaction to be brought into action, gas price (cost paid by the sender per computational step), and the gas limit (maximum number of steps a transaction is supposed to be executed in). In technical terms, the transaction can be defined as the product of gas price and the amount of gas used.

4.2. Node

The term node refers to the user or participant who is a part of the Blockchain platform. They form the building blocks of the Blockchain Infrastructure. When an attempt to add a new block to the chain is made, it is reflected on all the nodes in the system, and depending upon how authentic a transaction is, the nodes can together accept or reject the proposal. Nodes can either be online or offline. Online nodes are active participants in the network while offline modes need to catch up with the latest advances by downloading the new blocks that were added when they were in offline conditions. The process of updating the offline blocks is known as synchronization.

4.3. Mining

It is the process of adding transactions to the distributed public ledger technology, blockchain, and it is this process that facilitates the safe exchange of assets in the network. Miners are the nodes that are capable of mining. They have to solve a cryptographic puzzle for the creation of valid blocks and the miner who solves the puzzle first gets to add a block to the networked chain. They broadcast their block on the network which then requires verification from all the nodes in the network irrespective of whether they are simple nodes or miners. If the block is voted to be valid following the consensus mechanisms (which is explained in Section 4.7 of this Chapter), the block is added to the chain, otherwise, it is rejected.

4.4. Block

A 'block' can simply be defined as a collection of transactions that are bundled together logically. It is these blocks that are chained together to form Blockchain technology.

Structurally, a block consists of a block header and a block body [6]. The block header includes the Block Version, Merkle Tree Root Hash, Hash of parent block, Time Stamp, nBits, Nonce (Number used only once), and the Block Body includes all the transactions carried out in that block. Block Header includes the block metadata which can be visualized in Fig. (**1**) and better understood from the list that follows:

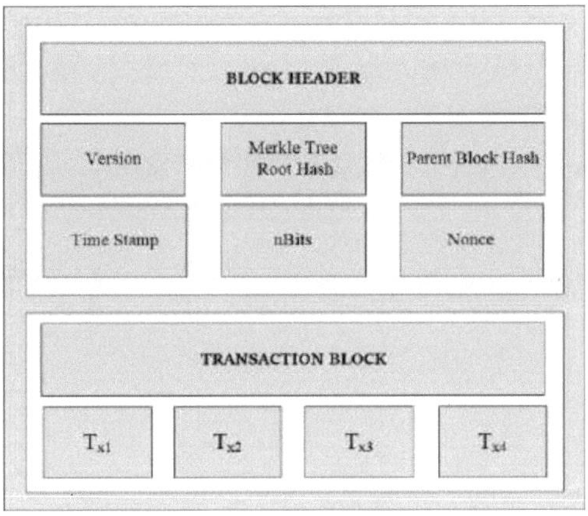

Fig. (1). Structure of a Block.

- Block version – It refers to the current version of the block structure.
- Merkle Tree Root Hash - A cryptographic hash of all of the transactions that a block contains.
- Hash of parent block – The hash value of the preceding/parent block, which is always linked to the succeeding/child block.
- Time Stamp - The exact time at which a block was created.
- nBits – It refers to the target, *i.e.*, the threshold value below which a block header hash must be for a block to be valid.
- Nonce ("number used once") - A random value that is added to a hashed block which, when re-hashed, matched the difficult restrictions.

Each block in the Blockchain is linked to two other blocks- one, its parent block, and two, its child block. It is to be remembered that there can only be one parent to a child block and a single child to a parent block as shown in Fig. (**2**).

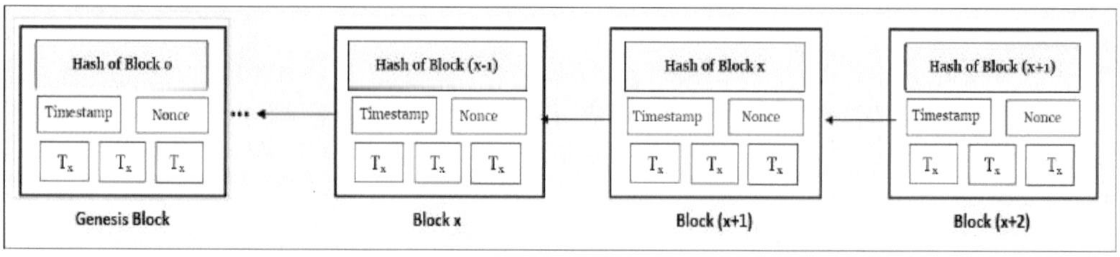

Fig. (2). How different blocks are linked together.

The first block to be added to a Blockchain network is known as "Genesis Block".

Types of Blocks:

- Main branch Blocks- They extend the longest chain in the network, *i.e.*, the main blockchain.
- Side Branch Blocks- Though they are currently not present practically, they are expected to be incorporated as a part of the main branch in a side chain soon, due to the growth of transaction rate.
- Orphan Blocks- Those blocks that point to a parent block that is unknown to the node processing it.

4.5. Hashing

Hashing is the process by which input of simple integers and strings is converted into a complicated, non-decipherable encrypted output using complex mathematical algorithms. Hashes of any length of input always give a fixed length of output and this makes it practically impossible to guess the original word. It is a 'one-way function' and can not be cracked. So how does it help in checking the authenticity of a message? Let's understand this with the help of an example. Suppose you want to download some important official document that is highly confidential. For this purpose, you will need a hash of the document and the digital signature of the sender which in turn is also hashed. The document message is encrypted and made it impossible to decipher using hashing algorithms. They act as a trap-door function that prevents it from being traced. The receiver decrypts the message using the same hashing function and signature and compares the two hash values. If the same hash value is produced, it can be said that the document and signature are both authentic. There are many algorithms available for this purpose, like different versions of the Secure Hashing Algorithm (SHA) – SHA1, SHA 224, SHA256, SHA512, *etc.*, Message Digest Algorithm (MD) – MD2, MD4, MD5, Keccak – Keccak-256, Keccak 512, *etc.*, Shake(Secure Hash Algorithm and KECCAK) with versions 128 and 256. Shake is different in the sense that it produces any length of the output.

Let us see how each of these algorithms produces different outputs for the same word. Suppose the word is "Abracadabra", the following Table **1** shows its corresponding hash value using a few of the many different algorithms available.

Table 1. Showing the different hash values produced using different hashing algorithms for the same message.

Algorithm Used	Message hash for "Abracadabra"
SHA256	46abe7c8d7f5033272383a4a2483ca72ca35c6bf7d8b4b9d60eee94fd7aebce2
SHA512	e31635ff8390c8df27ea5ecd810a73c92ba62a399fafe52b78467abf21d9e4adaf833 31238905f491bdcc1d7bfddf4d89074b4599638d4504c4eedfde45c62a9
MD5	53a5e9533a3a2dd2685f4f112b82379a
Keccak-256	cdbeda58b615b3bbdc510ac7b6aa14e618709a6c994e062e5e34e37e5992ab7a
Shake-256	abb7c5ab0ddcc178933e95cd40466fd2f6f7190ad1bdcb72e59e8fe447972f94da72 7056749cc535d94fead6a0ba697184427fd1fcf31ed5ef65e927ef943d00

The hash value for two messages will always be different. Therefore, hashing safeguards the privacy of the participants by ensuring secure transmission of the message intended for a particular recipient only.

4.6. Digital Signatures

The data to be transacted has to be secured using digital signatures which ensure that the data is not meddled with. The purpose of using digital signatures is to bind the signatory to the message which is to be sent. For this purpose, the participants use cryptography techniques which may either be public-key cryptography or private key cryptography. Digital signatures are the digital counterpart of handwritten signatures and should ideally be non-forgeable by any attacker. Let us gain an understanding of how digital signatures work. To sign a document, the sender uses two mutually authenticating keys, that is, the sender's private key and the receiver's public key. The mathematical algorithm used acts like a cipher, by encrypting the data and creating a hash of the message. Only the correct receiver can decode the document by using his private key and the sender's public key. If in any case the document changes after signing, the digital signature becomes invalid. There are several digital signature algorithms available.

Following Fig. (**3**) shows a flowchart of secure data transmission in the Blockchain platform.

4.7. Consensus

It is an important part of the blockchain architecture and is used for the verification and validation of transactions and blocks in the Blockchain is known as Consensus. It follows a set of self-enforced rules which every participant in the network has to abide by and thus helps in maintaining the integrity and synchronization of the nodes that are a part of this chain [7]. It also ensures that an identical and updated set of copies of the transactions is distributed among the participants. Its advantage is that it provides security, privacy, and transparency in the network. Some consensus algorithms are mentioned below:

- Proof-of-Work (POW)- The core idea behind this algorithm is to solve a complex mathematical puzzle that easily gives out a solution. The mathematical problem, in reality, uses a lot of computational power. The solution to the problem should be a number less than the hash of the block and the miner who solves the puzzle first is given some reward in terms of cryptocurrency. Ethereum, Litecoin, Dogecoin are few cryptocurrencies that use this algorithm.
- Proof-of-Stake (POS)- The essence of this algorithm is the same as a POW, but the approach is different. Here, there are 'validators' instead of miners who bet on the blocks they think will be added to the chain. Based on which block is added to the chair, their reward is proportionate to their investment and their stakes increase in value.
- Delegated Proof of Stake (DPoS)- The main idea behind this is that participants stake a few of their coins and elect delegates on their behalf. The weightage given to each delegate depends upon the investment made. It is thus one of the fastest consensus algorithms.
- Practical Byzantine Fault Tolerance (PBFT)- The basic idea behind this algorithm is that, depending upon the status of the ledger, the algorithm works even in the presence of a few faulty nodes or when a few nodes fail to respond. Hyperledger Fabric, Tendermint, Zilliqa are few platforms that use this algorithm [8, 9].
- Proof of Activity (PoA)- This is an energy-efficient and fast algorithm which uses a hybrid approach by clubbing the PoW and PoS algorithms. Here, validators or verified accounts are entrusted with the task of ensuring the correctness of the block.
- Proof of Capacity (PoC)- It is also called Proof of Space and is similar to the Proof of Work algorithm, where the computation of PoW is analogous to storage in PoC. The solution to the complex mathematical problems is accumulated in the storage used to produce blocks and the fastest one in computing the solution stands a better chance of creating blocks. The process which this algorithm follows is known as 'plotting'.

- Proof of Burn (PoB)- In this algorithm, instead of taking money, the participants burn their coins/ cryptocurrency by sending it to an address from where it is irretrievable. The greater the amount of cryptocurrency they burn, the greater is their chance of being selected for the next block.
- Proof of Elapsed Time (PoET)- It works by generating a random sleep time for each participant during which the particular nodes go into sleep mode. If a block is available when a particular node wakes up or becomes active, that participant is considered the lucky winner and gets a chance to commit a new block to the Blockchain.

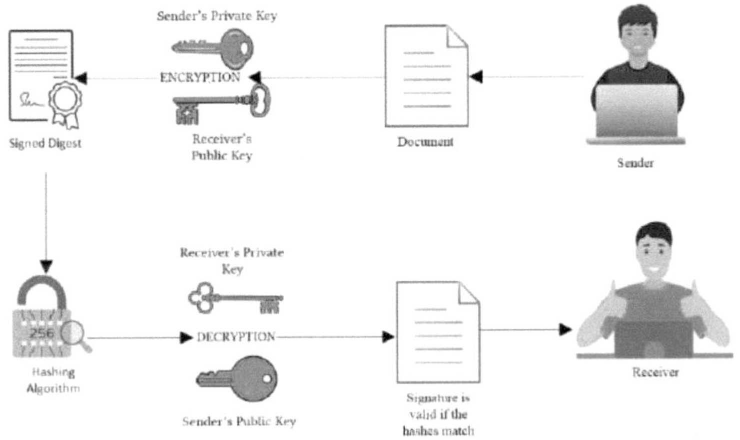

Fig. (3). How does Blockchain work?

Table **2** given below shows a comparison between the different consensus algorithms studied above.

Table 2. Tabular Comparison of different Consensus Algorithms.

Consensus Algorithm	Node Identity Management	Energy saving	Adversary tolerance power	Blockchain Type	Transaction Rate	Example
PoW	Open	High	<25% of Computing Power	Permissionless	Low	Bitcoin, Litecoin, Ethereum (till 2018)
PoS	Open	Medium	<51% of Stake	Both	High	Ethereum (since 2018)
DPoS	Open	Low	<51% of Validators	Both	Medium	Lisk, Bitshares, Waykichain, Steem

(Table 2) cont.....

PBFT	Permissioned	High	<33.3% of Faulty Replicas	Permissioned	High	Hyperledger Fabric
PoA	Open	High	<25% of Computing Power	Permissioned	Medium	Microsoft Azure, Decred
PoC	Open	Medium	<25% of Computing Power	Permissionless	Medium	SpaceMint, BurstCoin, Chia
Tendermint	Permissioned	High	<33.3& of Byzantine Voting Power	Permissioned	High	Tendermint
Ripple	Open	High	<20% of Faulty Nodes	Both	High	Ripple
PoB	Open	High	<51% of Stake	Permissionless	Medium	SlimCoin
PoET	Open	Low	<25% of Computing Power	Both	Medium	Hyperledger Sawtooth

4.8. Smart Contract

A contract, as we all know, is a legal bond between two parties. A smart contract refers to a piece of code that is stored on the Blockchain network and executed automatically when certain conditions are met. Colloquially, they are self-executing scripts encoding set protocols in Blockchain that digitally verify and implement the contract made between participants and ultimately help in transferring digital assets [10]. Smart contracts were first introduced by Ethereum and are written using the Solidity programming language. There are many tools available for authoring Smart Contracts, but the web-based tool Remix is the handiest among all.

Let's quickly perform a fun activity by creating and deploying a smart contract on an Ethereum test network. For this, we will first download the browser extension of MetaMask. MetaMask is a browser plugin that serves as an Ethereum Browser as well as a wallet. Once downloaded, we need to create a wallet. We can use any one of the test Networks available to get some Dummy Ethers in our wallet because the deployment of a smart contract cannot be done for free. (Ether is the cryptocurrency of Ethereum). For this, we need to select one of the test networks available as shown in Fig. (**4**) (I have used the Goerli Test Network because it is comparatively easier to get test Ethers on this network, but you can choose any) and open the Testnet Faucet browser of that network. By providing our account address, we can request them to give us test Ethers.

Having done this, we will open the remix.ethereum.org webpage and create our contract using the solidity language. Let us build a smart contract for the electricity bill. For this, we will create a new file with the '.sol' extension and follow the steps shown in Figs. (**5** and **6**).

Fig. (4). Steps to get Test Ethers in MetaMask wallet using Testnet Faucet.

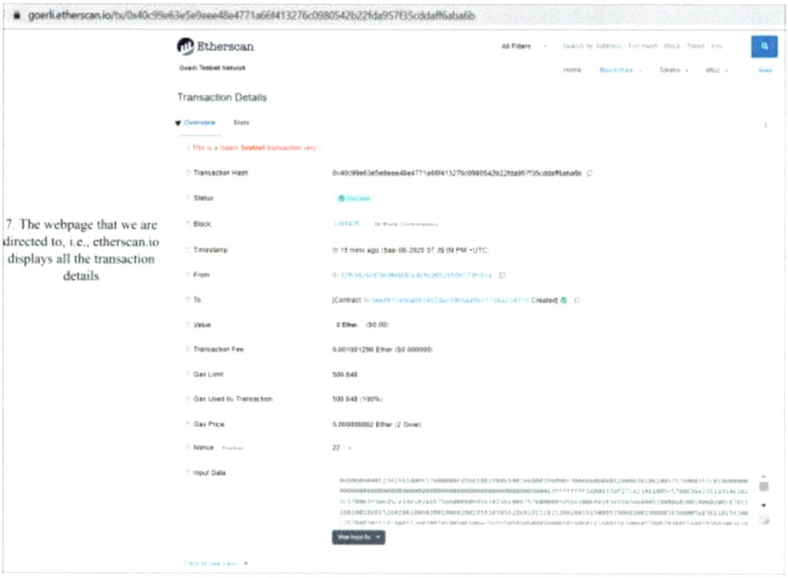

Fig. (5). Steps to be followed for the deployment of test Smart Contract on Remix IDE.

5. FEATURES

5.1. Distributed

It is a distributed technology that allows data/transactions to be synchronized and shared among all entities in the chain instead of being copied or transferred. What needs to be understood here is that due to the absence of a single data storehouse and transactions being distributed among all the entities, the records/ money can never be hacked or stolen. This also prevents load on a single server by distributing the computational power among the many computers on the network. Advantages:

- Better and more efficient outcome due to distributed computational power
- Ownership to all members is assured because they actively participate in all the transactions.
- Since the replica of each transaction gets stored on all the nodes, tampering with the data is impossible because any fraudulent activity can easily be detected.

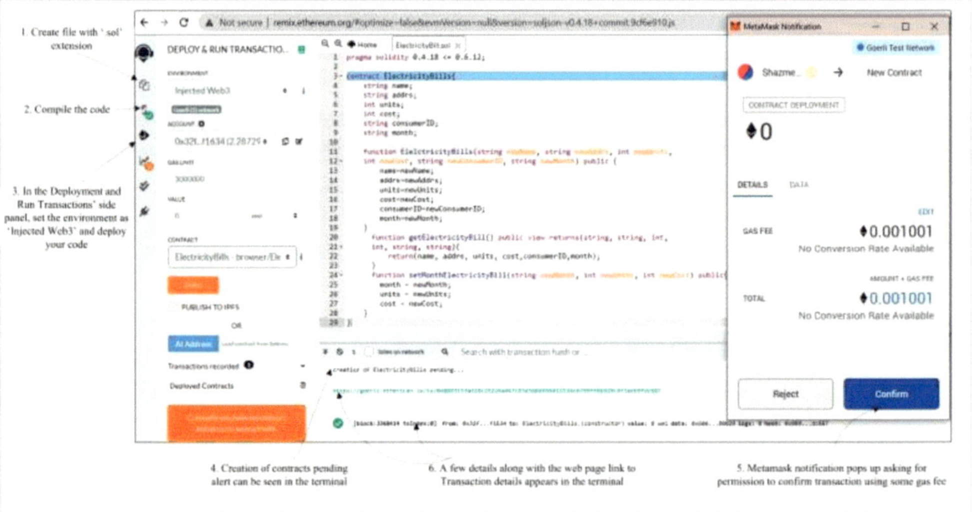

Fig. (6). Transaction details in the Etherscan Network.

5.2. Decentralized

It means that there is no need for a governing authority or third party to manage the data and transactions. This implies that it is an open ledger technology and ensures full integrity among all the members who are a part of the blockchain because every entity in the chain has the same copy of the ledger. By this feature, the users remain super active, alert, and always updated regarding all the transactions that take place [11]. To list a few advantages of these features:

- No need for third parties to drastically increases the speed of the transaction process
- Data will never be lost because each user has a copy of it
- Lower transaction cost
- No possibility of scams

Note: The two terms mentioned above might seem similar in context but in reality, they are very different. Decentralization relates to the level of control and the authority they share in decision-making whereas distributed network refers to the difference in location of the users. In a decentralized network, the decision is made based on the voting done by all the nodes. As stated earlier, if at least 51% of the participants vote in favor of something, that action is performed, or else it is rejected. But in a distributed system, the processing is shared among all the participants, but it might allow the decision to be made exclusively by a central authority. Blockchain incorporates both these features.

5.3. Immutable

Data once added to the Blocks can never be changed because it gets permanently stored on the Blockchain network forever. This means that data that was first added to the Bitcoin network when it was created is still safe and secure and can easily be accessed. What makes it different from Databases regarding this feature is that Databases allow us to Update and Delete data stored on their network, in addition to the creation and addition of data. However, this is not the case in Blockchain. While it allows us to Create and Add data, Updating and Deletion is not possible. It adds to its security because transaction records since Day 1 are stored just as they are and any attempt to tamper with the data goes in vain. Both the sender and receiver can rest assured that their data will never be meddled with.

5.4. Transparent

The addition of a single block or transaction between any two persons is reflected on all the blocks. Thus, nothing is hidden from anybody and changes are viewable publicly. It is one advantageous feature. Let's understand how. Imagine that a fraudulent participant has gained illegal access to the network and is pretending to be some other person. He can just not make any transaction because firstly, it needs to be validated by all, and secondly and most importantly, the private key is a unique key which is almost impossible to guess correctly, and in case a person tries a few keys, all these attempts are reflected on all the blocks and he can easily be traced.

5.5. Peer to Peer Network

Blockchain allows transactions to occur securely between two parties excluding the need of any third party. Each transaction is signed digitally by using some sort of Cryptographic Algorithm. This lets only the true receiver decipher the code with the knowledge of the sender's public key and his private key. Hashing algorithms used for signature generation are of immense importance because they act like a trapdoor and make them practically impossible for a cybercriminal to crack it.

6. TYPES AND PLATFORMS

This technology can be divided into 3 types [12]:

6.1. Public Blockchain

As the name suggests, this type is open to use by the general public and is not owned by any single authority. Anyone can participate in the consensus method of decision-making. All participants are given equal authority to decide the fate of the ledger by following the 51% rule, according to which if 51% of the participants vote in favor of a decision, for example, creation of a block, it is created, otherwise, the proposal is discarded. Each user actively participates in the transaction verification process. The users may or might not be rewarded for their involvement. To understand this clearly, imagine that you are a part of a public Blockchain network. A request for someone's new transaction pops up on your screen. To verify it, you are supposed to solve some mathematical problems and if you are the first one to give the correct answer, you are rewarded some money in terms of online Blockchain-based currency. The answers given by the other participants are equally important for decision-making, but they are not always rewarded. This type of Blockchain can be used to conduct votes during elections or in maintaining cryptocurrencies.

6.2. Private Blockchain

Private Blockchain, just like its name, are private. The accessibility and transactions are restricted to the members of the chain. Members may include organizations or some individuals who share personal data among themselves. The authority on data management is strictly monitored and controlled. This type of Blockchain might be used for some private bank, or a particular company to maintain their business records or a university to maintain the records of its students, staff, official documents, *etc*. It cannot be accessed by the general public. Platforms include R3 Corda, Ripple

6.3. Consortium Blockchain

It is also known as a semi-private or hybrid blockchain and incorporates both public and private blockchain networks. It can be perceived as a semi-decentralized network. It can be hosted on a private network where a few nodes can form a public blockchain just to incorporate its best features of stability, security, and verification. This Blockchain might be used for storing data of a mobile company for example, for which read-only permission is granted to the public but read and write access is provided to a few selected employees. Some notable platforms are Hyperledger, MultiChain, *etc*.

Following Table **3** briefly compares the three types of Blockchain:

Table 3. Comparison of the three types of blockchain.

Property	Public Blockchain	Private Blockchain	Consortium Blockchain
Access	Open	Limited to members	Partly open
Transparency	Completely transparent	Transparent only to users	Depends upon set rules
Decentralization	Yes	No	Partly
Reward	Participants rewarded for growing the chain	No incentives known	Might or might not reward participants (depends on set rules)
Speed	Comparatively slow	Faster	Somewhere in between
Efficiency	Low	High	High
Consensus Determination	All miners	Selected nodes	One authority
Use case	Almost every industry like cryptocurrency, supply-chain management, stock market, etc.	For organizations who need to keep their data private or carry out personal tasks	For organizations who want to make the best use of public blockchain features but want to keep their information completely private.
Platform	Bitcoin, Ethereum	Corda, Ripple	Hyperledger

7. HOW DOES IT WORK?

Having studied the basic elements of a Blockchain, we now know that all records in the ledger are stored in blocks that are secured by digital signatures made using cryptographic functions. Blocks are intangible and immutable. New blocks are created only when the old one runs out of memory. In a public Blockchain, when a request for new data to be added to the blockchain is received, the request is reflected on all the nodes in the network. If the transaction is approved following the consensus rules, it is validated by adding a timestamp and added to the blockchain network by linking it to the previous block. This decision as to which nodes will append the block is very critical because cybercriminals might be ready and lucky enough to cause the 51% attack. For this reason, the mechanism of the consensus algorithm being used also becomes extremely important. A transaction is made secure following the cryptographic algorithms. The main steps of how a Blockchain transaction is approved/ carried out are listed below:

Step 1: Transaction request is reflected on all nodes in the network.
Step 2: Consensus mechanisms are followed for its approval/ rejection.
Step 3: Transaction is approved and validated.
Step 4: Block gets added to the chain and the transaction is carried out.

8. APPLICATIONS, ADVANTAGES & CHALLENGES

8.1. APPLICATIONS

With its features and ability to carry out transactions within a short period, Blockchain is one such technology that can blend with almost all the technologies out there [13]. It is slowly impacting many different sectors, thereby making their task more efficient and secure. A few applications are listed below:

i. Blockchain-based Cryptocurrency- The most well-known example being Bitcoin, other cryptocurrencies like Litecoin and Ethers are also being developed. This can be attributed to the distributed, decentralization, immutability, and transparency features of this technology. DCEP by the Central Bank of China was launched on 29th August 2020 to develop an electronic cash infrastructure by providing anonymous digital wallets with no bank account [14].
ii. Secure sharing of Medical data- Healthcare is one sector where reliable activity tracking is needed and records need to be maintained perfectly. Introducing Blockchain technology in this field will make the best use of its potential and drastically improve healthcare facilities [15 - 18].
iii. In Supply Chain Management- Here Blockchain is needed to provide secure and complete information and to maintain proper integrity between the members, who need to be updated regularly about the products being

developed [19].

iv. In Business Applications- It helps save time and money and ensures proper management and safe monitoring of each step of progress [20].
v. In Elections- In democratic countries where elections take place to elect their leaders, Blockchain can be used to carry out fair elections where all records are maintained easily and the personal identity of the voters is not revealed [21].
vi. Government-based application for storing personal documents- Governments can use Blockchain platforms to store and exchange the personal documents of the people. Safe storage of these documents, especially in places that are prone to annual calamities like floods, is immensely helpful because the document is stored safely forever and can never be tampered with.

8.2. ADVANTAGES

The features of Blockchain technology already discussed in section 5 of this chapter can also be taken as its advantages. A few advantages have already been mentioned there. However, if you sit and think about it, you will realize that there are many more advantages to this technology that is reshaping the financial world. A few other advantages are mentioned below:

i. The biggest advantage is that it addresses the privacy and security concerns of the users by using cryptographic hash functions.
ii. Authentic transactions: Data once entered cannot be deleted or tampered with and also every block contains a permanent time-stamp of the transactions. This makes the whole process as authentic as any other and adds to the security and privacy features.
iii. Faster speed and Increased efficiency: Because the entire system is decentralized and distributed and not dependent on some central authority for transactions or data storage, the speed of the business being carried out drastically increases and the efficiency improves. This also means that time taken for one transaction reduces which is a major advantage because of time constraints in recent times.
iv. Easy to use: We got a brief exposure to the deployment of smart contracts in the network and saw how easy it is to work on this platform. We can safely carry out our transactions from anywhere and anytime, unlike financial organizations that have time restrictions.
v. Improved records and Better Traceability: As each block contains metadata including the Block version, timestamp, Merkle Tree Root Hash, Hash of parent block, bits, and Nonce (Number used only once), it becomes very easy and hassle-free to trace them even if they were generated 10 years ago. The fact that Blocks created since day 1 include a timestamp and are all intact and

can never be deleted or meddled with indicates that the records are all maintained in chronological order. This advantage can, among others, best be put to use in the healthcare sector where a proper record of a patient's medical history needs to be stored.

vi. Since transactions are added to a block only after the process of maximum trust verification by using consensus protocols to validate the entry, it eliminates risks like double-entry which can cause double payments to occur.

8.3. CHALLENGES

There is still a lot of excitement in the tech world about Blockchain Technology, and the excitement is only increasing every day. This technology is no doubt the most influential and thrilling in the 21st century, and we have already gone through quite a few applications and advantages of this technology. However, this technology is still in its developmental phase because of the few challenges it brings along with it, some of which are mentioned below:

i. Scalability- This is one of the biggest challenges, especially in public blockchains, which need to be resolved soon. Storage requirement has become an issue. Let us understand this with the help of the Bitcoin example. In Bitcoin, the size of one block is restricted to 1 MB and in general, a block is mined almost every 10 min. Also, a Bitcoin network has a limitation of 7 transactions/second, which is not capable of dealing with high-frequency trade. Also, larger blocks require more storage space and a slower rate of propagation [22]. This has the possibility of causing a shift to centralized networks that can maintain such a huge chain of transactions. This is causing a trade-off between security and block size, which is a major concern [23, 24].

ii. Limited Supply to increase demand- The total number of Bitcoins which will ever be available is 21 million. It has been predicted that the last of them will be mined in approximately 2140, and we have already mined 17 million bitcoins to date.

iii. Energy Consumption- This technology uses the Proof-of-Work mechanism for proper validation of the transactions and the ultimate addition to the network. This process uses a lot of computational power to reflect transactions on every node, solve complex mathematical problems required for the processing, and verification of transactions [25].

iv. Interoperability- Most Blockchain networks work in silos and are incapable of exchanging information with other Blockchain networks that are not a part of them. It can be speculated as one of the major reasons why most organizations are still not making a move towards this technology. Though attempts have been made towards resolving this issue, it has not helped much and a major portion of this problem still needs to be fixed.

v. Lack of trained professionals is yet another challenge, but that is gradually being fixed with increasing awareness regarding this topic.

9. FUTURE SCOPE

Though the pioneer implementer of this technology was the financial sector, it is expected to be adopted gradually by many other sectors. Some challenges need to be resolved, and it is expected to pave the way for new opportunities for scientists and researchers who work in this field. It is anticipated that the integration of this technology with other technologies like the Internet of Things, Artificial Intelligence, and Machine Learning will bring about incredible changes across the globe. Also, there is no standardization in terms of the Blockchain mechanisms followed and there are hundreds of different Blockchain platforms out there. Therefore, if a company wants to incorporate this technology in their workspace, they first need to find out which platform best suits their requirement. They can be done by Blockchain Testing wherein different parameters with special emphasis on the function to be performed is tested to check if the platform works as claimed by the developers [26, 27].

CONCLUSION

Blockchain technology can be perceived as a distributed decentralized ledger technology that is transparent and immutable and stores records as transactions in time-stamped blocks. It allows the users to make and verify transactions fast without the need for any central authority. Though this technology is still in its infancy and its first applications, starting with the development of Bitcoin, and limited to the financial sector, it is slowly creeping into all other sectors and has the potential to transform the traditional industries with its features. When clubbed with other technologies like the Internet of Things, Artificial Intelligence, and Machine Learning, it can bring about spectacularly impressive changes that add to the modernization of human lives. Having developed a fundamental idea about what Blockchain is and also its applications, advantages, challenges, and future trends, we can conclude the chapter with the famous actor Fred Ehrsam's remark, "While it may seem scarier in the earlier days, I think ultimately the blockchain creates a safer world."

CONSENT FOR PUBLICATION

Not applicable.

CONFLICT OF INTEREST

The author declares no conflict of interest, financial or otherwise.

ACKNOWLEDGEMENTS

We would like to acknowledge Director (Admin), Mr. Syed Sharique Hussain, Salfia Paramedical Institute Darbhanga, (SPI) Darbhanga, (director_admin@salfiainstitute.edu.in), Secretary, Engr Syed Shahid Hasnain, Academic Incharge, Dr. Aaliya Samreen, (aaliyasamreen@gmail.com), SPI Darbhanga, Admission Incharge, Mrs. Rana Kamal, SPI Darbhanga, Dr. Ashok Kumar Gadiya, Chairman, Mewar University, Chittorgarh, Rajasthan, Dr. A A A Faizi, Joint Secretary cum Director at Minority Welfare Department, Govt of Bihar, India, Additional DCP, Kumar RanVijay Singh, Noida, UP, India, Also, I would like to thanks our honorable Vice-Chancellor, Professor Afshar Alam, and Dr. Jawed Ahmed, Assistant Professor, Department of Computer Science, Jamia Hamdard, New Delhi, India.

REFERENCES

[1] M. Van Rijmenam, and P. Ryan, *Blockchain: Transforming your business and our world.* Routledge, 2018.
[http://dx.doi.org/10.4324/9780429457715]

[2] S. Nakamoto, *Bitcoin Whitepaper,* 2019. https://bitcoin.org/bitcoin.pdf

[3] M. Gupta, *Blockchain for dummies. Hoboken.* John Wiley & Sons: NJ, 2017.

[4] D. Efanov, and P. Roschin, "The all-pervasiveness of the blockchain technology", *Procedia Comput. Sci.,* vol. 123, pp. 116-121, 2018.
[http://dx.doi.org/10.1016/j.procs.2018.01.019]

[5] I. Bashir, *Mastering Blockchain: Distributed ledger technology, decentralization, and smart contracts explained.* Packt Publishing Ltd., 2018.

[6] M. Niranjanamurthy, B. Nithya, and S. Jagannatha, "Analysis of Blockchain technology: pros, cons and SWOT", *Cluster Comput.,* vol. 22, no. 6, pp. 14743-14757, 2019.
[http://dx.doi.org/10.1007/s10586-018-2387-5]

[7] G.-T. Nguyen, and K. Kim, *A Survey about Consensus Algorithms Used in Blockchain.,* 2018.

[8] M. Castro, and B. Liskov, "Practical byzantine fault tolerance", *in OSDI,* 1999.

[9] N. Stifter, A. Judmayer, and E. Weippl, *Revisiting Practical Byzantine Fault Tolerance ThroughBlockchain Technologies, in Security and Quality in Cyber-Physical Systems Engineering,* Springer, pp. 471-495, 2019.
[http://dx.doi.org/10.1007/978-3-030-25312-7_17]

[10] S. Wang, "Blockchain-enabled smart contracts: architecture, applications, and future trends", *IEEE Trans. Syst. Man Cybern. Syst.,* vol. 49, no. 11, pp. 2266-2277, 2019.
[http://dx.doi.org/10.1109/TSMC.2019.2895123]

[11] L. Madaan, A. Kumar, and B. Bhushan, "Working principle, application areas and challenges for blockchain technology", *in 2020 IEEE 9th International Conference on Communication Systems and Network Technologies (CSNT),* IEEE, 2020.
[http://dx.doi.org/10.1109/CSNT48778.2020.9115794]

[12] R. Andreev, "Review of blockchain technology: Types of blockchain and their application", *Intellekt. Sist. Proizv.,* vol. 16, no. 1, pp. 11-14, 2018.
[http://dx.doi.org/10.22213/2410-9304-2018-1-11-14]

[13] B. Bhushan, A. Khamparia, and K. M. Sagayam, "Blockchain for smart cities: A review of architectures, integration trends and future research directions", *Sustainable Cities and Society,* vol. 61, 2020.
[PMID: 102360] [http://dx.doi.org/10.1016/j.scs.2020.102360]

[14] Y. Li, *Emerging blockchain-based applications and techniques.* Springer, 2019.
[http://dx.doi.org/10.1007/s11761-019-00281-x]

[15] A. Hasselgren, K. Kralevska, D. Gligoroski, S.A. Pedersen, and A. Faxvaag, "Blockchain in healthcare and health sciences-A scoping review", *Int. J. Med. Inform.,* vol. 134, 2020.
[http://dx.doi.org/10.1016/j.ijmedinf.2019.104040] [PMID: 31865055]

[16] T. Kumar, "Blockchain utilization in healthcare: Key requirements and challenges", *in 2018 IEEE 20th International Conference on e-Health Networking, Applications and Services (Healthcom),* IEEE, 2018.
[http://dx.doi.org/10.1109/HealthCom.2018.8531136]

[17] M. Hölbl, "A systematic review of the use of blockchain in healthcare", *Symmetry,* p. 470, 2018.
[http://dx.doi.org/10.3390/sym10100470]

[18] A. Shahnaz, U. Qamar, and A. Khalid, "Using blockchain for electronic health records", *IEEE Access,* vol. 7, pp. 147782-147795, 2019.
[http://dx.doi.org/10.1109/ACCESS.2019.2946373]

[19] F. Longo, "Blockchain-enabled supply chain: An experimental study", *Comput. Ind. Eng.,* vol. 136, pp. 57-69, 2019.
[http://dx.doi.org/10.1016/j.cie.2019.07.026]

[20] V.J. Morkunas, J. Paschen, and E. Boon, "How blockchain technologies impact your business model", *Bus. Horiz.,* vol. 62, no. 3, pp. 295-306, 2019.
[http://dx.doi.org/10.1016/j.bushor.2019.01.009]

[21] T. Dimitriou, "Efficient, coercion-free and universally verifiable blockchain-based voting", *Comput. Netw.,* 2020.
[http://dx.doi.org/10.1016/j.comnet.2020.107234]

[22] Z. Zheng, "Blockchain challenges and opportunities: A survey", *Int. J. Web Grid Serv.,* vol. 14, no. 4, pp. 352-375, 2018.
[http://dx.doi.org/10.1504/IJWGS.2018.095647]

[23] A. Chauhan, "Blockchain and scalability", *in 2018 IEEE International Conference on Software Quality, Reliability and Security Companion (QRS-C),* IEEE, 2018.
[http://dx.doi.org/10.1109/QRS-C.2018.00034]

[24] Q. Zhou, "Solutions to scalability of blockchain: A survey", *IEEE Access,* vol. 8, pp. 16440-16455, 2020.
[http://dx.doi.org/10.1109/ACCESS.2020.2967218]

[25] J. Golosova, and A. Romanovs, "The advantages and disadvantages of the blockchain technology", *in 2018 IEEE 6th workshop on advances in information, electronic and electrical engineering (AIEEE).,* IEEE, 2018.
[http://dx.doi.org/10.1109/AIEEE.2018.8592253]

[26] A. Biswal, and B. Bhushan, "Blockchain for internet of things: architecture, consensus advancements, challenges and application areas", *in 2019 5th International Conference On Computing, Communication, Control And Automation (ICCUBEA),* IEEE, 2019.

[27] A. Malik, S. Gautam, S. Abidin, and B. Bhushan, *Blockchain Technology-Future Of IoT: Including Structure, Limitations And Various Possible Attacks,* pp. 1100-1104, 2019.
[http://dx.doi.org/10.1109/ICICICT46008.2019.8993144]

CHAPTER 6

Industrial Revolution: Blockchain as a Wave for Industry 4.0 and IIoT

Sukriti Goyal[1], **Nikhil Sharma**[1,*], **Ila Kaushik**[2] and **Bharat Bhushan**[3]

[1] *HMR Institute of Technology & Management, Delhi, India*

[2] *Krishna Institute of Engineering & Technology, Ghaziabad, U.P*

[3] *School of Engineering and Technology, Sharda University, Greater Noida, India*

Abstract: In ancient times, humans were much predisposed to utilizing their hand-created tools to finish any kind of work. From the last few years, businesses related to production have been expanding. People began to rely on tools, machines, and smart gadgets to process their work, as these kinds of tools help them to achieve their target in the given time. . Since the 18th century, the world has experienced a lot of revolutions in industry across the globe. This type of growth in technology has made a base for industrial revolutions. New technology was introduced called "blockchain."Probably, blockchain technology is the most disruptive technology in the modern digital economy. The ability of blockchain technology has been greatly described in many research works, media, and majorly in the fields of finance and payment. One existing research is at the organizational stage, where it implements the architecture for internet safety as well as inconvertibility. "Industry 4.0" and "IIoT (Industrial Internet of Things)" are involved in its rising applications. Thus, in this paper, current applications of blockchain in IIoT as well as Industry 4.0 setups, existing open issues, modern application sectors, challenges related to IIoT, and their solutions are illustrated. The main focus of this paper is to empower and facilitate research in this field, which will help the developers in blockchain acquisition as well as investment in the "Industry 4.0" and "Industrial Internet of Things" space.

Keywords: Agriculture industry, Blockchain, Education industry, Food supply chain, Healthcare industry, Industrial revolution, Industry 4.0, IoT (Internet of Things), Privacy, Security, Scalability.

* **Corresponding author Nikhil Sharma:** HMR Institute of Technology & Management, Delhi, India; E-mail: nikhilsharma1694@gmail.com

Sudhir K. Sharma, Bharat Bhushan, Parma N. Astya and Narayan C. Debnath (Eds.)

1. INTRODUCTION

Undoubtedly, blockchain technology is an unpretentious invention. Blockchain structured the backbone of a modern kind of internet by permitting digital information to be disseminated but not replicated. Genuinely, invented for the digital currency, *i.e.*, Bitcoin, the tech organization has now discovered other efficient usages of this technology [1]. Thus, in simple words, a blockchain is a time-stamped sequence of inconvertible collections of information that is handled by a network of computers and not owned by any individual entity [2]. Each of these digital blocks is defended and limited to each other by employing a public database (*i.e.*, chain) [3]. In the network, by using cryptographic principles to keep data sharing safe, blockchain technology gives a decentralized database or digital ledger of transactions to everyone [4]. Basically, this network is a series of computer systems that must allow sharing before it can be authenticated and stored. There are many core elements of blockchain, but only the three most necessary elements are described. The first element is a block in which every chain includes several blocks, and each block has three fundamental components such as the data stored in the block is the first component [5]. A whole number of 32-bit is known as a nonce. In the second component, when a block is generated, it is randomly created which further ~~then,~~ produces a block header hash [6]. In third, a number of 256-bit called hash is wedded to the nonce. It must begin with a large number of 0s that is, it will be enormously small [7]. A nonce creates the cryptographic hash after the generation of the first block of a chain. The data in the block is considered as signed and forever linked to the nonce as well as hash until it is mined [8]. The second element is a miner. Through a procedure known as mining, miners produce fresh blocks on the chain. In a blockchain, every block has its own unrepeatable hash as well as a nonce, but also, it references the hash of the preceding block in the chain [9]. So, It is not simple to mine a block, specifically on huge chains. To solve the complicated math problem of finding a nonce that produces an admissible hash, special software is used by miners, because the nonce is only 32 bits and the hash is 256 bits. There are approximately 4 billion plausible combinations of nonce-hash that must be mined just before searching the correction [10]. When that occurs, miners have to search the "golden nonce" and their data is included in the database. Any kind of modification is accepted by all the nodes of the network and the miner is rewarded financially after triumphing mining of a block [11]. The third element is Node. Decentralization is one of the most significant topics in blockchain technology. The chain cannot be owned by a computer system or a company [12]. Rather, it is a disseminated ledger through which nodes are linked to the chain. Nodes (in any form of electronic gadget) manage replicas of the blockchain as well as maintains the functioning of the network. A major application of blockchain technology is to record financial information with a protected sharing.

There have been efforts to enucleate as well as expand the usages of the blockchain technology beyond the field of finance and to other sectors namely, supply chain, automobile, healthcare, production, education, and banking [13]. It is widely classified that, "Blockchain 1.0" is typically linked with digital currency, for example, smart contracts, Bitcoin."Blockchain 2.0" is connected with the help of automated digital finance processes, and also, the popular technology *i.e.* "Blockchain 3.0". It is concentrated on considering the requirements of the digital community like smart homes, smart banking, smart cities, and Industry 4.0 [14]. The fourth industrial revolution is hugely powered by IoT and other associated technologies. Here is another concept of IIoT (Industrial Internet of Things) or Industrial IoT which has a more particular concentration while the fourth revolution of the industry is basically linked with an intelligent industry arrangement. The conversion from conventional industry to intelligent industry or IndustrialIoT is supported by the inter-associativity as well as the digitalization of our community and spreading of IoT gadgets [15].

The other sections of the chapter are organized as follows, Section 2 illustrated "Industry 4.0", its evolution from Industry 1.0 to 4.0, "Industrial Internet of Things (IIoT)" and major differences between the fourth revolution of industry and IIoT. Then, in section 3, some major applications of blockchain with some primary issues are described in different sectors such as healthcare and agriculture along with some of the existing open challenges in adopting blockchain in the IIoT technology. Modern application sectors in Industrial IoT or Industry 4.0, where blockchain technology is being executed for finding plausible solutions, are described in section 4. Furthermore, sections 5 and 6 present some of the major challenges related to the implementation of IIoT, and solutions to deal with the implementation issues in detail. And finally, a conclusion is discussed in section 7.

2. BACKGROUND MATERIALS

This section discusses the Evolution of Industry 4.0, and the comparison between IIoT and IoT.

2.1. Industry 4.0

In every day of humans' life, technology plays a significant role. It has made it plausible for data access to be much faster. The atmosphere of businesses is getting involved in this frequent evolution of technology. Gradually, the industrial field has been consolidating greater applications of automation and associativity. For 2020, "Industry 4.0" was proposed in the year 2011, at the Hanover event,

Germany. In the revolution of industry, Industry 4.0 implies tobe the modern stage that concentrates mainly on inter-associativity, ML (machine learning), real-time data, and automation [16]. Also, it is sometimes implied as IIoT or smart production. Before going too much deeper, it is advantageous to first know how production has evolved since the 1800s. There are four different industrial revolutions as shown in (Fig. **1**) that the world either has faced today [17].

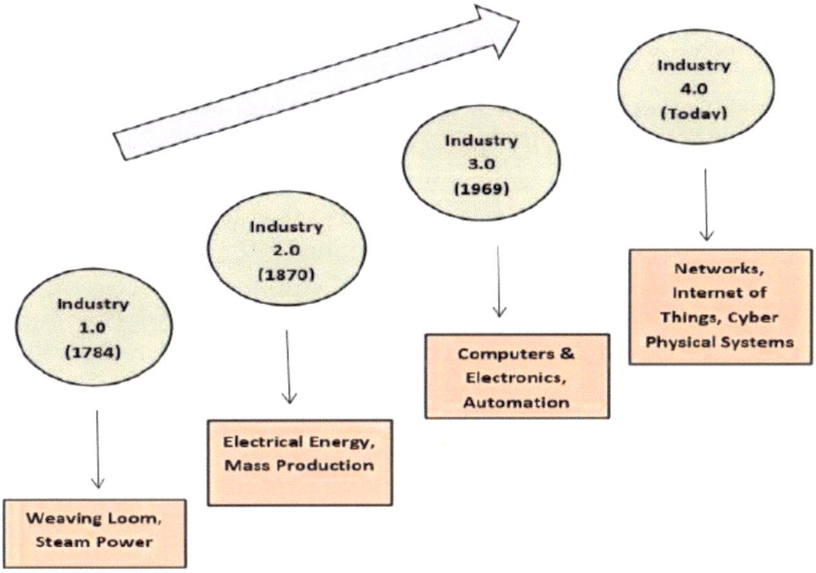

Fig. (1). Stages of revolution in industry.

2.1.1. The First Revolution of Industry

Between the late 1700s and the beginning of the 1800s, the first revolution of the industry occurred. During this time, production evolved from concentrating on manual exertion done by people and animals. It is supported by a more efficient type of exertion done by people through the usage of water as well as steam-powered engines and other kinds of machine weapons [18].

2.1.2. The Second Revolution of Industry

The world introduced a second revolution of the industry with the introduction of steel and the application of electricity in factories in the beginning stage of the 20th century. To raise the optimization and create factory machinery like mobile, electricity-enabled manufacturers were introduced in factories. And, during this stage, the concepts of mass manufacturing like the assembly line were proposed as a method to enhance productivity.

2.1.3. The Third Revolution of Industry

In the late 1950s, the third revolution of industry slowly started to rise as manufacturers and started unifying computer technology into their factories. During that period, they started experiencing a change that put less force on mechanical as well as analog technology, and more on digital technology including automation software.

2.1.4. The Fourth Revolution of Industry or Industry 4.0

From the last10 years, the fourth revolution of the industry has risen which is called "Industry 4.0". It mainly focuses on digital technology from the current 10 years to a complete modern stage with the support of inter-associativity through the Internet of Things (IoT). A more interconnected, vast as well as holistic strategy is offered by Industry 4.0 to production [19]. It links physical with digital technology and permits for better optimization and access across sectors, products, and people. Also, business owners are empowered by Industry 4.0 to monitor and understand every facet of their implementation and permit them to leverage instant information to enhance manufacturing, boost operations and raise growth.

2.2. IIoT

IIoT implies the extension as well as usage of the IoT in industrial fields and applications. Including a large concentration on big data, machine learning, and M2M (machine-to-machine communication), IIoT provides enterprises and factories to have better optimization, capacity, and stability in their implementations. Also, it encircles industrial applications, including healthcare gadgets, software-defined manufacturing procedures, and robotics too [20]. Generally, IIoT is the usage of smart actuators as well as sensors to boost production and industrial procedures. Sometimes, it is also considered as the "Industry 4.0" or "Industrial Internet". The main concept behind the IIoT is that smart machines are better than humans for evaluating data in real-time, and they are also preferred at interacting significant information that can be applied to make effective decisions faster and more precisely related to business [21].

2.2.1. IIoT versus IoT

Basically, both IIoT and IoT have many technologies that are known commonly, as M2M *i.e.* machine-to-machine communications, sensors and actuators, associativity, cloud platforms, and also, data analytics which can be applied for distinct objectives. The application of IoT is to link gadgets across many sectors namely, healthcare, enterprises, agriculture, automobile, customer and utilities, and also, including government and cities. Smart gadgets, fitness bands, and many other applications that normally don't generate emergency circumstances if something goes amiss are included in IoT gadgets. While, on the other hand, the IIoT links gadgets as well as machines which further helps in production and utilities. System failures and downtime in deployments of the IIoT can produce high-risk cases or even life-threatening circumstances. The application of IIoT is more focused on enhancing capacity and increasing health or safety, in opposition to the user-concentrated nature of applications of IoT [22].

3. MAJOR APPLICATIONS

IIoT plays important role in today's world. The involvement of IoT with the industry makes it more popular as compared to other technologies. It is involved in different fields like the health industry, agriculture, and many more. The major applications of IIoT are explained as follows:

3.1. Healthcare Industry

In the healthcare industry, the sensitive information of patients can be shared in an efficient way by applying blockchain technology, which can effectively boost the distribution of medical services. For instance, by decreasing the efficiency for dissimilar patients and also, decreasing the number of errors that occur during patient care [23]. To facilitate the controlling as well as management of diseases, blockchain-powered IoT has been applied in the healthcare sector. Wearable gadgets, smart medicines, and enhanced quality control are included in some of the illustrations of blockchain-enabled IoT [24]. They also permit for tracing clinical medicines during their evaluation, by testing their impact as well as their negative effects.

Here are some main applications of blockchain technology in the industry of healthcare:

3.1.1. Patient Record Management

One of the major issues experienced in handling the record of the patient is that the patient leaves their medical associated information disseminated across several suppliers of healthcare. The composition of EHRs (Electronic Health Records) is not easy to handle and cannot scatter across several industrial setups. Moreover, the issues lie between several healthcare organizations as well as service suppliers who generate more obstacles for the victorious for exchanging of information [25]. This deficit of adjusted management of data as well as information sharing refers to that these medical records are not unified, but instead are segmented. Blockchain technology supports in giving a design for data exchanging along with the safety of this information. In this manner, medical care suppliers can collect details from the patients which may comprise their name, DOB (date of birth), prescription adhered, past processes performed, and other necessary details. By using cloud computing, this information is then recorded on the networks in the current databases of organizations. After that, from each source of information, a cryptographic hash of the information is computed and then, transferred along with the patient's public ID which is to be recorded in the blockchain [26]. In this situation, smart contracts are a better option to handle the access of patient's information. The medical care providers can query the blockchain and then, place this info through an API without exposing the identity of the patient.

3.1.2. Securing Patient Data

In the field of healthcare, the security of data is a primary concern. Keeping the prominent healthcare data of patients secure and protected is the most famous blockchain medical application at this moment. The criminal theft credit card-related information as well as banking data, and also, health and genomic testing records. The capability of blockchain is to keep an undisrupted, decentralized as well as clear log of all the data of the patients which makes this technology rife for safety applications [27]. Moreover, blockchain remains private while it is transparent, concealing the recognition of any character with complicated and safe codes that can secure the susceptibility of healthcare data. Because of the decentralization feature of blockchain, patients, doctors, and healthcare suppliers are permitted to exchange similar data quickly and securely.

3.1.3. Industrial Implementations

Following are some famous industrial implementations of blockchain in the medical care industry.

i. MedRec: It is a famous instantiation of healthcare blockchain design for recording EHRs effectively as well as proficiently. The prototype of MedRec allows patients with one-stop-shop access to their healthcare history across several suppliers like smart contracts on an Ethereum blockchain aggregate data pointers into "patient-provider relationships". Reviewing, sharing, and posting of new records, via an efficient and easy-to-use user interface, are facilitated by MedRec too [28]. The interface also includes a notification system to alert users or patients when new data has been uploaded on their behalf or shared with them. In this implementation of blockchain, the EHR also has an emerged blockchain PHR (*i.e.* Patient Health Record) ability that allows the user and the several service suppliers in creating longitudinal medical data consisting of whole life medical situations for each patient.

ii. Medicalchain: It is a blockchain for EHR (*i.e.* electronic health records) which allows several medical care providers namely, hospitals, surgeons, professionals, pharmacists as well as insurers to request permission to access and communicate with healthcare data. Each of the communications is safe, secure, auditable as well as transparent, and also it is stored as a transaction on Medicalchain's disseminated ledger [29].

3.1.4. Challenges

Here are some of the complex issues that adopters in the healthcare industry could meet while applying blockchain into their systems.

i. Healthcare is disseminated: Providers of healthcare services are not streamlined in reference to managing the data. Without such a system, it would be a complicated job to get them to apply blockchain technology. Moreover, if any of the participants in the system are resistive to these modifications, then the utility of the entire system goes down.
ii. Deficiency of approved reliability : Healthcare is such a delicate as well as a disseminated sector that can't pass off modifications overnight. Thus, until the blockchain technology is triumphing implemented, it is tough to find if the acceptance of this technology will be feasible [30].
iii. Other Challenges: The implementation of blockchain technology needs the best architecture and inter-associativity, which startups cannot afford simply. Also, technical obstacles do not permit blockchain technology to apply to the healthcare sector completely. In some enterprises, the system of inter-linked gadgets is disrupted due to the scarcity of commands in the environment of blockchain.

3.2. Manufacturing Industry

The manufacturing sector is an essential participator in global GDP, which has always been persecuted with various challenges like inefficiency and data security. Though, similar to many industries, the manufacturing industry's apparent health is not essentially indicative of forthcoming success. Blockchain has the ability to radically convert it by providing visibility across every asset of manufacturing [31]. Some use-cases of the blockchain in the industry of manufacturing are discussed below.

3.2.1. Enhanced Data Protection

Interacting information like contact and invoice details in any supply chain can be very breakneck using conventional procedures. This is where the blockchain aids to keep the details safe with the best cryptography methods [32]. Since, in blockchain, information blocks are nothing but orderly recorded replicas of documents that are connected to the preceding block, which eliminates the chance of data getting attacked.

3.2.2. Manufacturing Plants

For scheduled maintenance, the Internet of Things and Machine Learning technologies are already used by some manufacturing plants. The details associated with the lifecycle of machine parts can be collected and stored in a network of blockchain, and replacement parts can be ordered by smart machinery and paid on a scheduled basis. Moreover, producers can record their data in the blockchain network and apply it to link their ERP systems with their suppliers' systems [33].

3.2.3. Developed Tracing as well as Traceability

An IoT-supported system can be implemented to trace the base of a manufacturing part. It improves transparency as well as traceability for everyone in the value chain. The data collected from IoT sensors can be recorded in the blockchain network, permitting for a shared view and also, assuring that there are no spaces in managing goods, as they move along with the supply chain [34]. Many processes included namely, documentations, getting certifications can also be enhanced significantly with the execution of the blockchain technology.

3.2.4. Credibility of Deliveries

Producers hugely depend on the quality of deliveries that they bought. Suppliers that are venerable, increasingly want their bands to be stored and popular. This requirement is confronted with the support of the blockchain where producers can get data related to their suppliers, so that, they confirm that they get what they claimed, and those deliveries are in the proper size, without any damage [35]. Also, the execution of smart contracts ensures the security of intellectual property as well as payments.

3.2.5. Efficient Inventory Management

The entries can be accessed by anyone in the network because blockchain technology allows the participants to link with every stakeholder in the supply chain, including suppliers, disseminators, or retailers. This implies, everyone holds a replica of the record, thereby avoiding confusion generated in the procedures of the supply chain. This aids to design and handle inventory superior.

3.2.6. Challenges

Blockchain has the ability to enhance various aspects of the manufacturing sector and make it more credible, cost-efficient, as well as fast. With a lot of advantages, several issues are also faced by the industries when it comes to leveraging blockchain technology into their manufacturing businesses. Business owners require to analyze the scalability of their businesses and to understand whether the acquisition of blockchain technology will be advantageous for them or not. Also, to get advantages from the blockchain in the manufacturing industry, it will need broad enhancement that will involve every participant of a chain. Each producer may be a segment of various blockchains, therefore, the setup required to handle all these chains is challenging. So, various executions of those blockchains have to be standardized as well as interoperable for a consolidated unification of these blockchains. Since various enterprises are generating possessory blockchains, interoperability would be a large issue to realize [36].

3.3. Agriculture Industry

Agriculture business relies on several exterior components (like temperature, climate, humidity, the perfection of reap, and many more), as well as complicated delivery chains that could be made circumstantially transparent by executing blockchain. This technology permits end-to-end transactions which occur transparently, without the requirement of an inter-medium such as a middleman or bank in the field of agriculture. By removing the requirement of a central organization, blockchain modifies the manner which granted faith– rather than banking organization. Faith is placed in cryptography as well as end-to-end infrastructure. It also helps to restore the faith between both the manufacturers and customers, which can decrease the costs of transactions in the agriculture market.

A credible technique of tracking transactions between nameless participators is offered by the blockchain [37]. Blockchain supplies transparency among all involved communities, facilitates the set of credible information, and gives solutions to problems related to the quality of food and safety, which are hugely concerned by customers, organizations, and the government.

Some use-cases of blockchain technology in the agriculture sector are described below.

3.3.1. Production of Crop and Food

From farmer to producer and grocer, blockchain technology combined with the Internet of Things to reshape the food production market. Blockchain is ready to make farming a sustainable job by utilizing farming sources containing labor, water, as well as fertilizer, by implementing a simplified technique [38].

3.3.2. Preventing Weather Crisis

While producing distinct kinds of crops, farmers generally have to meet unpredictable weather circumstances. Thus, foreshowing as well as monitoring weather situations are necessary to crop production. Many of the crops produced in the United States (US) cannot endure due to intense spring rains. Also, lack of transparency in the recent food chain ecosystems can consequence in obscure and huge surge pricing. Customers do not have any idea when did the crops confront lousy weather circumstances and what led to the enhanced costs. Farmers, producers, and other stakeholders will be capable to get a straightforward understanding of the price distinctions in the market of food dissemination. From the blockchain ledger, authenticated organizations can track the weather situations, so that, farmers can quickly get the claims of crop insurance through smart contracts.

3.3.3. Food Supply Chain

Tracing a food supply chain is delicate to retracing the source from where the food has been produced. It is necessary to assure that the delivered food is safe to eat. But when it comes to the manner, the supply chain of food becomes an issue for the food originators as well as retailers to validate the origination of the products. With the integration of blockchain technology, it has become plausible to bring faith and transparency in the food delivery chain atmosphere, assuring food safety for each person.

3.3.4. Handling Agricultural Finance

Some of the innumerable issues occurring between formal financial meetings and smallholders are a shortage of transparency, credit histories, and problems in contract enforcement. The incapability to get financial services can have an unfavorable influence on the performance of agricultural value chains due to which manufacturers cannot increase their yields and purchasers meet problems [39]. Blockchain generates fairness in the procedure of agricultural finance via transparency as well as shared control accessibility.

3.3.5. Challenges

The information entering into the chain of blocks is assumed to be transparent as well as public, and it could be an issue to persuade and embolden small-scale consumers to accept the concept of blockchain technology. Most of the existing solutions are based on this gathered data through IoT sensors. Hence, additionally, paying for the subscription of the blockchain, the included organizations have to compensate for the implementation of the Internet of Things. Secondly, collecting the info uploaded to a blockchain platform can be very expensive, which will be an obstacle to the acceptance of blockchain in the agriculture industry. Thirdly, a blockchain does not straightly seamlessly combine with current legacy systems and constructing a structure to apply the blockchain technology, which is often time-consuming. Thus, the complications present in the blockchain will be a preservative to the illustration of solutions based on this technology in the agricultural field.

4. OPEN ISSUES AND MODERN APPLICATION SECTORS

In this part of the chapter, some of the recent major issues in the acquisition of blockchain in the Industrial Internet of Things technology get discussed along with modern application sectors in Industrial IoT or Industry 4.0 where blockchain technology is being executed for finding plausible solutions.

4.1. Open Challenges related to Adoption of Blockchain Technology in IIoT

The Open Challenges related to Adoption of Blockchain Technology in IIoT are explained as follows:

4.1.1. Energy and Cost Efficiency

As the size of blockchain gets increases, more powerful miners have to be appointed for implementing the consensus mechanism such as Proof-of-Work. Rather than recording the complete data of blockchain, some energy-adept protocols of consensus can record only the most current data of transactions on the blockchain. However, still, energy and resource-constrained industrial IoT gadgets are overpowered by large amounts of commercial information produced [40]. Hence, the structure of more adept consensus algorithms is still a major issue.

4.1.2. Regulations

A central organization, commercial standard as well as government regulations must be enforced since the blockchain technology implements in a decentralized manner without depending on any kind of the third party.

4.1.3. Resource Constraints

Existing blockchain workings needed constant network connectivity, and the gadgets of industrial IoT did not always ensure long-lasting network connections. Hence, the execution of blockchain is an issue in this situation. Moreover, high network overhead is incurred by the blockchain which is again a problem for unification into industrial IoT [41]. Due to the resource extents of IoT gadgets as well as networks, the degree of decentralization plausible in existing executions of blockchain technology combined with the IoT networks [42].

4.1.4. Security and Confidentiality

Already, IoT networks are prone to several protection perpetrations namely, eavesdropping perpetrations and replay perpetrations. Along with these threats, blockchains bring several safety risks. Some of the familiar safety threats in the technology are message hijack, confidentiality leakage, smart contract program risks, *etc.*

4.1.5. Scalability

In the blockchain, the problem of scalability is a primary disincentive in broad compliance. Each completely taking part as a node that is needed to hold a replica of blockchain in existing executions of blockchain technology. In opposition to conventional databases, this moves to large storage overhead [43]. Particularly, in the case of industrial IoT, the number of sensor nodes as well as the amount of information produced get increasing, therefore the issue becomes aggravated.

4.2. Modern Application Fields in IIoT where blockchain is being implemented

In IIoT, there are various application fields where blockchain is being implemented as explained below.

4.2.1. Taxi Industry

Existing services of ride-sharing like Uber, Ola operate with a concentrated structure, implementing algorithms from their dispatch centers to monitor their fleet of cabs. The blockchain technology could supply a decentralized as well as disseminated technique to the current model with cab drivers and riders for producing a more consumer-driven customer location. To work on a huger scale, through faith and better coverage, drivers can also cooperate. They can also form a repeating list of clients whom they can depend upon for daily income, and the consumers will have a river that they can bank upon.

4.2.2. Music Industry

The integrity of a copyrighted product is assured by a smart contract. These smart contracts describe and automate the communications as well as connections between the stakeholder of a product. Also, it helps in assuring that the product, a consumer is purchasing, is authorized, and not just an exquisite replica. In the sector of music, music rights management is an efficient use case of smart contracts [44]. Because of the Internet improvement as well as numerous online music streaming features in the past 10-15 years, the music industry has been experiencing a primary modification. The procedure of royalty assessment in the music industry has always been a complex job. However, in the development of Internet services, this method has become even more complicated [45]. Blockchain can assist to make the royalty payment procedure secure as well as transparent by handling a precise and extensive decentralized database for recording complete data (in a disseminated ledger manner) of music rights ownership.

4.2.3. Education Industry

The potency of distance learning based on the web helps in the requirement for a self-reliant as well as the transparent manner of checking up educational data and transcripts of students. For educational documents, a platform based on blockchain technology could work as a scrivener and can produce a form for academic organizations and proprietors to get safe transcripts as well as all the recorded data. The circumstantially functional characteristic of employment indicates that more specializations are needed as career paths digress across institutions and disciplines [46]. Now, in this scenario, blockchain can become the base of academic proof, providing proprietors information required to find whether the CV of an applicant is precise or not.

4.2.4. Drone Industry

The drone industry is the modern industry where blockchain technology is being attempted as well as tested. Drones (also known as UAVs *i.e.* Unmanned Aerial Vehicles) are being appointed on a huge scale for civilian motives, digressing from their conventional usage in the military sector. Safety of UAV network is a significant field, with a lot of research works in this sector. In a study [47], a combination of blockchain technology with UAV networks is proposed, where each unmanned aerial vehicle in the network will operate as a node of the blockchain. This proposal is considered to secure the network from intrusion perpetrations where the perpetrators attempt to intercept interactions as well as the control commands to take control of each and every node in the network [48].

5. CHALLENGES IMPLEMENTATION

The physical world is converted into computerized. An eruption of smart gadgets and modern technologies has enabled humans to be in frequent interaction with one another anytime. Huge volumes of information are simply handled as well as evaluated with data metric technology. Out of modern as well as trending technologies, one such technology is the Industrial of Things (IIoT) which is also called Industry 4.0 or Industrial Internet. The technology can introduce amazing gadgets, enhanced analytics, and the people embraced at work. On concatenating M2M interaction with big data analytics in the industry, Industrial IoT can run unexcelled stages of optimization, producibility, and outcomes. Almost all the companies are refracted towards the Internet of Things enhancement organizations to achieve the technology unified into their works. With the advancement of the IIoT, it has become demonstrable in handling real-time dynamics of data analytics in the commercial field. However, there are some challenges that are holding the implementation of the industrial internet of things. The major challenges recently confronted by industries are illustrated in (Fig. **2**).

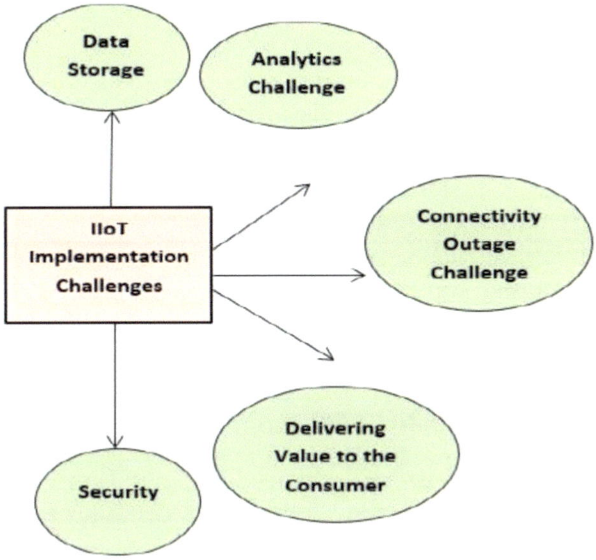

Fig. (2). Challenges related to IIoT implementation.

5.1. Data Storage

Data storage is one of the primary challenges for businesses. In today's world, all presumed activities largely depend on the saved data from the past. No organization lives with an ancient conventional procedure to unravel the data which typically would be evaluated high-frequency info, and then throw it away [49]. IIoT helps to gather a large amount of data that have sensitive pertinency to forthcoming assets of the enterprise outside of the OT network. Thus, it becomes a requirement for any business to prearrange for safe storage of info before going through the complete industrial internet of things in the long run [50].

5.2. Analytics Challenge

In this challenge, if the internet of things solution is executed in the business, its original ROI value is determined through actionable insights implied from the gathered IoT content. This could only be plausible with the support of a high-performance analytics platform that can manage the huge amount of info included to the solution. It is necessary for the data analytics team to include processing, cleaning, as well as representation of data while executing the structure of IoT. This ascertains leaving sufficient space for extendibility component to concatenate real-time or predictive analytics simply to a solution of IoT [51].

5.3. Connectivity Outage Challenge

There is a stable requirement for undisturbed connectivity if an organization is thinking to go industrial IoT. Even while using the Internet connection, its presence of 100% is approximately impracticable. At one point in time, the connectivity is lost either for maintenance purposes or for some other purpose [52]. Hence, if an organization is thinking to bring IIoT technology into their systems, then the crucial requirement is to be available with an uninterrupted connection.

5.4. Delivering Value to the Customer

The design to execute solutions of industrial IoT can hugely influence capacity, consumer gratification, as well as productivity in the long run. Having industrial IoT is a huge deal and the complete process requires deep understanding. Businesses generally design for modern technology to bridge the space of understanding the consumers' problem statement. Thus, it becomes highly necessary for consultants of the internet of things to find out the major performance pointers to measure and enhance through an IoT solution [53].

5.5. Security

In history, there had been several cases of cyber-perpetrations recorded. Thus, it is so much necessary to protect sensitive information from cyber crimes than handling general networks of IT. And, hence, this had been the hugest challenge of the industrial internet of things for the implementation as well as technology, since a usual risk can destroy the business [54]. In case, if an enterprise prearranges to reduce such problems with industrial IoT [55], this would mean proposing new protection tools to the network which implies progressed cost as well as heavy maintenance. Hence, many enterprises are generally avoiding the concept of the industrial internet of things until they are prepared with a solid security or protection arrangement in place [56].

6. SOLUTIONS TO DEAL WITH INDUSTRIAL IOT IMPLEMENTATION CHALLENGES

To deal with the challenges of industrial internet of things implementation, there are various solutions, as presented in (Fig. **3**), that businesses, organizations, or companies can apply in their systems.

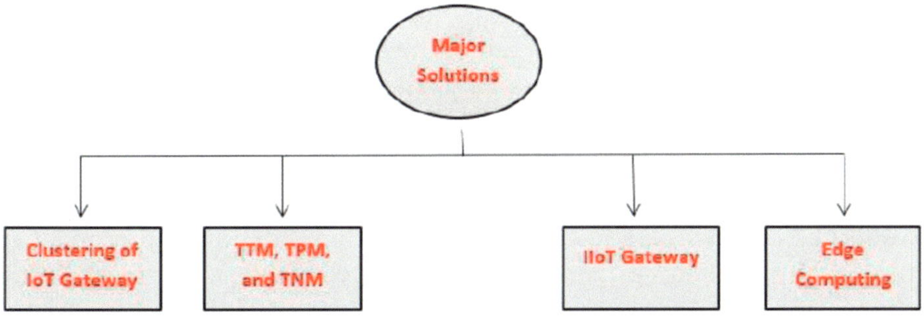

Fig. (3). Solutions to handle IIoT implementation challenges.

6.1. Clustering of IoT Gateway

Internet of Things gateway grouping assures the unification of IT systems, namely ERP systems and CRM applications with OT systems like SCADA and MES systems. Also, it assures the consistency of cloud interaction and recording odd info, which resolves the issue of OT as well as IT convergence [57].

6.2. TTM, TPM and TNM

To reduce security problems, commercial units can bring into operation trusted terminal module (*i.e.* TTM), trusted perception module (*i.e.* TPM), and trusted network module (*i.e.* TNM). Additionally, there are numerous data concentrated protection solutions that assure the security of data encryption while in transit state or in a rest state, which consists of Safe Web Gateway, Web Application Firewall, and also, Application Transmission Controller.

6.3. IIoT Gateway

Industrial internet of things gateway can support the current gadget architecture to safely link to any commercial architecture. For example, a gateway of IoT can link the disseminated control systems straightly with the cloud platform using industrial protocols namely, OPC, wireless technology, MODBUS, ISA100, and PROFIBUS for edge to gateway connection. This works as a solution for the issue of device-to-device interaction [58].

6.4. Edge Computing

Edge computing technology permits only reasonable data to transmit further for analytics rather than transferring a group of data on the cloud platform. In edge computing technology, a particular number of gateways having distinct operations are linked with each other to generate a bunch of gateways and this bunch leads to disseminated edge computing [59]. In this, disseminated edge nodes permit the processing of data near the edge as well as near the source before transferring it to the cloud, which decreases delay as an output [60]. After that, all the filtered info can be straightly transmitted to the fog node and conjugation of fog nodes permit disseminated fog computing. This will assist in speedy data sharing, real-time data evaluation, and allowing faster defect response time.

7. CONCLUSION

As a result of the forthcoming fourth revolution of industry, also called Industry 4.0, modern deleterious technologies are being presumed to be consolidated in the atmosphere of businesses. One of these solutions is “Blockchain technology”, which targets to unify heterogeneous systems and handle industrial transactions. While blockchain technology plays an important character, it is delicate for the holistic enhancement of Industrial IoT or Industry 4.0. IIoT endeavors for huger amounts of automation in modern society. According to experts, IIoT or Industry 4.0 technology will definitely develop production stages even further with time. It is considered that industrial IoT will ultimately become the driving force of innovations behind several kinds of revolution. In this chapter, we have discussed the applications of blockchain in IIoT in detail along with the detailed presentation of Industry 4.0 and IIoT. Furthermore, challenges associated with the implementations of IIoT and solutions to deal with those challenges are also illustrated.

CONSENT FOR PUBLICATION

Not Applicable.

CONFLICT OF INTEREST

The author declares no conflict of interest, financial or otherwise.

ACKNOWLEDGEMENTS

Declared none.

REFERENCES

[1] D. Puthal, N. Malik, S.P. Mohanty, E. Kougianos, and G. Das, "Everything You Wanted to Know About the Blockchain: Its Promise, Components, Processes, and Problems", *IEEE Consumer Electronics Magazine,* vol. 7, pp. 6-14, 2018. [http://dx.doi.org/10.1109/MCE.2018.2816299]

[2] https://www.industryarc.com/Report/7385/industrial-internet-of-things-(IIoT)-market-report.html

[3] A. Arora, A. Kaur, B. Bhushan, and H. Saini, *Security Concerns and Future Trends of Internet of Things. 2019 2nd International Conference on Intelligent Computing, Instrumentation and Control Technologies (ICICICT),* 2019. [http://dx.doi.org/10.1109/icicict46008.2019.8993222]

[4] J. Lin, W. Yu, N. Zhang, X. Yang, H. Zhang, and W. Zhao, "A Survey on Internet of Things: Architecture, Enabling Technologies, Security and Privacy, and Applications", *IEEE Internet of Things Journal,* vol. 4, pp. 1125-1142, 2017. [http://dx.doi.org/10.1109/JIOT.2017.2683200]

[5] D. Miller, "Blockchain and the Internet of Things in the Industrial Sector", *IT Prof.,* vol. 20, pp. 15-18, 2018. [http://dx.doi.org/10.1109/MITP.2018.032501742]

[6] J. Huang, L. Kong, G. Chen, M. Wu, X. Liu, and P. Zeng, "Towards Secure Industrial IoT: Blockchain System with Credit-Based Consensus Mechanism", *IEEE Trans. Industr. Inform.,* vol. 15, pp. 3680-3689, 2019. [http://dx.doi.org/10.1109/TII.2019.2903342]

[7] Y. Xu, J. Ren, G. Wang, C. Zhang, J. Yang, and Y. Zhang, "A Blockchain-Based Nonrepudiation Network Computing Service Scheme for Industrial IoT", *IEEE Trans. Industr. Inform.,* vol. 15, pp. 3632-3641, 2019. [http://dx.doi.org/10.1109/TII.2019.2897133]

[8] W. Liang, M. Tang, J. Long, X. Peng, J. Xu, and K. Li, "A Secure FaBric Blockchain-Based Data Transmission Technique for Industrial Internet-of-Things", *IEEE Trans. Industr. Inform.,* vol. 15, pp. 3582-3592, 2019. [http://dx.doi.org/10.1109/TII.2019.2907092]

[9] H. Yao, T. Mai, J. Wang, Z. Ji, C. Jiang, and Y. Qian, "Resource Trading in Blockchain-Based Industrial Internet of Things", *IEEE Trans. Industr. Inform.,* vol. 15, pp. 3602-3609, 2019. [http://dx.doi.org/10.1109/TII.2019.2902563]

[10] S. Zhao, S. Li, and Y. Yao, "Blockchain Enabled Industrial Internet of Things Technology", *IEEE Transactions on Computational Social Systems,* vol. 6, pp. 1442-1453, 2019. [http://dx.doi.org/10.1109/TCSS.2019.2924054]

[11] J. Al-Jaroodi, and N. Mohamed, "Blockchain in Industries: A Survey", *IEEE Access,* vol. 7, pp. 36500-36515, 2019. [http://dx.doi.org/10.1109/ACCESS.2019.2903554]

[12] T.M. Fernández-Caramés, and P. Fraga-Lamas, "A Review on the Application of Blockchain to the Next Generation of Cybersecure Industry 4.0 Smart Factories", *IEEE Access,* vol. 7, pp. 45201-45218, 2019. [http://dx.doi.org/10.1109/ACCESS.2019.2908780]

[13] A.K. Goel, A. Rose, J. Gaur, and B. Bhushan, "Attacks, Countermeasures and Security Paradigms in IoT", *2019 2nd International Conference on Intelligent Computing, Instrumentation and Control*

Technologies (ICICICT), 2019.
[http://dx.doi.org/10.1109/icicict46008.2019.8993338]

[14] F. Shrouf, J.B. Meré, and G. Miragliotta, "Smart factories in industry 4.0: A review of the concept and of energy management approached in production based on the internet of things paradigm", *2014 IEEE International Conference on Industrial Engineering and Engineering Management,* pp. 697-701, 2014.
[http://dx.doi.org/10.1109/IEEM.2014.7058728]

[15] https://www.iot-now.com/2018/10/12/89230-iot-iiot-connected-industry-industry-4-0-come-together - create-new-model-business/

[16] D. Preuveneers, and E.I. Zudor, "The intelligent industry of the future: A survey on emerging trends, research challenges and opportunities in Industry 4.0", *J. Ambient Intell. Smart Environ.,* vol. 9, pp. 287-298, 2017.
[http://dx.doi.org/10.3233/AIS-170432]

[17] Z. Li, J. Kang, R. Yu, D. Ye, Q. Deng, and Y. Zhang, "Consortium Blockchain for Secure Energy Trading in Industrial Internet of Things", *IEEE Trans. Industr. Inform.,* vol. 14, pp. 3690-3700, 2018.

[18] J. Kang, R. Yu, X. Huang, S. Maharjan, Y. Zhang, and E. Hossain, "Enabling Localized Peer-to-Peer Electricity Trading Among Plug-in Hybrid Electric Vehicles Using Consortium Blockchains", *IEEE Trans. Industr. Inform.,* vol. 13, pp. 3154-3164, 2017.
[http://dx.doi.org/10.1109/TII.2017.2709784]

[19] J. Wan, J. Li, M. Imran, and D. Li, "A blockchain-based solution for enhancing security and privacy in smart factory", *IEEE Trans. Industr. Inform.,* 2019.
[http://dx.doi.org/10.1109/TII.2019.2894573]

[20] Y. Yu, R. Chen, H. Li, Y. Li, and A. Tian, "Toward data security in edge intelligent Iot", *IEEE Netw.,* vol. 33, pp. 20-26, 2019.
[http://dx.doi.org/10.1109/MNET.001.1800507]

[21] L. Xu, W. He, and S. Li, "Internet of Things in Industries: A Survey", *IEEE Trans. Industr. Inform.,* vol. 10, pp. 2233-2243, 2014.
[http://dx.doi.org/10.1109/TII.2014.2300753]

[22] J.M. Müller, D. Kiel, and K. Voigt, "What drives the implementation of Industry 4.0? The role of opportunities and challenges in the context of sustainability", *Sustainability,* vol. 10, p. 247, 2018.
[http://dx.doi.org/10.3390/su10010247]

[23] C. Esposito, A. D. Santis, G. Tortora, and H. Chang, "Blockchain: A panacea for healthcare cloud-based data security and privacy?", *IEEE Cloud Computing,* vol. 5, no. 1, pp. 31-37, 2018.
[http://dx.doi.org/10.1109/mcc.2018.011791712]

[24] H. Wu, "Toward blockchains for health-care systems: applying the bilinear pairing technology to ensure privacy protection and accuracy in data sharing", *IEEE Consumer Electronics Magazine,* vol. 7, no. 4, pp. 65-71, 2018.
[http://dx.doi.org/10.1109/mce.2018.2816306]

[25] M. A. Salahuddin, A. Al-Fuqaha, M. Guizani, and K. Shuaib, "Softwarization of Internet of Things Infrastructure for Secure and Smart Healthcare", *Computer,* vol. 50, no. 7, pp. 74-79, 2017.
[http://dx.doi.org/10.1109/MC.2017.195]

[26] T. Nugent, D. Upton, and M. Cimpoesu, "Improving data transparency in clinical trials using blockchain smart contracts", *F1000 Res.,* vol. 5, p. 2541, 2016.
[http://dx.doi.org/10.12688/f1000research.9756.1] [PMID: 28357041]

[27] Q. Xia, E. B. Sifah, K. O. Asamoah, J. Gao, and X. Du, "MeDShare: Trust-Less Medical Data Sharing Among Cloud Service Providers via Blockchain", *IEEE Access,* vol. 5, pp. 14757-14767, 2017.
[http://dx.doi.org/10.1109/ACCESS.2017.2730843]

[28] *MedRec,* 2016. https://medrec.media.mit.edu/ [Online; accessed 12- April-2019].

[29] *Medicalchain,* 2019. https://medicalchain.com/en/ [Online; accessed 12-April-2019].

[30] T. Bocek, B.B. Rodrigues, and T. Strasser, "Blockchains everywhere - a use-case of blockchains in the pharma supply-chain", *2017 IFIP/IEEE Symposium on Integrated Network and Service Management (IM),* 2017.
[http://dx.doi.org/10.23919/INM.2017.7987376]

[31] D. Kiel, C. Arnold, and K. Voigt, "The influence of the Industrial Internet of Things on business models of established manufacturing companies – A business level perspective", *Technovation,* vol. 68, pp. 4-19, 2017.
[http://dx.doi.org/10.1016/j.technovation.2017.09.003]

[32] Y. Sun, L. Zhang, G. Feng, B. Yang, B. Cao, and M. Imran, "Blockchain-Enabled Wireless Internet of Things: Performance Analysis and Optimal Communication Node Deployment", *IEEE Internet of Things Journal,* vol. 6, pp. 5791-5802, 2019.
[http://dx.doi.org/10.1109/JIOT.2019.2905743]

[33] P. Nash, *Challenges of the Industrial Internet of Things,* 2017. [Online]. Available: https://www.invma.co.uk/blog/iiot-challenges

[34] P.J. Zelbst, K.W. Green, V.E. Sower, and P. Bond, "The impact of RFID, IIoT, and Blockchain technologies on supply chain transparency", *J. Manuf. Tech. Manag.,* 2019.
[http://dx.doi.org/10.1108/JMTM-03-2019-0118]

[35] M. Isaja, and J. Soldatos, "Distributed Ledger Architecture for Automation, Analytics and Simulation in Industrial Environments", *IFAC-PapersOnLine,* vol. 51, pp. 370-375, 2018.
[http://dx.doi.org/10.1016/j.ifacol.2018.08.321]

[36] A. Gottheil, *Can Blockchain Address the Industrial IOT Security?,* 2018. [Online]. Available: http://iiot-world.com/cybersecurity/canblockchain-address-the-industrial-IOT-security

[37] F. Yiannas, "A New Era of Food Transparency Powered by Blockchain", *Innov. (Camb., Mass.),* vol. 12, no. 1-2, pp. 46-56, 2018.
[http://dx.doi.org/10.1162/inov_a_00266]

[38] M. P. Caro, M. S. Ali, M. Vecchio, and R. Giaffreda, "A case study for grain quality assurance tracking based on a blockchain business network", *arXiv preprint,* 2018.
[http://dx.doi.org/10.1109/IOT-TUSCANY.2018.8373021]

[39] P. Lucena, A.P. Binotto, F.S. Momo, and H. Kim, "A case study for grain quality assurance tracking based on a blockchain business network", *arXiv preprint,* 2018.

[40] F. Wang, Y. Yuan, J. Zhang, R. Qin, and M.H. Smith, "Blockchainized Internet of Minds: A New Opportunity for Cyber-Physical-Social Systems", *IEEE Trans. Comput. Social Systems,* vol. 5, pp. 897-906, 2018.
[http://dx.doi.org/10.1109/TCSS.2018.2881344]

[41] C. Manchanda, N. Sharma, R. Rathi, B. Bhushan, and M. Grover, "Neoteric security and privacy sanctuary technologies in smart cities", *2020 IEEE 9th International Conference on Communication Systems and Network Technologies (CSNT),* 2020.
[http://dx.doi.org/10.1109/csnt48778.2020.9115780]

[42] H. Jaidka, N. Sharma, and R. Singh, "Evolution of IoT to IIoT: Applications & Challenges", *SSRN Electronic Journal,* 2020.

[43] E. Pasquali, *Industrial Iot and the (Data) Sharing Economy,* 2018. [Online]. Available: http://iiot-world.com/connected-industry/industrialiot-and-the-data-sharing-economy

[44] R. Sethi, B. Bhushan, N. Sharma, and R. Kumar, "Applicability of Industrial IoT in Diversified Sectors: Evolution, Applications and Challenges", *Studies in Big Data Multimedia Technologies in the Internet of Things Environment,* pp. 45-67, 2020. 45-67.
[http://dx.doi.org/10.1007/978-981-15-7965-3_4]

[45] L. Urquhart, and D. McAuley, "Avoiding the Internet of Insecure Industrial Things", *ArXiv,* 2018. [http://dx.doi.org/10.1016/j.clsr.2017.12.004]

[46] I. Brass, L. Tanczer, M. Carr, M. Elsden, and J.J. Blackstock, "Standardising a moving target: The development and evolution of IoT security standards", *IoT,* 2018.

[47] A. Kuzmin, and E. Znak, "Blockchain-base structures for a secure and operate network of semi-autonomous unmanned aerial vehicles", *2018 IEEE International Conference on Service Operations and Logistics, and Informatics (SOLI),* IEEE, pp. 32-37, 2018. [http://dx.doi.org/10.1109/SOLI.2018.8476785]

[48] T. Varshney, N. Sharma, I. Kaushik, and B. Bhushan, "Authentication & encryption based security services in blockchain technology", *2019 International Conference on Computing, Communication, and Intelligent Systems (ICCCIS),* 2019. [http://dx.doi.org/10.1109/ICCCIS48478.2019.8974500]

[49] L. Bassi, "Industry 4.0: Hope, hype or revolution?", *2017 IEEE 3rd International Forum on Research and Technologies for Society and Industry (RTSI),* pp. 1-6, 2017.

[50] L. Zhou, D. Wu, J. Chen, and Z. Dong, "When Computation Hugs Intelligence: Content-Aware Data Processing for Industrial IoT", *IEEE Internet of Things Journal,* vol. 5, pp. 1657-1666, 2018. [http://dx.doi.org/10.1109/JIOT.2017.2785624]

[51] V. Domova, and A. Dagnino, "Towards intelligent alarm management in the Age of IIoT", *Global Internet of Things Summit (GIoTS),* pp. 1-5, 2017.

[52] I.A. Brusakova, A.D. Borisov, G.R. Gusko, D.Y. Nekrasov, and K.E. Malenkova, "Prospects for the development of IIOT technology in Russia", *2017 IEEE Conference of Russian Young Researchers in Electrical and Electronic Engineering (EIConRus),* pp. 1315-1317, 2017.

[53] A. Sajid, H. Abbas, and K. Saleem, "Cloud-Assisted IoT-Based SCADA Systems Security: A Review of the State of the Art and Future Challenges", *IEEE Access,* vol. 4, pp. 1375-1384, 2016. [http://dx.doi.org/10.1109/ACCESS.2016.2549047]

[54] D. Quarta, M. Pogliani, M. Polino, F. Maggi, A.M. Zanchettin, and S. Zanero, "An experimental security analysis of an industrial robot controller", *2017 IEEE Symposium on Security and Privacy (SP),* pp. 268-286, 2017. [http://dx.doi.org/10.1109/SP.2017.20]

[55] Z. Guan, X. Lu, N. Wang, J. Wu, X. Du, and M. Guizani, "Towards secure and efficient energy trading in IIoT-enabled energy internet: A blockchain approach", *Future Gener. Comput. Syst.,* 2019.

[56] E. Uhlmann, E. Hohwieler, and C. Geisert, "Intelligent production systems in the era of Industrie 4.0 – changing mindsets and business models", *Journal of Machine Engineering,* 2017.

[57] M. Banerjee, J. Lee, and K.R. Choo, "A blockchain future for internet of things security: a position paper", *Digital Communications and Networks,* vol. 4, pp. 149-160, 2017. [http://dx.doi.org/10.1016/j.dcan.2017.10.006]

[58] T. Varshney, N. Sharma, I. Kaushik, and B. Bhushan, "Architectural model of security threats & their countermeasures in IoT", *2019 International Conference on Computing, Communication, and Intelligent Systems (ICCCIS),* 2019. [http://dx.doi.org/10.1109/ICCCIS48478.2019.8974544]

[59] T. Sharma, S. Satija, and B. Bhushan, "Unifying blockchian and IoT: Security requirements, challenges, applications and future trends", *2019 International Conference on Computing, Communication, and Intelligent Systems (ICCCIS),* 2019. [http://dx.doi.org/10.1109/ICCCIS48478.2019.8974552]

[60] B. Chen, J. Wan, L. Shu, P. Li, M. Mukherjee, and B. Yin, "Smart Factory of Industry 4.0: Key Technologies, Application Case, and Challenges", *IEEE Access,* vol. 6, pp. 6505-6519, 2018. [http://dx.doi.org/10.1109/ACCESS.2017.2783682]

CHAPTER 7

Enhancement of Iot Security Solutions Using Blockchain Technology

K. Sheela[1,*] and **C. Priya**[2]

[1] *Department of Computer Science, Vels Institute of Science, Technology and Advanced Studies (VISTAS), Chennai, India*

[2] *Department of Information Technology, Vels Institute of Science, Technology and Advanced Studies (VISTAS), Chennai, India*

Abstract: A blockchain is a growing list of records, called blocks, which are linked together using cryptography. Each block contains a cryptographic hash of the previous block, a timestamp, and transaction data. It is a decentralized, distributed and public digital ledger that is used to record transactions across many computers called nodes. Blockchain, in collaboration with the technologies like Artificial Intelligence, the Internet of Things, Big data, *etc.*, provides more effective outcomes by minimizing manpower with an increase in its feasibility. IoT is all about expanding the power of the internet beyond computers and smartphones to a whole range of other things, processes, and environments. Our day-to-day life can be made interesting with the applications of IoT-enabled devices in the home, agriculture, logistics, industries, healthcare sectors, and so on. They can be combined with the disciplines like data collection, management of huge data, storage of data, data analytics, *etc.* These IoT devices are embedded with sensors that are vulnerable to hackers and malware. At present, we cannot give complete assurance of the security of the access and data associated with the devices as it is possible for an intruder to misuse or mishandle the scheduled process. But, in association with blockchain technology, we can acquire solutions for problems related to security.

Keywords: Application, Authenticity, Blockchain, Banking sector, Consensus, Corda, Crypto-currency, Cryptography, Distributed, Ether, Ethereum, E-governance, Hashing, Healthcare, IoT, Platforms, Proof of work and stack, Security, Smart contract, Smart city.

1. INTRODUCTION

IoT devices have become a regular component in our day-to-day life. We can see that the devices which are connected to the internet are gradually increasing by

* **Corresponding author K. Sheela:** Department of Computer Science, Vels Institute of Science, Technology and Advanced Studies (VISTAS), Chennai, India; E-mail: ksheela.research@gmail.com

Sudhir K. Sharma, Bharat Bhushan, Parma N. Astya and Narayan C. Debnath (Eds.)

paving the way for a digital environment. The traditional database provides a centralized architecture, whereas blockchain provides a distributed peer-to-peer network. In simple terms, blockchain is a collection of data stored in a database that maintains the continuously growing records in a distributed, peer-to-peer network node [1]. This makes the Blockchain and IoT to get integrated to provide even better services. Generally, IoT devices are liable to many kinds of security attacks [2]. The following are some of the attacks which occur to the devices connected to the internet.

Brute Force Attack: It is the process of trying all the possibilities of the password given by the authorized user.

The Man in the Middle: In this kind of cyber-attack, an intruder involves himself in the communication and gain access to the messages transferred. It is also possible for him to alter the messages which lead to miscommunication.

Denial of Service: This attack is used to slow down the process which also affects the reputation of an organization. Distributed Denial of Service (DDoS) may also occur to engage the resources in unnecessary services and makes the network resources unavailable for the appropriate activities. One of the methods to overcome this is proof of Activity which is the combination of PoS and PoW [3].

Eavesdropping: It is also known as sniffing or snooping attacks. It is the process of stealing the information while it gets transmitted over the network by devices like a smartphone, computers, or other connected devices.

Sybil Attack: It is the process of creating large numbers of pseudonymous identities to hide real identities and slow down the process. It entirely damages the operation of the network.

These attacks can be overridden by collaborating blockchain technology with the Internet of Things having the features like decentralized framework, immutability, reliability, autonomous behavior, and so on [4]. Every transaction in the blockchain is cryptographically sealed using public/private keys. Every transaction must be defined and authenticated. With these transactions, blocks must be created, validated, and linked (chained) [5] to enhance the security level of the transactions.

Blockchain technology, in collaboration with technologies like Artificial Intelligence, Internet of Things [IOT], Bigdata, *etc.* provides more effective end results by minimizing the manpower with an increase in its feasibility. Certainly, Blockchain entitles IoT devices by providing security and authentication with transparency in IoT ecosystems. We can easily predict that IoT will become a part of our day-to-day life in our near future with its huge development and collaboration with effective technologies like blockchain technology. Fraudulent activities may also occur in the localization of IoT devices where the location of the connected device might be tampered with to provide erroneous data. It can be overridden by this blockchain technology [2]. It is well-known specifically for its unique features like decentralized and distributed nature, hashing and cryptographic techniques, and smart contracts maintained between them. Let us have a deep look into this collaboration in this chapter.

1.1. Contribution of the Work

This chapter elaborates on security enhancement solutions and sheds light on the platforms where blockchain technology can be implemented.

Furthermore, it consolidates the features of these technologies and

highlights the study on collaborating Artificial Intelligence, Blockchain, and the Internet of Things for a sustainable environment.

It also encapsulates research directions along with certain guidelines.

1.2. Paper Organization

In section 2, we have discussed the platforms which can be used for implementing blockchain technology along with IoT integration. Further, in section 3, a number of techniques for imposing security for an operation have been explained with diagrams and tabular columns. A detailed explanation of IoT implemented with blockchain technology in various fields like smart city, healthcare, e-governance, education system, waste management, supply-chain management, *etc.*, has been elaborated in section 4.

2. PLATFORMS TO IMPLEMENT BLOCKCHAIN TECHNOLOGY AND ITS USES

By considering the nature of the Blockchain, it has been classified into three types, namely private, public, and consortium. A private blockchain is a restricted one. The user, who can access the data, will be assigned by a network administrator and others will be restricted from accessing it. There is no restriction of access in the public blockchain. The consortium is a semi-restricted blockchain where access permission will be given with certain restrictions to work with the blockchain platform [6]. A platform is an environment in which a piece of software can be executed. Many platforms have been designed to support and develop blockchain technology. These platforms are classified into two categories, namely permissioned and permission-less: The following are some of the most effectively used platforms for this technology:

Ethereum– It is a permission-less, decentralized application (DApp). It uses Ether as its cryptocurrency (ETH).

Hyperledger fabric – It is a permissioned blockchain where only known identities could be able to participate.

Ripple – It is most essentially designed for transactions on payment.

Quorum – It is an enterprise-focused version of ethereum.

Corda – Initially, it was designed for the financial sector. But nowadays, it has also been implemented in other sectors too.

EOS – It eliminates fees for all of its users.

Open chain – It was highly designed for managing digital assets.

Stellar – It deals with all the transactions and exchanges between cryptocurrencies and fiat-based currencies. To achieve the desired consensus, it uses Stellar Consensus Protocol (SCP).

There are many other types of platforms available to implement blockchain technology. The above mentioned are the platforms that are highly popular and user-friendly platforms of this technology. Table (**1**) provides a clear comparison between the top 5 blockchain platforms in the most efficient forums [7].

Table 1. Comparison between top-five blockchain platforms.

Blockchain	Ethereum	Hyperledger Fabric	Corda	Ripple	Quorum
Industry focus	Cross-Industry	Cross-Industry	Finance purpose	Finance purpose	Cross-Industry
Governance	Ethereum Developers	Linux Foundation	R3 Consortium	Ripple Labs	Ethereum Developers and JP Morgan Chase
Smart contract service	Yes	Yes	Yes	No	Yes

(Table 1) cont.....

Blockchain	Ethereum	Hyperledger Fabric	Corda	Ripple	Quorum
Language for smart contract	Solidity	Java, Node.js, Go	Kotlin, Java	No	Solidity
Ledger type	Permissionless	Permissioned	Permissioned	Semi-Permissioned	Permissioned
Cryptocurrency	Ether (ETH)	None	None	Ripple (XRP)	None
Consensus algorithm	Proof of Work (PoW)	Pluggable Framework	Pluggable Framework	Probabilistic Voting	Majority Voting
Transaction performance	Scalable	Very Scalable	Very Scalable	Very Scalable	Very Scalable

2.1. IoT and Its Integration

Internet of Things promotes connectivity between humans and devices in our day-to-day life and enables a wide range of customized services to the end-users who might suffer from a lack of security. This issue can be overridden by the integration of blockchain technology. Each and every communication made by device 1 with other devices will generate a transaction. These transactions between the service provider and the acceptor will be stored in the blockchain which maintains a public digital ledger [8]. Blockchain in collaboration with IoT has achieved many targets like energy consumption, data aggregation, scalability, security and privacy, access control, authentication, non-repudiation, and so on with a great increase in efficiency and productivity [9].

3. TECHNIQUES USED FOR IMPOSING SECURITY

As we already know, Blockchain is a distributed and decentralized network, which furnishes privacy and security along with transparency and immutability. From its decentralized nature, it is clear that there is no central authority to validate or verify the transactions. Even then blockchain assures its verification and security with the consensus protocol. To maintain its reliability, we can use distributed digital ledger along with cryptographic techniques.

3.1. Consensus

It is a common agreement that has to be satisfied by all the connected nodes of the blockchain network in a distributed ledger [10]. It has been classified as follows.

- **PoW** – **Proof of Work** algorithm is used to confirm the transactions and provides a new block to the chain. It brings out the concept of mining. The person who does mining is known as a miner. Mining is the process of validating the transactions and maintaining them on a global ledger called a blockchain.

- **PoS – Proof of Stake** has been created as an alternative for PoW. Here, the available balance of bitcoin will be considered instead of considering the resources to solve the puzzles. For example, a miner who holds only 4% of bitcoin in his account can only mine 4% of the blocks.
- **PBFT – Practical Byzantine Fault Tolerance** occurs in a decentralized, distributed system like blockchain technology. There is a possibility for the participants to communicate with each other in an uncontrolled, open, and permission less system. There is a chance for an assumption that the transaction could be malicious if it does not reach the destination in the mentioned span of time. It can be overridden by having at least 2/3 of the most reliable network nodes. If the majority of the system decides to act maliciously, then it reaches 51% attack.

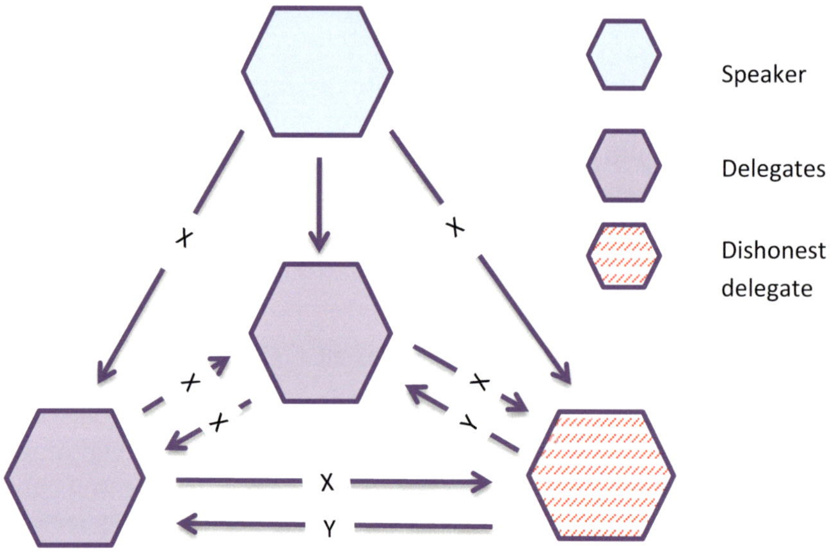

Fig. (1). Byzantine Generals Problem.

From the given Fig. (**1**), we can notice that the dishonest delegate modifies the original message and sends it to other delegates. The problem occurs if other delegates trust and act according to the information shared by the dishonest one. To avoid such cases, blockchain implements certain consensus like PoW, PoS, and so on in order to select the most reliable network nodes. Here, every transaction of a single node will be automatically reflected in all other nodes. Therefore, there is no chance for modification.

- **PoB**–Proof of Burn is fondly referred to as Proof of Work with less energy consumption. It does not require huge computational resources. Miners have to burn a certain amount of their own crypto-currencies like native coin or bitcoin to determine their commitment towards the network to gain the virtual mining, power (it was compared to virtual mining rig) to mine and validate the transactions. Similar to PoW, PoB also provides rewards to the miners for their effort in a specified period of time. Most of these rewards will cover the initial investment of the burned coins.
- **PoC** – PoC stands for Proof of Capacity. The name itself clearly depicts that it is highly concerned with the capacity of the node. Greater the hard drive capacity, the greater the chance to become a miner or validator of the upcoming block.
- **DAG**–Directed Acyclic Graph is a finite directed graph with no cycles. In order to promote blockchain technology in a more practical way, DAG has been suggested. It holds a series of nodes in a topological order connected together in the ledger. This newly proposed structure in the blockchain is termed the tangle. Each transaction must be validated by two former transactions [11].
- **Pluggable Consensus** –The ordering of transactions is consigned to a modular component for consensus which will be logically decoupled from peers that execute transactions and maintains a ledger. Its platform relies on Byzantine Fault Tolerant (BFT) ordering [12].

Table (**2**) clearly describes the functionalities with the merits and demerits of consensus protocols in blockchain technology [13].

Table 2. Comparison between the consensus protocols.

Protocol	Function	Language	Resource utilized	Processing Speed	Efficiency	Drawbacks
PoW	Used to assure the transactions and build new blocks to the chain.	Solidity, Python, Java, *etc.*,	Elevated	Slow	Stunted	Higher the power consumption, lowers the security
PoS	Available balance of bitcoin plays a major role	Native	Stunted	Fast	Elevated	Only wealthy stakeholders can enjoy the consensus control
PBFT	Voting mechanism will be considered to assure the integrity and origin of the transaction	Java and Go lang	Elevated	Elevated	Elevated	Excessive communication overhead

(Table 2) cont.....

Protocol	Function	Language	Resource utilized	Processing Speed	Efficiency	Drawbacks
PoB	PoW with less energy consumption. It involves coin burning strategy.	Solidity, Go lang, C++	Moderate	Moderate	Stunted	Wastage of resources
PoC	Increased hard drive capacity increases the chance of being a miner	-	Elevated	Stunted	Elevated	Only nodes with greater capacity receive more stake
PoET	Each node produces a random number to evaluate its waiting time	Python	Elevated	Medium	Elevated	Chances repeatedly fall for the same node to be the leader
DAG	It has no cycles. Every node must be validated with 2 former nodes	-	Stunted	Elevated	Elevated	Must be in a topological order

- **PoET** – In Proof of Elapsed Time, each node participating in the network is required to wait for a specified period of time. The first node which completes the designated waiting time wins the mining authority for a new block. Each node in the network generates an arbitrary waiting time and sleeps for that specified duration. The node which wakes up first will grab the chance for mining the block. The same process will be repeated for all the upcoming blocks.

3.2. Ledger

In general, a ledger is termed as a record-keeping system where we can maintain all the financial transactions (credit or debit) of a person or a business for future reference. It can be differentiated into two types.

Centralized ledger - Common server manages the entire process

Distributed ledger - No single point of storage

Blockchain facilitates distributed digital ledgers with its decentralized nature. A distributed ledger is a database that is contemporized and accessed across different areas. Any change made by one user will be automatically reflected to all other connected nodes. That modification will be approved only if 51% of nodes accepting it. If not, that particular action will be prohibited. This process reduces cyber attacks and fraudulent activities which might occur in the network. It has greater potential to restructure the way institutions, governments and corporations work. When we think about scalability, blockchain works very well and fast with the least number of users on the network. The greater number of nodes reduces the speed of the transaction [14].

3.3. Cryptography

Cryptography facilitates secure communication. The meaning for the term "crypt" is "hidden" and "graph" means "writing" i.e. hidden writing. Hence the communicated message will be understood only by an intended receiver. It uses two special keys called private and public keys along with two most specific features called encryption and decryption. Encryption is the process of converting plain text into ciphertext and decryption is the process of converting the ciphertext into plain text (readable form). This encryption and decryption will be done with the private and public keys of the node. Data Encryption Standard (DES), Triple DES, two fish encryption, Advanced encryption standard (AES), the RSA algorithm are some of the most commonly used encryption algorithms.

The public key cryptography and consensus mechanism of blockchain, applied by the crypto-currency transaction are unbreakable for any fraudulent transactions [15]. In cryptography and cybersecurity, a man-in-the-middle attack is considered a widely performed attack where the hackers can easily monitor or alter the contents of the communication. This can be avoided by including features like private and public keys for authentication, using sensors linked with communicating devices with the help of TensorFlow, Raspberry pi, to implement IoT and blockchain for enriching the level of security in a transaction and uses MQTT (Message Queuing Telemetry Transport for transferring message between devices [16].

3.4. Hashing

Blockchain is usually comprised of a list of blocks connected with each other. It is not possible to alter the order of the blocks as they are interlinked to each other. Each block has a unique hash value associated with it. The hash value of one block will be linked with the next block. Therefore, every block will have its own unique hash value along with the previous block's hash value. Fig. (**2**) depicts the structure of blocks with their hash values where there is no possibility to rearrange the order of blocks [17]. A series of hashing algorithms were proposed and named Secure Hash Algorithm (SHA). SHA-1 was announced in 1993 which produces 160-bit hash but proved to have weak collision avoidance.

SHA-2 was announced in 2001. SHA 2 includes SHA-224, SHA-256, SHA-384,SHA-512. They are named by considering the length of hash bit or message digest generated by them.

SHA-3 came into existence to tighten the security level. But it made the process slow in software. Though the concerned security was given, it was comparatively slower than SHA-2.

Hash: 3346 Hash: 5456 Hash: 8856

Previous Hash: 0000 Previous Hash: 3346 Previous Hash: 5456

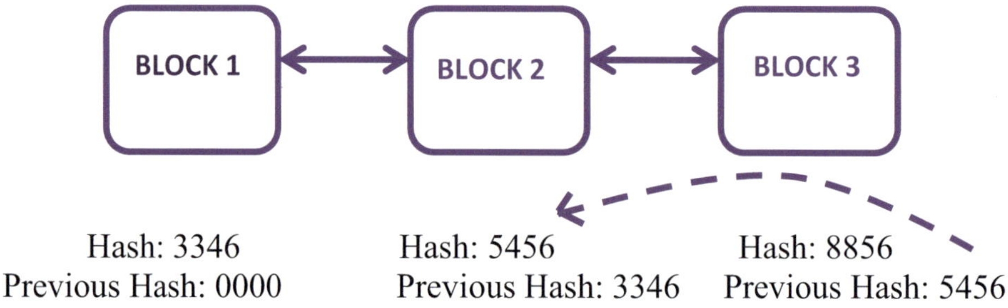

Fig. (2). Blocks with their hash values.

Fig. (3). Generated hash value for a given string "Integration of blockchain and IOT".

IoT with blockchain improves network connectivity using peer-to-peer communication directly without relying on any third party. Blockchain technology with its security features avoids cyberattacks [18].

SHA-256 is the most commonly used hashing technique. This algorithm returns a hexadecimal representation. Therefore, it returns 64-bit hash values for every given input irrespective of the size of an input. In Figs. (**3**) and (**4**), we can see that the inputs are not in the same length, but the hash values are 64 bits.

Fig. (4). Generated hash value for a given string "BC and IOT".

Also, it must be noted that the string in Fig. (**4**) is a substring of Fig. (**3**). But we could not find any resemblance in their hash value which seems to be completely unique. Every transaction in blockchain technology will be stored in all the nodes connected to it, which can be termed as a full node. In full mode, huge storage space will be consumed which may not satisfy few users. Therefore, Lightweight nodes have been created which send their data to the full nodes instead of maintaining all the duplicate records in it. This will be suggested for devices with less computational power [19].

3.5. Smart Contract

A smart contract is a digital contract with the security coding of a blockchain. They are almost similar to the traditional contract. These smart contracts will be executed exactly by the rules coded by the coder when it is created. It directly controls the transfer of digital assets between the nodes at certain conditions. In the case of IoT, we can maintain a smart contract between devices and gadgets which we are using in our day-to-day life. While considering the operational mechanism of smart contracts, we can observe that its life cycle into five stages [20].

Negotiation – Analyses the needs for implementing smart contract

Development – Plans for the functionalities to get implemented

Deployment – Creates the contract between the parties involved in the transaction

Maintenance –This phase manages and maintains the data associated with it.

Learning and self-destruction – Organizes the entire process in a systematic manner. Self-destruction can also be implemented once the entire process is done.

Smart contract promotes automation. Many companies and organizations are putting efforts to include smart contracts into their regular practice by ignoring the traditional contracts [21]. No mishandling can be done when we are relying on a smart contract. This can be implemented using solidity language in the blockchain. Solidity is specifically created for maintaining smart contracts.

4. IoT IMPLEMENTATION

Blockchain technology can be integrated with the Internet of Things (IoT) to enhance its applications in the real world. In recent times, this technology has responded constantly to the issues related to privacy and security, trust, reliability, single point of failure, and scalability by empowering peer-to-peer contract behavior, without the intervention of third parties. To overcome the vulnerability in security issues, we use cryptographic concepts like private and public keys with Public Key Infrastructure (PKI) for the secure distribution of keys to generate and verify digital signatures [22]. It can be implemented in few fields where green engineering can also be achieved. Certain applications are as follows:

4.1. Data Storage In A Distributed Manner

Initially, data will be shared through a cloud, and the permission and access controls will be managed by a centralized server where there is a chance for a single point of failure. Hence, we can shift towards a decentralized storage network called the blockchain. It can collaborate with IoT devices like sensors which can identify and alert the users at the time of immoral activities. This alert system can be used in many real-time applications in our day-to-day life.

4.2. Decentralized Energy Production And Consumption

Usually, energy resources are produced in different locations and they can be consumed by the people irrespective of locations until the resources exist. This energy production requires authentication for the producers to incentivize them for their efforts. There is a chance to forge people without recognizing their work or people may consume the energy resource and deny/pretend as if they have not consumed it. In such cases, we can implement blockchain technology to have a transparent transaction.

4.3. Selective Offloading To Minimize The Data Path

The concept of decentralization minimizes the data path. It is essential to redesign the network architecture to randomly offload computing and storage devices connected with IoT in order to minimize the expense and resource utilization. Every transaction will be recorded in the distributed ledger which lets all the connected nodes to be aware of the entire structure. Each datum will be stored in all the nodes in an encrypted format which can be decrypted only by the authorized user.

4.4. Iot In Home Appliances

Nowadays, home appliances are getting connected to the internet to access from anywhere and anytime. It is necessary for things to have secure communication with their owner. We can implement blockchain technology in this area to provide authenticated service with no interference. In smart homes, every device connected to the internet will periodically store its data in cloud storage for better efficiency to provide details upon query by the authority. For example, the security camera can be accessed or viewed from anywhere by the owner of the house without any fear of intruders [23].

4.5. E-Governance

Government portals are fully centralized. It can include this technology to improvise its sectors in a more efficient way. It includes other biometrics, IT details, education system, and so on. This decentralized method vanishes a single point of failure and guarantees secure storage of data. This process also promotes green engineering by accomplishing many essential aspects of our environment. Nowadays, technologies are playing a predominant role in achieving the objectives of green engineering by reducing the human intervention where we may come across fraudulent activities. When we discuss e-governance with blockchain technology, e-tendering will be an essential step in its progress in the business field. E-tendering promotes the online bidding process by providing more trust and efficiency with its distributed nature [24]. Blockchain can be integrated with IoT in many fields of governance.

4.6. Education System

Education and employment longed to achieve a flawless confluence between students, educational institutions, and companies which essentially improve the efficiency and transparency of education and employment. Students can be the administrator for their own data in this technology.

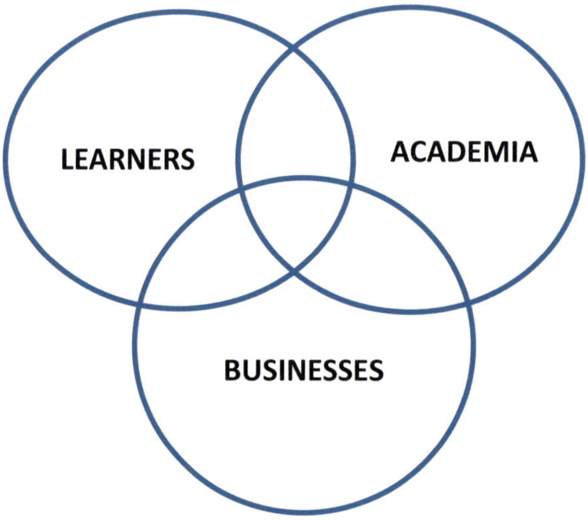

Fig. (5). Perspective views on education.

So that, he can monitor the changes done to his record by an authorized user without permitting any intruders [25]. Education institutions are maintaining students' credit systems to assess their regular activities on the campus with which they can grade the student's overall performance. It is necessary to carry that information from one institution to another (wherever he/she goes) to showcase the credits gained by them. This can be done with the help of blockchain technology where data cannot tamper, accessible by authorized users, secure storage, and so on. Blockchain can also be used for accreditation of educational institutions where the complex task of verifying the quality and qualification of the staff employed. In Fig. (**5**), it is depicted that the education system can be viewed from three perspectives. It can be accomplished by learners, academicians, and business people. Whatever might be the field, people willing to develop themselves will never stop learning. If an institute owns a channel for online classes, only authorized users can access it. This restriction can be provided by the institution while deciding the beneficiaries. Also, it is possible to implement this technology for copyright and the digital right protection for an individual's work. As there are many chances for plagiarism to occur, we can able to avoid it by using these kinds of blockchain platforms for recognizing one's efforts. In this era, pilot development is needed for technology deployment.

4.7. Healthcare

Blockchain holds enormous applications in the healthcare sector. As a decentralized and distributed technology, it serves in different fields of this sector. It mainly ensures secure data sharing, maintenance of the medical history of patients, fee transactions, drug supply chain, and so on. This data sharing can occur in two ways, either locally or globally. If a medical record of a patient is transferred from one clinic/hospital to another in the same location, then it is termed local sharing. If data gets shared from country to country, then it is known as global sharing. With this platform, there is no need for a patient to carry his/her entire medical records while travelling to some other places.

Table 3. Blockchain-based applications for the healthcare sector.

Applications	Description
Data sharing	It must provide security for all the stored data and it must be securely transmitted to the authenticated user as per the request. The data can also be shared globally.
Medical record maintenance	Every medical data must be securely available for constant support for patients irrespective of time.
Management of drug supply-chain	It includes the entire chain of a product starting from the base material.
Bill payments	All the transactions can be managed by blockchain technology to accomplish a flawless service. For example, medical billing.
Research or clinical trials	It must be accountable for pivotal clinical and research trials.
Accessibility	It gives assurance for patients in managing their health records with extremely safe access controls.

Table (**3**) illustrates the applications of blockchain technology in the healthcare sector. All data will be securely available on this platform. Without the knowledge of a user, it is impossible for an intruder to collapse the data. Hence, patients are the owner of their medical records. The basic architecture of collaborating blockchain technology with its IoT presents four layers for its working.

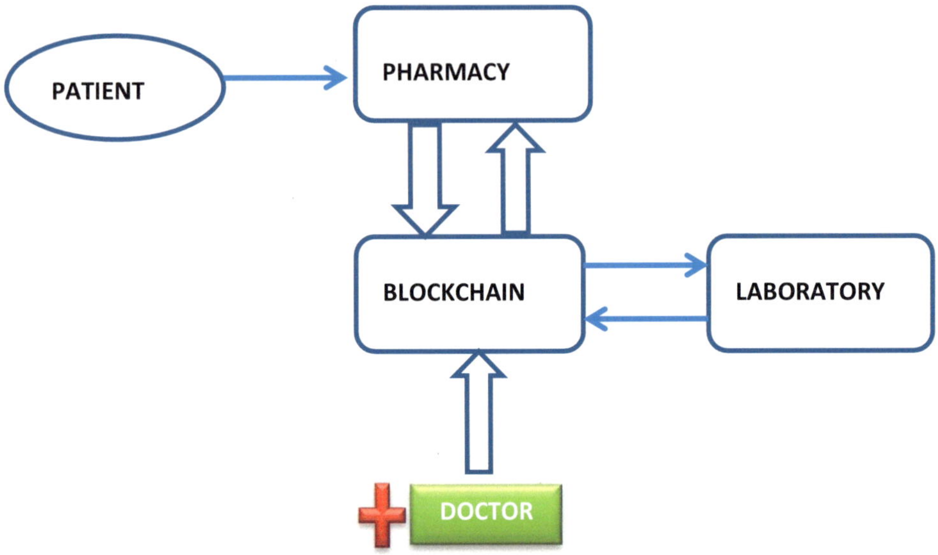

Fig. (6). Smart contract between healthcare people.

The layers are 1) IoT at e-healthcare, 2) Platform for blockchain, 3) Connectivity and 4) IoT devices. Also, the nodes connected to this technology can either be a full node (by storing the entire copy of the blockchain) or a lightweight node (by storing only the current status and last recent transaction in the blockchain) [26]. Fig. (**6**) illustrates the smart contract between the people of the healthcare sector where the data will be interconnected with respect to the patient's knowledge. With the presence of this smart contract, we do not need to rely on any third party's monitorization. Blockchain technology provides a personalized platform to store all the health records under a single roof by promoting record tracking and accessing [27].

4.8. Secure Payment Processing

Blockchain technology agrees to provide secure, fast, minimal charge for national and international payment processing services by utilizing the encrypted distributed ledgers which provide trusted real-time verification for transactions without any intermediaries as they are maintaining smart contracts with the beneficiaries. Usually, the bank plays the centralized role in a transaction where a certain percentage of the amount will be automatically detected as a service charge. This can be avoided in the case of decentralization. Countries like Japan,

Europe, China, and Texas have already introduced this technology in international payment processing and trade finance. As they are maintaining smart contracts, miner plays the role of checking authentication by collecting a very small unit of digital currency. Trade finance will be conducted *via* Digital Trade Chain Consortium in the form of Distributed Ledger Technology.

Industries also started accepting digital currencies using blockchain technology to avoid unnecessary charges and to provoke greater security. The following are some of the companies which widely accept these crypto-currencies.

AIRFOX: The company is located in Boston, Massachusetts. It facilitates the world to make payments, receive mini loans, and transfer money all over the world.

CIRCLE: It is located in Boston, Massachusetts. The circle pay function is accessible in 29 countries and in Euros, British pounds, and U.S. dollars. Every transaction is encrypted on blockchain to ensure safety.

ZCASH: It is located in Denver, Colorado. It has created its own crypto-currency with the name of zcash to help people in paying for goods and services.

RIPPLE: This company is located in San Francisco, California. The company's RippleNet platform serves quick transactions of payments and requires a lower capital amount for cross-border payment.

VEEM: It is located in San Francisco, California. It provides blockchain-backed payment platforms to serve small businesses in sending and receiving money in local currency. It ensures a transparent history of all incoming and outgoing payments in small businesses too.

IVY: It is located in Beverly Hills, California. Businesses use IVY tokens to facilitate digital asset transformation and provide access to 24 know-your-customer (KYC) access points to have a transparent transaction from the secure access points.

This technology supports the growth of existing business models using cryptographically secured transactions in a distributed P2P network. In the financial sector, we have efficient platforms like Hyperledger Fabric, Ethereum, Corda, FinTech, DLT (Distributed Ledger Technology), and so on [28]. Blockchain technology is entering into all sectors by extending its wings to bring betterment to our society.

4.9. Supply-Chain Management and Logistics

Blockchain does not fail to enter the field of commerce too. The term Supply-chain management refers to the management of goods and services and also the processes involved in converting raw materials into a final product. By keeping this chain transparent, we can gain a competitive advantage in the market. The supply chain usually collides with business functions among the network of its trading partners. This may be vulnerable to certain attacks or risks to occur in the transaction. Hence, risk assessment is essential and it can be done by following the upcoming steps:

- Initially, supply chain partners or traders must be identified. Then the contracts will be built through them.
- Prepare a process map that shows all the information related to the transaction and its flow in the network. This helps to identify the risk factor.
- Classify and observe the vulnerabilities
- Develop an action plan to overcome the risk by including each step to be included in our process like RFID (Radio Frequency Identification) which spots the risk and captures the data automatically according to the vehicle movement.
- Finally, implement the developed plan into reality to monitor and control risk factors in the supply chain [29].

This supply chain can be clubbed up with blockchain technology to provide the best service to the users. Initially, let us see four main functionalities of blockchain as follows:

Transparent transactions: Blockchain has no intermediaries. Also, it does not have any central authority to act as a server. Hence, it is completely transparent.

Preapproved transaction fees: While making a cross-border payment, the commission for a transaction (transaction fee) will be deducted only at the end of the process. Also, this transaction fee will be initially shown to the user and deducted only after the transaction gets successfully completed.

Auditability: Every transaction is instantly visible to all authorized parties which means, it is tamper-proof and no one can delete or modify the data associated with it.

Reliability: As it maintains a distributed digital ledger, there is no single point of failure. Hence they are immutable and eliminate the risks of fraudulent behavior. It includes three major use cases.

Traceability – It is essential to track the product from its base to the final outcome. IT helps in ensuring its standard.

Transparency – By capturing the data points like certifications and claims, it enables trust, and also open access will be provided to authorized users. Everything will be registered on a blockchain platform where the verification has to be done. These kinds of verifications are carried out by miners.

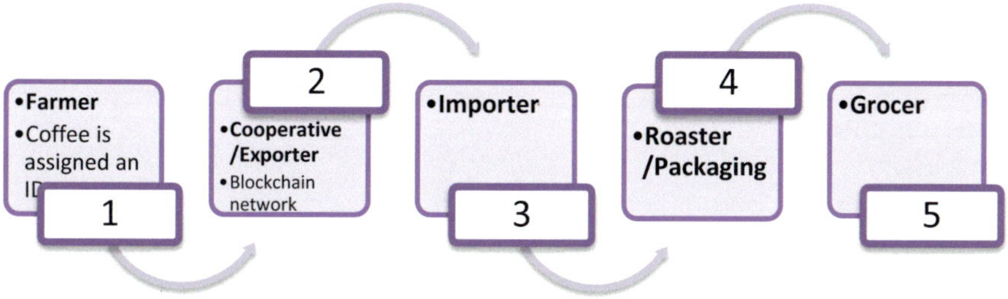

Fig. (7). Working procedure of coffee supply chain with blockchain.

Trade ability – It is a key concept of tokenization where the token value will be assigned for each property and stakeholders in a specific range. Blockchain technology assures ownership and license for a product. These tokens are tradeable with which the owner of an asset can transfer the property's ownership without the physical asset changing hands.

For example, IBM Coffee machine. Yes. IBM blockchain has designed a machine using its application to track its entire supply chain. Once we requested a supply chain, it shows the details of the process from the date and place of the coffee bean's growth, grinding, and filling it into the machine, and all these details are clearly shown to the customer. Fig. (7) shows the steps involved in the coffee supply chain using blockchain technology. It has to be noted that every block is broadcasted and validated by everyone. Logistics is the process of detailed organizing and performing tasks like transferring products or goods from one location to another. It can be accommodated with blockchain technology with respect to its end-to-end delivery to proceed in a more secure way. This supply-chain management and logistics can be done in many sectors like the food value chain, finance and payment, healthcare, power generation fields, real estate, and so on.

4.10. Smart City

A smart city can be defined as an urban area that uses information and communication technology (ICT) in a more efficient way to enhance its operational efficiency. The utilization of ICT can be combined with blockchain technology to promote green engineering in many ways. Smart city includes many applications like:

- Smart vehicles
- Digital Identity
- Smart parking
- Waste management
- Smart parking
- Smart lighting
- Smart sanitation and sensor utilizations
- Smart environment

4.10.1. Smart Vehicles

It includes many features like evidence catcher, prevents accidental situation, vehicle tracker (with GPS), and so on. In the case of the evidence catcher, consider an example where two vehicles are met with an accident and a mistake was on both sides. No one volunteers to be a witness to an accident. In such a case, a camera affixed to a vehicle covers the incident and pays a loyalty solution. Even then, there is a chance of losing the camera's data with an intruder's effort. To avoid this, we can make use of blockchain technology where there is no single point of failure. Secondly, we can track every vehicle through GPS. Instead of waiting for public vehicles like buses, we can track it on our own to reach the vehicle on time. It offers uninterrupted tracking of passengers or vehicles. Also, all information about the driver and the vehicle can be clearly tracked in a secure platform for future references. On other hand, vehicle sharing can also be promoted during transportation [30]. In order to keep it highly secure, blockchain technology is taken into consideration. An example of a smart city is Estonia. It includes all the features of a smart city at its best.

4.10.2. Digital Identity

Nowadays, technological involvement has become increasingly common everywhere. Digital identity refers to an identity of an authorized user [31]. In the blockchain, it can be provided by the two special keys named private and public keys. The private key is to identify a single user. It will never be shared with others. The public key will be provided to all the users of a community to share with each other while having transactions. The public key of the users will be known to each other. Authentication is necessary for all the fields like healthcare, banking, transportation, asset maintenance, and so on. This process of providing keys for identification will be implemented by blockchain technology to own a secure digital identity. This identification can be made common for all the purposes of blockchain usage depending on the requirements.

4.10.3. Smart Parking And Lighting

This includes the combination of blockchain and the Internet of Things (IoT) in order to increase smartness in public activities. Vehicles can be attached with sensors and cameras, to automatically drive and park the vehicles. In such cases, it is not necessary to depend on the drivers. Smart roads can be implemented in order to timely inspect the conditions of the road and its facility to avoid road accidents. This smart parking requires certain entities like KDC (Key Distribution Center), parking lot owners, PIR (Private Information Retrieval) along with a consortium blockchain network. KDC plays a vital role in invoking a smart parking system with this technology where the key generation will be done for authentication of vehicle, drivers, owners of parking lots, *etc.*, Payment processing for the lots can also be done for this parking system [32]. Also, street lights can be affixed with sensors to automatically on and off lights when the target time reaches. These applications will reduce unnecessary manpower by promoting green engineering. The services will be mainly shared among three participants, namely, owning organization, technology, and human.

Fig. (**8**) depicts that all the three will be interconnected with each other to share the data or information within them. Organizing party interconnects with the stakeholders dynamically [32]. It gives transparency and protects from liability, unskilled service providers, and fraudulent activities. The technology assures the availability and accessibility of the systems and also real-time awareness and smart computing technology will be taken into progress. Human power trusts the security and privacy policies and believes in the reliability of sharing services. This can be achieved by blockchain technology.

4.10.4. Waste Management And Smart Sanitation

It is possible to generate blockchain-based waste management and sanitation system. Waste management can be classified into two phases. The first phase includes collection and transport. It is the phase where the garbage and waste materials are collected and shifted to their destination in a regular interval. The second phase includes disposal and recycles where the collected trash will be vanished or treated for further use [33]. Waste management supports smart sanitation by considering this technology along with the Internet of Things (IoT). Tracking can be familiarly done with the help of IoT in a distributed platform to follow sanitation practices. In this portal, we will be having users like customers, municipality employees, supervising inspectors, contractors, police, and admin. These members will be assigned to one group or zone. This can be done for all the zones to connect the progress. The inspection process must be carried out at a regular interval. If not, people can file a complaint with the proof available in distributed ledger technology (DLT) against the inspector or any other employee who is responsible for the fault. In the waste management sector, it is indispensable to monitor the full cycle from how they have been gathered to how they are being discarded. Regular inspection helps in maintaining our environment in a clean and neat manner. Every data must be tracked using blockchain technology, which can not be altered. This procedural activity reduces the involvement of manpower and promotes green engineering.

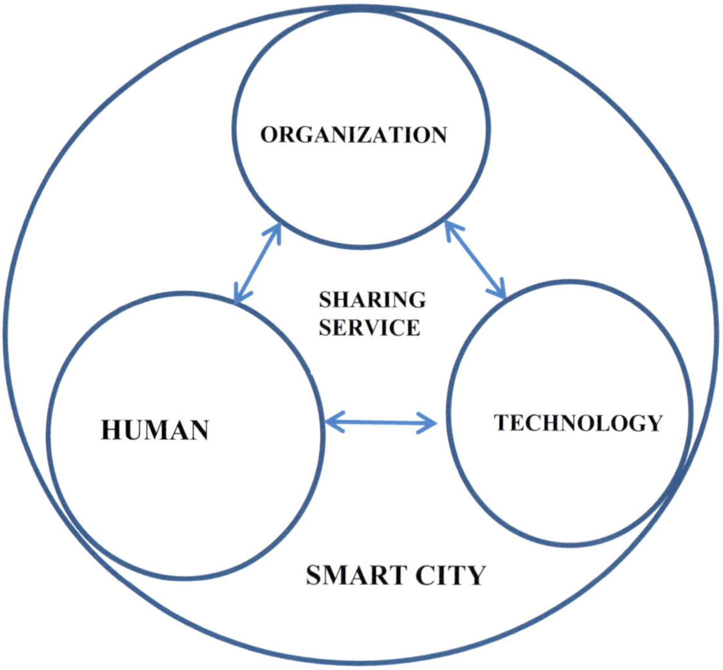

Fig. (8). Sharing services of smart city.

4.10.5. Smart Environment

We can integrate this blockchain technology with IoT to provide great inventions in favor of our society which facilitates a smart environment. It accumulates identification and alarming of forest fire, excessive air pollution (can attempt to control CO_2 emission from factories and toxic gases from vehicles), early detection of earthquake and landslide and monitoring the snow level to get escaped from natural calamities. This is slightly an advanced feature to implement in real life with the inclusion of blockchain technology. Also, it helps in creating awareness to people regarding the controlling measures that can be followed to minimize the level of pollution in our environment. It paves way for Industry 4.0 by enhancing its benefits for industries like manufacturing or production. Without neglecting the transportation sector, blockchain and IoT provides the best, even in the case of TDG (Transportation of Dangerous Goods) [34]. Hence, it is clear that it promotes technical properties in real-time by sharpening its security level.

4.10.6. Blockchain In Tourism And Travel Management

Blockchain in tourism is still in its infant stage. Even in this stage, 13 platforms have been created and developed their own coins or tokens. Few of them have been created based on ethereum and few with their own format. DApps are considered the latest application of blockchain technology [35]. Tourism companies are also taking efforts to implement DApps to have better interaction with their customers. For example, Travel Block is a coin designed by the tourism sector based on ethereum with low cost as a highlight for their business models. In travel management, the ticket booking process for all kinds of transport vehicles can be done in a secure way without any interruptions with the help of blockchain technology. Process tracking and scheduling process can also be done with their transparent nature. The travel plan of the customers can be securely maintained in the travel management system of the company. This prevents crashes during travel with the help of the automatic reporting system. Entire tour details of the customers they served have to be completely managed and maintained by Travel Advisory System (TAS) in a blockchain platform for further reference [36].

CONCLUSION

In this chapter, we have proposed the benefits of integrating blockchain technology with the Internet of Things (IoT) from the basics by explaining aspects, including blockchain platforms, consensus, crypto-currencies, digital ledger, hashing, along with their application areas. It also explains the security measures considered with these technologies to enhance its performance in all aspects. With this integration, we can clearly conclude that there will be no single point of failure and no possibilities for repudiation. Hence, accessing our data or records from any device irrespective of time and location will be supported without bothering about data security. These two integrated technologies can fix any field like supply chain, healthcare sector, education, smart city, travel management, and so on. These technologies promote abundant development in our environment in all aspects.

Many research works are conducting in various countries to merge this technology with others to increase the efficiency of the processes. IoT with blockchain technology has started penetrating almost all the fields in our day-to-day life. Many security measures are still considered to enrich the security of these blockchain-enabled IoT systems. As further work, blockchain with IoT can be implemented in all the fields without any interruption, as it is under progress in our country. Therefore, it must be included in all the sectors of our environment. Researchers can make it possible by implementing this technology in a user-friendly manner in daily life in order to preserve the record in a secure way. We can conclude that the development and deployment of blockchain technology with other technologies like Artificial Intelligence, Machine Learning, Internet of Things, and Image processing are essential to address the specific demands of our future.

CONSENT FOR PUBLICATION

Not Applicable.

CONFLICT OF INTEREST

The author declares no conflict of interest, financial or otherwise.

ACKNOWLEDGEMENT

Declared none.

REFERENCES

[1] M.S. Urmila, B. Hariharan, and R. Prabha, "A comparitive study of blockchain applications for enhancing internet of things security", *2019 10th International Conference on Computing, Communication and Networking Technologies (ICCCNT),* pp. 1-7, 2019. [http://dx.doi.org/10.1109/ICCCNT45670.2019.8944446]

[2] O. Cheikhrouhou, and A. Koubâa, "BlockLoc: Secure localization in the internet of things using blockchain", *2019 15th International Wireless Communications & Mobile Computing Conference (IWCMC),* pp. 629-634, 2019. [http://dx.doi.org/10.1109/IWCMC.2019.8766440]

[3] Z. Zheng, S. Xie, D. Hongning, X. Chen, and H. Wang, "An Overview of Blockchain Technology: Architecture, Consensus, and Future Trends", *2017 IEEE International Congress on Big Data*

(BigData Congress), pp. 557-564, 2017. [http://dx.doi.org/10.1109/BigDataCongress.2017.85]

[4] Alam T., "Blockchain and its role in the internet of things (IoT)", *ArXiv, abs/1902.09779. International Journal of Scientific Research in Computer Science, Engineering and Information Technology,* pp. 151-157, 2019.

[5] S. Gupta, S. Sinha, and B. Bhushan, "Emergence of Blockchain Technology: Fundamentals, Working and its Various Implementations (April 6, 2020)", *Proceedings of the International Conference on Innovative Computing & Communications (ICICC),* 2020. Available at SSRN: https://ssrn.com/abstract=3569577 [http://dx.doi.org/10.2139/ssrn.3569577]

[6] A. Malik, S. Gautam, S. Abidin, and B. Bhushan, *Blockchain Technology-Future Of IoT: Including Structure, Limitations and Various Possible Attacks*, 2019, pp. 1100-1104. [http://dx.doi.org/10.1109/ICICICT46008.2019.8993144]

[7] https://www.leewayhertz.com/blockchain-platforms-for-top-blockchain-companies/

[8] M. Conti, "A survey on security and privacy issues of bitcoin", *IEEE Comm. Surv. and Tutor.,* 2018. [http://dx.doi.org/10.1109/COMST.2018.2842460]

[9] S.K. Singh, S. Rathore, and J.H. Park, "Block IoT Intelligence: A Blockchain-enabled Intelligent IoT Architecture with Artificial Intelligence", *Future Gener. Comput,* vol. 110, pp. 721-743, 2020.

[10] https://www.geeksforgeeks.org/consensus-algorithms-in-blockchain/

[11] J. Huang, G. Chen, M-Y. Wu, and X. Liu, "Mechanism", *IEEE Transactions on Industrial Informatics,* vol. 15, no. 6, 2019.

[12] Available from https://hyperledger-fabric.readthedocs.io/en/release-2.2/whatis.html#:~:text=a%20 separate%20channel.-,Pluggable%20Consensus,Specifically%2C% 20the%20ordering%20service

[13] B. Bhushan, A. Khamparia, K. M. Sagayam, S. K. Sharma, M. A. Ahad, and N. C. Debnath, *Blockchain for smart cities: A review of architectures, integration trends and future research directions, Sustainable Cities and Society,* vol. 61, 2020. [PMID: 102360]

[14] L. Madaan, A. Kumar, and B. Bhushan, "Working principle, Application areas and Challenges for Blockchain Technology 2020", In: *IEEE 9th International Conference on Communication Systems and Network Technologies (CSNT)*, 2020, pp. 254-259. [http://dx.doi.org/10.1109/CSNT48778.2020.9115794]

[15] N. Arunkumar, and P. Sivaprakasam, "Blockchain Technology in Data Management", In: *2020 Fourth International Conference on Computing Methodologies and Communication (ICCMC)*, 2020, pp. 199-206. [http://dx.doi.org/10.1109/ICCMC48092.2020.ICCMC-00039]

[16] T. Faika, T. Kim, J. Ochoa, M. Khan, S. Park, and C. S. Leung, "A Blockchain-Based Internet of Things (IoT) Network for Security-Enhanced Wireless Battery Management Systems", *2019 IEEE Industry Applications Society Annual Meeting,* pp. 1-6, 2019. [http://dx.doi.org/10.1109/IAS.2019.8912024]

[17] K. Sheela, and C. Priya, "Enabling the efficiency of Blockchain Technology in Tele-Healthcare with Enhanced EMR", *2020 International Conference on Computer Science, Engineering and Applications (ICCSEA),* pp. 1-6, 2020. [http://dx.doi.org/10.1109/ICCSEA49143.2020.9132922]

[18] A.M. Al-madani, and A.T. Gaikwad, "IoT Data Security *Via* Blockchain Technology and Service-Centric Networking", In: *2020 International Conference on Inventive Computation Technologies (ICICT)*, pp. 17-21.

[19] A. Ghosh, S. Gupta, A. Dua, and N. Kumar, "Security of crypto currencies in blockchain technology:

state-of-art, challenges and future prospects", *Journal of Network and Computer Applications,* vol. 163, .
[http://dx.doi.org/10.1016/j.jnca.2020.102635]

[20] S. Wang, L. Ouyang, Y. Yuan, X. Ni, X. Han, F. Wang, and , "Blockchain-Enabled Smart Contracts: Architecture, Applications, and Future Trends", *in IEEE Transactions on Systems, Man, and Cybernetics: Systems,* vol. 49, no. 11, pp. 2266-2277.
[http://dx.doi.org/10.1109/TSMC.2019.2895123]

[21] A. Shojaei, I. Flood, H. Izadi Moud, M. Hatami, and X. Zhang, *An Implementation of Smart Contracts by Integrating BIM and Blockchain* , 2019.
[http://dx.doi.org/10.1007/978-3-030-32523-7_36]

[22] Kim Seong-Kyu, Kim Ung-Mo, and Huh Jun-Ho, "A Study on Improvement of Blockchain Application to Overcome Vulnerability of IoT Multiplatform Security", *Energies,* vol. 12, no. 3, p. 402, 2019.
[http://dx.doi.org/10.3390/en12030402]

[23] Mohanty S., Ramya K., Rani S., Gupta D., Shankar K., Lakshmanaprabu S., and Khanna A., "An efficient Lightweight integrated Blockchain (ELIB) model for IoT security and privacy", *Future Gener. Comput. Syst.,* vol. 102, pp. 1027-1037.

[24] O. Pal, and S. S. Singh, "Blockchain Technology and It's Applications in E-Governance Services", *International Journal of Recent Technology and Engineering,* vol. 8, pp. 2277-3878, 2019.
[http://dx.doi.org/10.35940/ijrte.D8599.118419]

[25] U. Rahardja, A.N. Hidayanto, T. Hariguna, and Q. Aini, "Design framework on tertiary education system in indonesia using blockchain technology", In: *2019 7th International Conference on Cyber and IT Service Management (CITSM)*, 2019, pp. 1-4.
[http://dx.doi.org/10.1109/CITSM47753.2019.8965380]

[26] P. P. Ray, D. Dash, K. Salah, and N. Kumar, "Blockchain for IoT-based healthcare: Background, consensus, platforms, and use cases", *IEEE Systems Journal,* vol. 15, no. 1, pp. 85-94, 2021.
[http://dx.doi.org/10.1109/JSYST.2020.2963840]

[27] A. Khatoon, "A Blockchain-Based Smart Contract System for Healthcare Management", *Electronics,* vol. 9, no. 1, p. 94, 2020.
[http://dx.doi.org/10.3390/electronics9010094]

[28] Aggarwal S., Chaudhary R., Aujla G., Kumar N., Choo K.R, Zomaya A. Y., and , "Blockchain for smart communities: Applications, challenges and opportunities", *J. Netw. Comput. Appl.,* vol. 144, pp. 13-48.

[29] Min Hokey, "Blockchain technology for enhancing supply chain resilience", *Business Horizons,* vol. 62, Elsevier, no. 1, pp. 35-45, 2019.

[30] H. Treiblmaier, A. Rejeb, and A. Strebinger, "Blockchain as a driver for smart city development: application fields and a comprehensive research agenda", *Smart Cities,* vol. 3, pp. 853-872.
[http://dx.doi.org/10.3390/smartcities3030044]

[31] A. Melhem, O. AlZoubi, Mardini W., and Yassein M.B., "Applications of blockchain in smart cities", *DATA 19,* 2019.

[32] W. A. Amiri, M. Baza, K. Banawan, M. Mahmoud, W. Alasmary, and K. Akkaya, "Privacy-Preserving Smart Parking System Using Blockchain and Private Information Retrieval", In: *2019 International Conference on Smart Applications, Communications and Networking (SmartNets)*, 2019, pp. 1-6.
[http://dx.doi.org/10.1109/SmartNets48225.2019.9069783]

[33] M. Lamichhane, O. Sadov, and A. Zaslavsky, "Smart waste management system: a fusion of IoT and blockchain technology", In: *Dependable IoT for human and industry: modeling, architecting, implementation,* Kharchenko V., Kor A.L, Rucinski A., Eds., River Publishers: Gistrup, Denmark,

2018, pp. 351-366.

[34] A. Imeri, N. Agoulmine, and D. Khadraoui, "A secure and smart environment for the transportation of dangerous goods by using Blockchain and IoT devices", In: 7th *International Workshop on ADVANCEs in ICT Infrastructures and Services (ADVANCE 2019)*, Praia, Cape Verde., 2019. (hal-02439984)

[35] Kichan Nam, and Christopher S. Dutt, "Blockchain technology for smart city and smart tourism: Latest trends and challenges", *Asia Pacific Journal of Tourism Research,* 2019. [http://dx.doi.org/10.1080/10941665.2019.1585376]

[36] S. Singh, and P.K. Sharma, "Convergence of blockchain and artificial intelligence in IoT network for the sustainable smart city", *Sustainable Cities and Society,* vol. 63, 2020. [PMID: 102364]

CHAPTER 8

Secured IoT Model for Sensitive Data Transmission Using Blockchain Technique

Vejendla Lakshman Narayana[1,*], **R.S.M. Lakshmi Patibandla**[2] and **Arepalli Peda Gopi**[1]

[1] *Vignan's Nirula Institute of Technology & Science for Women, Peda Palakaluru, Guntur-522009, Andhra Pradesh, India*

[2] *Department of IT, Vignan's Foundation for Science, Technology and Research, Andhra Pradesh, India*

Abstract: Global progress in terms of technology involves dumb physical objects that communicate and solve intelligent species problems for us. The thrilling world of the 'network of things' or the Internet of Things (IoT) is certainly a safe place to feel and fulfill our needs. Communication technologies for machine-to-machine(M2M) enable autonomous networking between devices without human intervention. Such autonomous control is of vital importance for a range of Internet of Things (IoT) implementations, including smart manufacturing applications, healthcare systems, and home automation, to name a few. The Internet of Things has attracted almost everyone's attention because of its ability to track and influence the environment. One of the key features of any IoT system is its ability to connect and exchange data with other devices. In particular, IoT devices are using wireless networking to communicate with other devices. In this test, it tells us how IoT technology can communicate with our lives. The proposed method uses Secured IoT Model for Efficient Data Transmission using Blockchain Technique(SIoTM- EDTB) to provide security to the data during transmission. The proposed model is compared with the traditional method, and the results depict that the proposed model exhibits better performance.

Keywords: Attacks, Blockchain, Data loss, Data transmission, Security model.

1. INTRODUCTION

The IoT is a new computing paradigm aimed at turning ordinary daily objects into intelligent objects. IoT was described as one of today's transformative innovations that will change our vision, interpretation, and reaction to the changes in the environment around us. Advancements in omnipresent and widespread compu-

* **Corresponding author Vejendla Lakshman Narayana:** Vignan's Nirula Institute of Technology & Science for Women, Peda Palakaluru, Guntur-522009, Andhra Pradesh, India; E-mail: lakshmanv58@vignannirula.org

ting, integrated devices, communication, Sensor networks, and Internet-based protocols underlie the development and enablement of IoT in ordinary devices [1]. As a result, these technologies are usually known as technology enabling IoTs [2]. The authors examine, with a special focus on their characteristics, capabilities, strengths, and issues of different wireless communication technologies widely used in IoT devices.

The IoT paradigm is not a new technology but rather a combined 20 nations of approaches that benefit from research developments in semi-controllers, networking, and the processing of information [3]. If you are able to take a data center, you can use IoT to produce context-centric data and transmit it to another device or cloud where it is processed and mined to extract secret knowledge [4]. If you are able to accept the data center, you can use IoT to create new devices as well as new physical objects. This will then enable new technologies and applications to be created. In facilitating the wireless sharing between the IoT devices and the portal, and then the gateway to the remote repository via Internet, Machine-to-Machine (M2M) communication technologies play a vital role. In view of the limited battery capacity of IoT equipment, it is clear that the energy efficiency of wireless communication is very important: both duty cycle and energy-recovery solutions are extensively examined.

The Internet of Things is focused on conventional telephone networks and other knowledge providers. IoT is an extension of the Internet. The Internet terminal is a computer (PC, server) running all sorts of programs [5]. The Internet is nothing more than the encoding and transmission of data between the machine and the network [6]. There is no other terminal (hardware) on the Internet. The Internet is still the main concept for IoT. Unlike the Internet, there are not only PCs and servers, but even built-in computer systems and their help sensors can be viewed as terminals [7]. It can link all sorts of independent objects and make them work together in order to achieve a functional interconnection network.

Blocks are the technology's main principles. In the scheme, there are small collections of transactions. Each new block contains a reference to the previous transaction, including the previous transaction's SHA-256 hash [8]. This creates a 'chain' of connections . Blocks are difficult to build computationally and need several specialized processors and a considerable amount of time to produce. Due to the difficulty in creating a block and to the interference from one block, you need to manipulate the previous block and follow the chain to alter it altogether.

The proposed model introduces Secured IoT Model for Efficient Data Transmission using Blockchain Technique. In the proposed model, data transmission is secured as the blockchain technology is used for locking the completed transmission so that nodes' behavior is also monitored [9 - 12]. The introduction section gives a brief introduction of IoT and Blockchain and the remaining chapter is organized as a literature survey and then the proposed model that explains the process of secure data transmission framework, and then results are discussed and finally the conclusion of the chapter is given.

2. LITERATURE SURVEY

The new wireless communications system for green intelligent cities has been proposed by Bedogni *et al.* [6]. As IoT devices are used to plan, manufacture information, and monitor the energy supply and demand of households, IoT plays a key part in their plan. Although it was not mainly aimed at analyzing the communication systems used in IoT, they were assessed because they played a major role in the final implementation. The evaluation conducted in that work is quite superficial and focuses not on contact but the transfer of wireless power [13 - 15]. Moreover, not all available technologies are taken into consideration for assessment since they primarily focus on the SDN (SDN) architecture for heterogeneous IoT applications.

The study examined systems like cellular networks, short-range multi-shop technologies, and low-power (LPWA) technologies in order to use them for intelligent city implementation. The key weakness of these communication technologies is the failure to implement large-scale in restricted fields [16]. It was also suggested that these limitations can be resolved with various network optimization methods, including cell zooming, HetNets implementation, and context-aware content delivery [17 - 19].

The survey is similar to our study, although it has quite a different subject since it is based primarily on cellular technology and examines in detail the state-of-art criteria for 5 G; our work offers, compared to this, a more general classification of the M2M scenario (*e.g.* in the light of shorter distance 110 and capillary technology). Data sensor management and information extraction are very important in the second group [20 - 22].

The industry has been carefully studying and classifying industrial context-conscious technologies and applications ranging from localized products to manufacturing and healthcare [23 - 25]. Crowdsensing techniques are explored on the convergence of IoT, context-aware computing, and mobile devices.

3. PROPOSED MODEL

Blockchain – a decentralized dispensed headline – is a breakthrough technology capable of addressing IoT security challenges. A blockchain-based IoT network approach will solve numerous problems facing the current model and increase security.

Blockchain has the following features as an important instrument in the fight against IoT cyber threats.

3.1. Decentralizing

Data is saved at various nodes around the world on the blockchain ledger, preventing a single failure point. Every node must accept and validate it before adding any data to the network. Therefore, no change is permitted without the general approval of all network participants. This method is called peer communication and is aimed at ensuring blockchain transactions by malicious parties. There is no risk that an individual will perform the middle assault if the hackers record data and sent it from the server to the computer because there is no single server.

3.2. Media Connections

Blockchain is public and is open to everyone on the network. The common history of stored blocks and transactions can be seen by all network participants, but a private key is required for access. This provides full access to all activities while maintaining secure data. It cannot be altered if a piece of information is stored in a blockchain.

3.3. Safe Information

In order to protect data, blockchain uses advanced encryption algorithms privately. This is done mainly to ensure that there is no risk to financial activities. IoT devices can send and receive information in the way financial transactions allow secure data communication between connected objects using the blockchain model.

The security of IoT is a major issue of privacy. Free Internet access to data allows users to be collected and monitored by monitoring agencies without their consent. The recent growth of IoT can easily lead to undesirable circumstances by data collection activities. One viable solution is to enable users to control their own data and to ensure confidentiality. This defines loosely how much data these programs need to work properly or in all the situations is actually agreed by the customers. On the other hand, in our environment, IoT devices often abuse the concept by collecting information without user permission.

Therefore, greater protection of privacy is needed to maintain the privacy of IoT users ' personal information. A new solution to limit user contacts to share the minimum amount of information needed is the Delegation Method. Let consumers find others on the platform that best suits their preferences without corresponding to their preferences.

To reveal to everybody this knowledge. Another concept underway is the privacy coach, in which the essence of this concept lies in a system that can scan and retrieve tags of embedded devices. If the object's privacy policy does not correspond to the user's preferences, the user refuses to use the object. In other circumstances, scanned items explicitly transmit their privacy policies and request the users' consent. The privacy coach will act as a physical space, malicious, and unwanted scanning defensive mechanism.

Various attack forms are based on a Cisco model because it is a common model that is very similar to the ISO / OSI model. The below-mentioned attacks can be perpetrated and presented a real challenge on Smart Home devices.

3.4. Edge Nodes Assaults

This section provides an in-depth overview of different attacks, including nodes, against the first layer of the reference model.

3.5. Denial of Installations

Denial-of-service attack, shortened by do-s, is normally a type of attack that usually inundates traffic-driven servers, devices, or networks to overload victims 'resources and prevent legitimate users from using them. DoS maybe three different attacks in the IoT world against edge computing nodes.

Battery drainage: IoT device size limits lead to small, very limited capacity batteries. Battery drainage attacks have become a powerful tool, leading indirectly to serious implications such as node failure and function failure. For instance, the entire fire alarm system will be disabled if an intruder discovers a way to deplete the battery of an intelligent SMD detector. If no battery in such a system can be replaced or recharged, an attacker could cause a node to be destroyed in the network. It can be done by sending a large number of arbitrary traffic to a node and forcing it to perform controls, such as authentication and checksum of packets.

Deprivation of sleep: is a specific type of DoS attack vaguely similar to the attack on battery drain by the battery of the node. Battery-powered devices with limited energy capacity are vulnerable to this attack. The attacker sent a valid number of requests in a timely manner to avoid sleep or twelve node functions. The battery-driven attack, because the packets are actual, is a much harder one to detect. External attacks are the most common DoS type for stopping edge nodes and forcing an outage. It prevents machines from operating normally and, in some cases, shuts off operations completely. This can be done because of accidental fabrication errors, the battery attacks mentioned above, unauthorized physical access to the device, or the injection of code. Stuxnet, which has inserted a malicious code that avoided an abnormative behavior in Iran that could not shut down in a state of emergency, is a well-known example of a failed attack.

3.6. Strong Node Management

Access to the network physically is an opening for further attacks. Direct node manipulation attacks can be divided into two categories according to the type of operation carried out by the attack node. Each such attack may cause severe damage and often lead to considerable network performance reduction. Node replication is an attack-type where an attacker replicates a node identification number by adding a new node to an existing set of nodes. Newly added nodes are often malicious, which makes it easy for the attacker to corrupt or misdirect the replica packets. This attack allows the assailant to access cryptographic shared keys or, by executing node revocation protocols, to even relocate access to valid and authorized nodes.

Camouflage attacks are used to insert or hit a node that is accepted to hide on the edge. This malicious node is used in normal mode in which packets identified as active are received, processed, or sent back. Only traffic analysis and data collection are performed through passive mode. Node functions are defined. Node corruption is a common attack to access the underlying node network unauthorized. Malicious nodes inserted into the network will gain access to other nodes which could control the whole system for the assailant. The malware node may also be used to insert false data in the device or prevent true messages from being transmitted.

3.7. Attacks Routing

Attacks in the routing process ask how packets are routed to the communication layer. An attacker can spoof, redirect, error, or completely drop the packet out of the network by such an attack. The routing information can be simply changed to create routing loops or error messages. Routing attacks can be subsequently split into several different categories.

The Gray Hole Attack is called a variation of the attack, in which nodes selectively drop certain packets. Wormhole attacks are much more dangerous than Black and Gray Hole attacks since they can be performed in all communications even with authenticity and secrecy. The heart of this attack is that packets are received and then tunneled to another location in the network. Basically, wormhole nodes create away in a network that is shorter than the original. Therefore, the tunnel must be a quick connection to create the illusion that both wormhole nodes are very similar.

3.8. Solution IoT Blockchain

It should be noted that in particular when the global P2P framework develops across the entire IoT ecosystem, the above mechanisms (P2P network involvement, support of acceptable P2P protocols, peer-functionality endorsing, support for consensus algorithms, PoW, and other associated mechanisms) give rise, are somewhat complex. Because of the conventional limitations of IoT nodes as set out in section 2, the use of a fully-fledged blockchain network within an IoT generic framework may not always be feasible; certain key or institutional applications such as smart grids, ITSs, e-health, insurance, or smart contract environments may, however, have sufficient capacity to support the required functions of P2P. Another alternative is to establish P2P networks with a limited local range instead of a global one; this requires less consolidated bandwidth and far-reaching assurance of a stable distribution over large networks for the messages supported – finding, transaction querying, invocation, synchronization, and consensus.

The Stage of The Gateway:

Individual users generate data not always secured for integrity, but once the data enters the gateway, it is integrated with data from other users into the blockchain.

The Photo Picture:

This is a case in point. One reason is that there is no computing capability to generate hashes of (possibly large) data blocks for individual end nodes.

Standard Website:

In this case, individual website users (*e.g.* sensorsorrobotsonthe floor) generate data that isn't automatically secured for system integrity. However, the data are integrated into the blockchain along with information from other users of the website once the data entered into the local focus node (*e.g.* layer 2 switch, Wi-Fi connection point, router, firewall, *etc*.). One reason for this approach is because individual end nodes cannot compute (possibly large) blocks of data, but the NE based on the site will be capable of computing.

3.9. Strong IoT Protection with Blockchain Technology

For the stable application of IoT, the following points should be considered.

3.9.1. Secure Communication

In order to process the transaction, the IoT devices must communicate and save it in a repository. Ledgers can also be used to store encryption keys to ensure secure transfers. An encrypted message is sent to the IoT system via a public key of the destination device that is then saved on a blockchain network. The sender then asks his node to obtain the public key of the recipient from the headline. And the transmitter encrypts the message with the public key of the recipient, so only the recipient can decrypt the message with his private key.

3.9.2. Consumer Authentication

Before sending it to other users, the sender will sign the message digitally. In order to validate the digital signature of the received letter, a receiver would then receipt the public key from the ledger. The following are the work on digital signatures:

- Sender calculates the hash of a private key-encrypted message.
- The message will be sent along with a digital signature.
- The receiver will then decrypt the digital signature by means of a public sender key stored in the directory to retrieve the sender hash value.
- The message is true only if the hash and the hash of the message that is measured are identical.
- Recovered confidence is enhanced if each sender's digital signature is stored in the directory.

3.9.3. Finding a Broad Legal IoT

Once a new IoT system is introduced, a list of confident nodes on the network is requested by root servers. This computer then registers in a node and the information exchange starts. In order to secure root server name resolution,

DNSSec must be introduced, preventing attacks by spoofing. Any contact made must be effectively authenticated and encrypted. This can be done based on the following:

- Credentials are already mounted during configuration on the computer.
- The IoT device owner may issue credentials.

3.9.4. IoT Configuration

Blockchain technology greatly helps to build a safe and reliable IoT device setup. Approaches that seem important in this regard are:

- On a ledger, you can host IoT features, such as setup data and the latest version of the validated firmware. During bootstrap, your blockchain node must be set up from the ledger. The setting needs to be encrypted in the booklet so that information contained in the public leader does not discover the topology or its properties of the IoT network.
- The hash value for each device can be stored in the ledger of the most recent configuration file. The IoT device has the latest and most trustworthy configuration file to be downloaded at every fixed time interval using a cloud service. The app can then retrieve and match the hash value stored in the database using a blockchain node API. Administrators are thus able to regularly uninstall bad settings and restart all IoT systems on the network with the latest and most trusted settings.
- Securing the IoT network with a blockchain network is a decentralized system with no single authority able to approve any transaction. A copy of the ever-growing data chain will come from every computer. This means all network members must verify it whenever someone wants to access the system and transact. The transaction is placed in a block and forwarded to all the nodes on the network after confirmation. All this ensures that unauthorized sources do not violate security and make the system safer.

4. RESULTS

The proposed model is implemented using an NS2 simulator for creating IoT nodes that are used for secured data transmission. The proposed model introduced a Secured IoT Model for efficient data transmission using Blockchain Technique. The proposed model is compared with the traditional models and the results show that the proposed model exhibits better security in the transmission of data using the blockchain technique. The proposed model is compared with the traditional models in terms of data transmission rate, security levels, attack identification levels, accuracy levels, and throughput. The parameters used for creating an IoT simulation are depicted in Table **1**.

Table 1. Parameters used.

No. of Nodes	50,100..300
Area Size	500 X 500
MAC	802.11
Simulation Time	200 sec
Traffic Source	CBR
Packet Size	512
Transmit Power	1.500w
Receiving Power	0.675w
Transmission Range	100m
No.of Sinks	5

The Data Transmission rate of the proposed and the Traditional Trusted Node-based Transmission Method (TTNTM) are depicted in Fig. (**1**). The data transmission rate of the proposed model is high when compared to the existing method. As the proposed model considers only authorized nodes, the data transmission rate is high. All the nodes will transfer the data to its neighbor nodes without causing any data loss. The proposed model uses blockchain to record all the data transmission instances and then analyze the generated blocks to identify the nodes that are malicious.

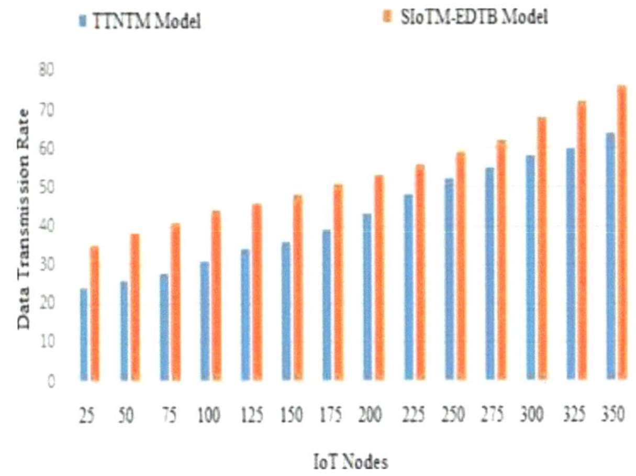

Fig. (1). Data transmission rate.

The proposed model uses blockchain techniques to record the completed transaction. As blockchains are used the security of the proposed model is high when compared to the existing method. When a block is created, the transaction is recorded and it is immutable. There is no chance to modify its contents. All the generated blocks are interlinked with each other. The security levels of the proposed and the existing methods are depicted in Fig. (**2**).

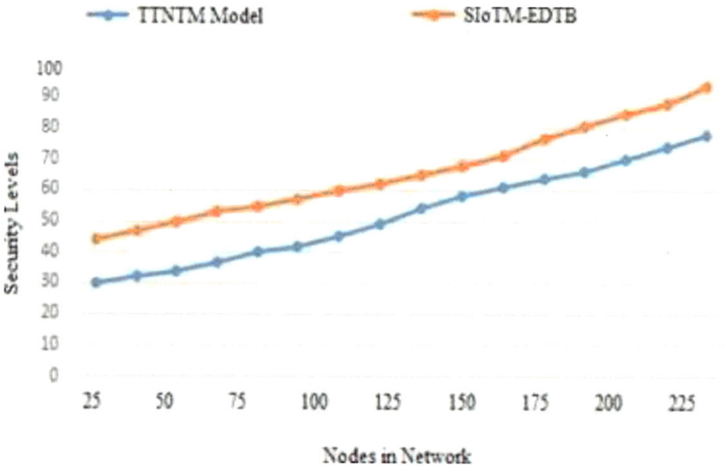

Fig. (2). Security levels.

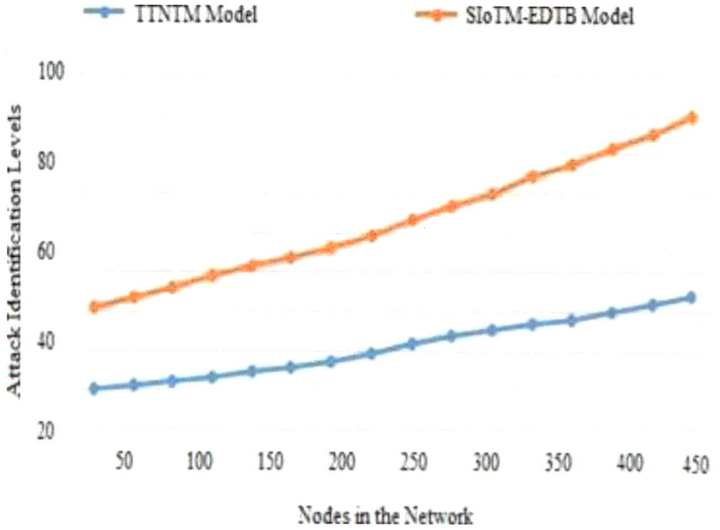

Fig. (3). Attacks identification levels.

As IoT undergoes several attacks, the blockchain model is used for efficient identification of attacks and where the attack has happened. The Attack Identification levels of the proposed model are high than the proposed model. In the proposed model, blocks are generated for every transaction, and they are analyzed for the identification of the behavior of nodes. The block values depict that which nodes are causing data loss and nodes causing malicious actions are easily identified. The attack identification levels are depicted in Fig. (**3**).

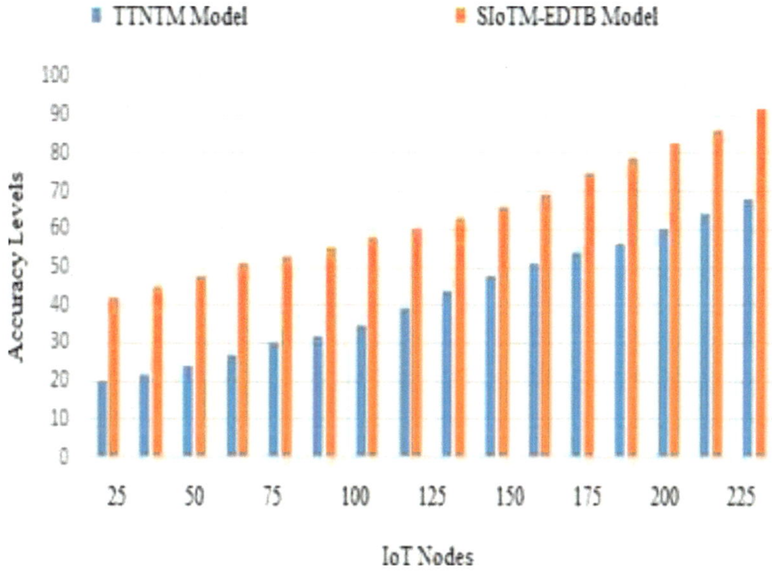

Fig. (4). Accuracy levels.

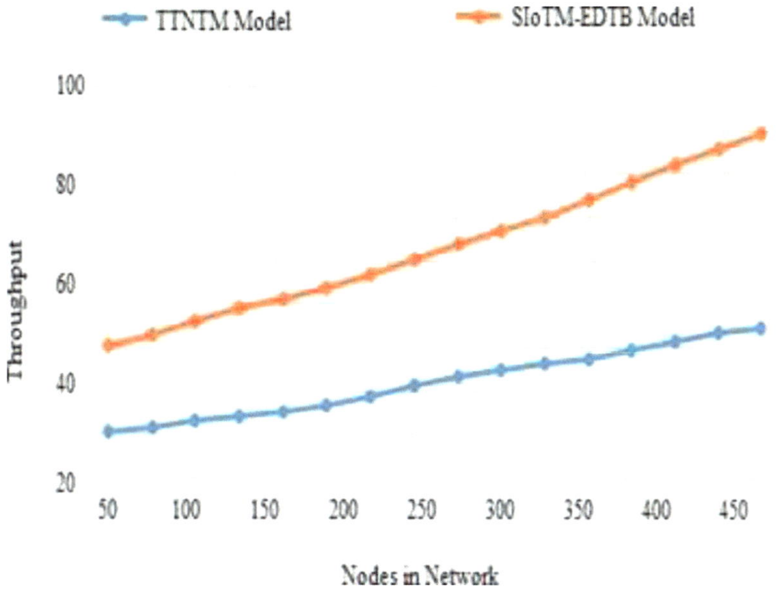

Fig. (5). Throughput.

After every successful data transmission, the blockchain will record every transaction till the process is completed. The accuracy levels of the proposed model are illustrated in Fig. (**4**). The accuracy of the proposed model is high than the existing method. The proposed node identifies the malicious nodes so that the data transmission rate can be improved. A node that is malicious is not allowed to be involved in data transmission.

The system usage of the proposed model is also high as the proposed model uses IoT nodes and also considers blockchain for recording the transactions. The throughput levels of the proposed and existing methods are depicted in Fig. (**5**). The proposed model uses generated blocks to analyze the nodes' data receiving and transmitting rate. The proposed model removes the nodes that are malicious so that the data transmission accuracy is high.

CONCLUSION

Internet of Things is the key path people can take. Some major companies are beginning to deliver various kinds of services to our everyday lives, such as Smart Home, Health Monitor, and so on, to improve the quality of human life by using the Internet of Things. It's a big step forward for computer science technology as a whole. However, it has two sides. There are several issues on which we can attract our attention to. As we all know, IoT is the next version of the Internet, but it's all focused on the Internet. The protection concern should still be an i mportant point that needs to be looked into. Telecommunications technology has also limited the growth of telecommunications. In addition, we should pay attention to problems, such as latency, transmission costs, and so on. An example of an IoT application has been listed in the article. It explained how a simple IoT might already have an effect on people's lives. However, attention should be given to future jobs. The cognitive IoT method is more complex, but it is more successful to see how IoT can accomplish the ultimate aim of the Internet of Things. The creation of a real cognitive IoT framework should be considered as a future task. In the future, a central head node can be assigned to analyze the remaining nodes so that the complexity and congestion in the network can be reduced.

CONSENT FOR PUBLICATION

Not applicable.

CONFLICT OF INTEREST

The author declares no conflict of interest, financial or otherwise.

ACKNOWLEDGEMENTS

Declared none.

REFERENCES

[1] L. Madaan, A. Kumar, and B. Bhushan, "Working principle, Application areas and Challenges for Blockchain Technology", In: *2020 IEEE 9th International Conference on Communication Systems and Network Technologies (CSNT)*, 2020, pp. 254-259. [http://dx.doi.org/10.1109/CSNT48778.2020.9115794]

[2] S. Gupta, S. Sinha, and B. Bhushan, "Emergence of Blockchain Technology: Fundamentals, Working and its Various Implementations (April 6, 2020)", In: *Proceedings of the International Conference on Innovative Computing & Communications (ICICC)*, 2020.

[3] A. Malik, S. Gautam, S. Abidin, and B. Bhushan, *Blockchain Technology-Future Of IoT: Including Structure, Limitations And Various Possible Attacks,* pp. 1100-1104. [http://dx.doi.org/10.1109/ICICICT46008.2019.8993144]

[4] Bhushan B., Sahoo C., and Sinha P., "Unification of blockchain and internet of things (biot): requirements, working model, challenges and future directions", *Wireless Netw,* vol. 27, pp. 55-90, 2021. [http://dx.doi.org/10.1007/s11276-020-02445-6]

[5] B. Bhushan, A. Khamparia, K. M. Sagayam, S. K. Sharma, M. A. Ahad, N. C. Debnath, and , "Blockchain for smart cities: A review of architectures, integration trends and future research directions", *Sustainable Cities and Society,* vol. 61, 2020. [PMID: 102360]

[6] L. Bedogni, F. Malabocchia, M. Di Felice, and L. Bononi, , Indoor Use of Gray and White Spaces: Another Look at Wireless Indoor Communication, IEEE Vehicular Technology Magazine (2017) XX12–XX12doi:10.1109/ MVT.2016.2598414. 1830,

[7] G. Longoria, F. Akhtar, and L. Shi, "Wireless power transmission in smart cities: The wlshood wireless smart neighborhood", In: *6th International Conference on Smart Cities and Green ICT Systems*, Porto, Portugal, 2017. [http://dx.doi.org/10.5220/0006364003170322]

[8] F. Chiariotti, M. Condoluci, T. Mahmoodi, and A. Zanella, "Symbiocity: Smart cities for smarter networks", *Trans. Emerg. Telecommun. Technol.,* vol. 29, no. 1, 2017. [http://dx.doi.org/10.1002/ett.3206]

[9] C. Cachin, "Architecture of the hyperledger blockchain fabric", In: *Workshop on Distributed Cryptocurrencies and Consensus Ledgers*, 2016.

[10] M. Conoscenti, A. Vetro, and J.C. De Martin, "Blockchain for the Internet of Things: A systematic literature review", In: *Proceedings of the 13th IEEE/ACS International Conference of Computer Systems and Applications, AICCSA 2016, IEEE*, Agadir, Morocco, 2016. [http://dx.doi.org/10.1109/AICCSA.2016.7945805]

[11] A. Dorri, S.S. Kanhere, and R. Jurdak, *Blockchain in internet of things: Challenges and Solutions,* 2016. https://arxiv.org/abs/1608.05187

[12] A. Dorri, S.S. Kanhere, and R. Jurdak, "Towards an optimized blockchain for IoT", In: *Proceedings of the 2nd IEEE/ACM International Conference on Internet-of-Things Design and Implementation, IoTDI 2017, ACM*, Pittsburgh, PA, USA, 2017.

[13] M. Conoscenti, A. Vetro, and J.C. De Martin, "Peer to peer for privacy and decentralization in the internet of things", In: *Proceedings of the 39th IEEE/ACM International Conference on Software Engineering Companion, ICSE-C*, IEEE, Buenos Aires, Argentina, 2017. [http://dx.doi.org/10.1109/ICSE-C.2017.60]

[14] M. Crosby, P. Pattanayak, S. Verma, and V. Kalyanaraman, "Blockchain technology: Beyond bitcoin", *Applied Innovation,* vol. 2, pp. 6-10, 2016.

[15] D. Wörner, and T. Von Bomhard, "When your sensor earns money: Exchanging data for cash with Bitcoin", In: *Proceedings of the 2014 ACM International Joint Conference on Pervasive and Ubiquitous Computing, UbiComp*, ACM, 20142014. [http://dx.doi.org/10.1145/2638728.2638786]

[16] V. Lakshman Narayana, "Secure data uploading and accessing sensitive data using time level locked encryption to provide an efficient cloud framework", *Ingenierie des Systemes d'Information,* vol. 25, no. 4, pp. 515-519, 2020.

[17] V. Lakshman Narayana, "A Time Interval based Blockchain Model for Detection of Malicious Nodes in MANET Using Network Block Monitoring Node", In: *International Conference on Inventive Research in Computing Applications (ICIRCA).* Publisher: IEEE, 2020, pp. 852-857. [PMID: 9183256]

[18] V. Lakshman Narayana, "Enhanced path finding process and reduction of packet droppings in mobile ad-hoc networks", *Int. J. Wireless and Mobile Computing,* vol. 18, no. 4, pp. 391-397, 2020.

[19] V. Lakshman Narayana, *A Time Interval based Blockchain Model for Detection of Malicious Nodes in Manet Using Network Block Monitoring Node.* IEEE Xplore, 2020.

[20] V. Lakshman Narayana, "A Trust Based Efficient Blockchain Linked Routing Method for Improving Security in Mobile Ad hoc Networks", *International Journal of Safety and Security Engineering,* vol. 10, no. 4, pp. 509-516, 2020.

[21] C. Goursaud, and J. M. Gorce, "Dedicated networks for IoT: PHY / MAC state of the art and challenges", *EAI Endorsed Transactions on Internet of 1825 Things,* vol. 1, no. 1, pp. 1-11, 2015. [http://dx.doi.org/10.4108/eai.26]

[22] J. Cowan, Wireless rebrands as Ingenu and launches US-wide M2M wireless public network (2015),

[23] H. Kim, "A Study of Digital Currency Cryptography for Bbusiness Marketing and Finance Security", *Asia-pacific Journal of Multimedia Services Convergent with Art, Humanities, and Sociology,* vol. 6, no. 1, pp. 365-376, 2016. [http://dx.doi.org/10.14257/AJMAHS.2016.01.42]

[24] P. Vasin, *Blackcoin's proof-of-stake protocol v2,* 2014.

[25] G. Wood, "Ethereum, A secure decentralised generalised transaction ledger", *Ethereum Project Yellow Paper,* vol. 151, 2014.

CHAPTER 9

Transforming OTT Digital Platform Business Using Blockchain Technology

J.S. Shyam Mohan[1,*], Nagendra Panini Challa[2], Pasumarthy Swathi[1] and **Nuggu Kowshiki[1]**

[1] *Department of Computer Science and Engineering, Sri Chandrasekharendra Saraswathi Viswa Mahavidyalaya (SCSVMV), Tamil Nadu 631561, India*

[2] *Department of Information Technology, Sri Vishnu Engineering College for Women, Bhimavaram, Andhra Pradesh 534202, India*

Abstract: Technology is becoming an indispensable part of our lives. It plays an important role in health, banking, and education. Organizations have started adopting these technological developments to satisfy customer needs. The rise of the Over-th--Top (OTT) digital platforms has created an economic platform in which the digital content, services, and offerings are facilitated by intermediaries and has changed the way of interaction. The blockchain serves as a means for creating a digital platform by creating trust among the intermediaries. Organizations should carry out innovative technology practices to be successful in a competitive environment. This chapter examines the gap between blockchain platforms and the role of the digital transformation process. It thereby provides researchers a holistic approach for studying the impact of blockchain on OTT platforms.

Keywords: Blockchain technology, Digital technology, Over-the-Top.

1. INTRODUCTION

Over-the-Top (OTT) is a term used in the media industry when TV is used to reach individuals' homes through physical links and boxes, and advanced content was conveyed through the web 'over the top' of the links and boxes. OTT has two products, the content and the viewers or the subscribers. Data collected from various locations is processed using Big Data analytics for enhancing and improving the customer viewing experience. Compared with steady competition from traditional television, the future of OTT platforms across the world looks bright.Traditional TV has started innovating by adapting to newer technologies to reach out to a wider range of audiences. Over the last decade, traditional TV has

* **Corresponding author J.S. Shyam Mohan:** Department of Computer Science and Engineering, Sri Chandrasekharendra Saraswathi Viswa Mahavidyalaya (SCSVMV), Tamil Nadu 631561, India; Tel: ???????; E-mail: jsshyammohan@kanchiuniv.ac.in

Sudhir K. Sharma, Bharat Bhushan, Parma N. Astya and Narayan C. Debnath (Eds.)

started including OTT platforms as a part of their service offered to the consumers. AIB Research states that the video market across the world will keep on increasing at a fast pace with over-the – Top (OTT). By 2022, the OTT market will produce massive revenue of $51.4 billion with a surge CGAR (Compound Annual Growth Rate) of 10%. Subscribers will enjoy most of the benefits of OTT provided if they subscribe to the OTT platforms. In countries like North America and Europe, TV channel broadcasters are providing OTT services to their customers to withhold them consistently. Virtual Multichannel Video Programming (vMVPD) is provided at relatively cheaper prices to all the subscribers [1]. Globally, the number of subscribers opting for OTT is increasing when there has been a decline in traditional TV. The Average Revenue per User (ARPU) for pay channels is expected to go down four times, probably by 2022. Thus, there is no doubt that OTT players are marching towards increasing their revenue by adding more number of subscribers. Amazon, Apple, DAZN, Facebook, Google, and Netflix have started investing in setting up their own production houses. There is a great demand for content in OTT platforms owned by broadcasters, going ahead to have deals between broadcasters and OTT providers [2]. Table (**1**) shows the industry report of FICCI- E&Y for the period 2020 [3].

Table 1. The FICCI-E&Y M & E Industry report 2020.

Customer Segment	**No. of Users (in Millions) in a Particular Year**		
	2018	**2019**	**2022**
Digital Content (users consume content only on digital platforms, do not access television)	2.5	8	14
Tactical Digital (Consume Pay-TV and at least one paid OTT service)	12	34	91
Bundled Digital (Consume Pay-TV bundled with telecom)	218	262	363
Mass consumers (Consume Pay TV & occasionally some free OTT content)	426	316	176
Free consumers (Do not pay for content)	180	190	220

The worldwide income for the OTT market is expected to increase from $62.0 million (in 2018) to $149.7 (in 2024), making it with an increase of 15.8% in compound annual growth rate (CAGR) [4]. Indian users are more inclined to freely available content than subscription platforms. Keeping this in mind, OTT players have come up with a pay-per-user model called subscription-based video on demand (SVOD) business models on a monthly or yearly basis. Simultaneously, many OTT players are trying to promote advertising – based on the video on demand (AVOD), while other OTT players are adhering to free business models and planning them to convert into paid users. A blockchain describes an ever-growing set of shared, maintained, digital records and verified by several participants. There is a myriad of blockchain species, but this one definition is suitable for most scenarios [5, 6]. Each set of digital records in a blockchain is grouped into dependent blocks in order. This means that attempting to modify a transaction in any block would usually require modifying all of the following blocks, a computation-intensive task that is economically feasible by design, taking into account a new block is added within minutes. This process makes the data more sure and as time goes by, more blocks are added. Since this unique record set is maintained continuously in several places or distributed, it is highly fault tolerant; there is no central party that attacks, shuts down, coerced, or (in many cases) sues [7]. This decentralization is absolutely essential to do this work; a blockchain 100% owned by a single entity provides barely incremental benefit. Blockchain technology owes its origin to the Bitcoin cryptocurrency. Ensuring consent around a permanent digital ledger without the participation of a trusted central authority was needed (such as a bank, e-payment provider, or government) in order to create "digital currency" [8, 9]. Without an authoritative party to keep the register, you had to design something really innovative so that someone couldn't copy and paste the way they spend their digital money twice. This feature of blockchain technology, or the ability to have a unique and truly owned digital resource, is a vitally important characteristic for brands and marketers. The "digital scarcity" of the blockchain technology not only supports the value of Bitcoin, but it also provides brands with a real bridge between the finite physical world and a numerically infinite world. Many companies see blockchain as an open platform [10]. Open blockchains, like those that support Bitcoin cryptocurrency and Ethereum network, rely on a new model to make up for the lack of a trusted broker. On the other hand, with their exploration of closed or "authorized" blockchains, financial institutions are fall to the top to adopt a technology that an anonymous individual or group invented to help render these institutions useless after the 2008 crash. Even in this digitally sterile implementation, banks can enjoy advantages such as quick settlement times and more quickly agreed trade finance terms by inheriting at least some of the characteristics of an open blockchain, such as immutability and decentralization.

In recent years, British Columbia has gained prominence in the industry and gradually to be recognized as a game-changer for many industries such as the service, financial, and manufacturing sectors [11]. Due to its specific features such as privacy, security, smart contracts, scalability, and the ability to resolve file double-spending problems, the need to make SCM more efficient becomes essential. The BC implementation improves the transaction between two or multiple parties in terms of confidentiality, monitoring, transparency, and enforceability in smart contracts. Long-term use of BC technology makes the SC system more energy-efficient, affordable, and oriented towards high performance. The application of BC technology can be used to improve efficiency and efficient use of resources and this latest technology help establish a CSS. British Columbia is an emerging technology and researchers and industry professionals seek to implement British Columbia in the field of SC. This technology is in its early stages and so far limited work has been done. Here are the main gaps in the BC region, particularly in the SSC [12]. Our society should evolve towards 2030 as a more digital, data-driven, and intelligent solution-inspired society, which needs an almost instantaneous wireless connectivity. So several novel applications that provide such interaction and integration are destined to emerge in the next decade. Like, some key trends that should emerge in the near future are: virtual and augmented reality, 8K video streaming, holograms, remote surgery, industry 4.0, smart homes, fog computing, integrated artificial intelligence services, unmanned aerial vehicles, and autonomous vehicles, to name a few. These, in turn, will ask for much more mobile networks in terms of reliability, latency, and higher data rates than 5G [13]. For providing video streaming, over-the–Top (OTT) services overlap with complementary software solutions like the quality of experience (QoE) and quality of service (QoS). Most OTT vendors have their proprietary software and use a combination of servers, networks, and intelligent software to determine the quality of services in real-time [14]. Consumers demand watching personalized videos from a variety of content available to them on their own devices at their convenient time. OTT platforms have revolutionized to satisfy consumer demands. The videos that are watched on OTT platforms will be a revenue-generating model. Growth in GDP per capita increases with the increase in the number of smartphone users, *etc.* that would ultimately make the OTT market increase its revenue. OTT has some challenges to overcome like piracy, censorship, and low internet speed, *etc.*

This chapter focuses on the following aspects but not restricted to:

- Provide a better understanding of OTT applications and their implementation in blockchain technology.
- Suggest that blockchain technology provides an effective way of royalty payments to the copyright owners without the involvement of a third party.
- Describes the rise of OTT applications and their usage statistics in India during 2018-2020 and proposes the implementation of blockchain for ensuring security and privacy.

The rest of the chapter is organized as section 2 gives an overview of the rise in OTT contents in India. Section 3 defines blockchain and smart contracts. Section

4 states the proposed blockchain business models, benefits, and challenges. Section 5 highlights transforming OTT digital platform business using blockchain technology as a theoretical perspective. Disruptions of blockchain technology as a game-changer in OTT platform business and their real-time applications are mentioned in section 6. Section 7 explores Machine Learning (ML) adoption in Blockchain (BC) - Research Issues and Challenges followed by a conclusion.

2. RISE IN CONTENT FOR VIDEO STREAMING APPLICATIONS FOR THE CUSTOMERS

Over the years, the number of subscriptions for OTT platforms grew to 285% worldwide. Netflix was the top application rated by the annual consumer during the period 2016 to 2019. The launch of Disney+ has also added further revenue to this market. When compared with other countries, India has the highest number of consumers using OTT platforms. During the year 2018-2019, OTT platforms played a vital role in India. TV content has been the greatest classification of utilization in the course of the last year. There is no negative development in TV viewing till today; hence get up to speed seeing is probably the most grounded guarantee of OTT contributions. Live streaming has attracted many consumers during the cricket seasons and even some shows like "Game of Thrones". Television broadcasters have come up with new weapons that streamed the live content on their OTT platforms. The live streaming of the content has attracted many consumers. Occasions like elections and terrorist attacks created a huge demand in the OTT platforms. Video content consumption in OTT platforms has created a demand for more live and content-based aspects. However, there is no censor board for videos in OTT platforms like special shows, *etc.* have violence and vulgar contents that can be streamed in OTT but can not be telecasted on TV. Indian platforms like ALTBalaji have attracted many consumers. Apart from ALTBalaji, Netflix and Amazon too attracted many Indian viewers. Another important aspect of OTT platforms is that the platforms are trying to strengthen their video content dependent on the existing library that was aired on TV. India has many channels, contributing countless long periods of video content consistently. Content has demonstrated its value on one stage, is syndicated to another stage, hence reiterated content is still sought after. Content is streaming all over the stages, and customers are continuously exploring all the available platforms of their choice. There is a demand for newly added videos. The video content produced originally will define the growth of the particular OTT. With internet access becoming cheaper, more people are showing interest in OTT platforms; particularly the semi-urban and rural areas have access to content. The majority of these consumers are subscribers of OTT. In today's scenario, even rural and non-urban viewers are also showing interest in OTT. A combination of regional content will guarantee an AVOD platform for local markets. If any OTT provider provides the regional content, then they will be the game changer in OTT platforms in the Indian market. The content environment for OTT stages started developing in 2018 with the concurrence of publicly supported content, free content, and studio-created content, film content, and TV content. The Indian market is providing more entrants to provide more content similar to TV. The majority of the consumers on OTT platforms worldwide are Indian consumers. FM Radio has been delivering music for decades and providing music on the go. The emerging OTT platforms have started keeping the younger consumers engaged with their high consumption. The content market is anticipating a major change. Many OTT platforms are keen on delivering specials that were split into episodes that are trying to attract more subscribers. Gaming and live content streams are developing; the rise of tech-driven content like nonlinear content, intuitive accounts, different stage stories, and vivid content will be explored by the OTT content makers in the future. Globally, all the OTT players are trying to provide curated content based on viewer choices. As a result, major players have started investing to build a content pipeline. The investments of Netflix are 3x more than the investments made by Amazon and Hulu (BCG December 2018). The normal cash spent on content for OTT platforms is higher than the TV markets in India. Time spent on Video Streaming Apps globally went up 140% in 2018 versus 2016 in countries like Australia, India, Indonesia, South Korea, and Thailand (App Annie, The state of the mobile 2019). Table (**2**) shows the OTT Platform revenue generation model. Table (**3**) shows the list of OTT platforms available in India.

Table 2. Over the Top Platform - Revenue generation model.

Country	Description
China	To contribute 76% of the total revenue in 2021
South Korea	Average revenue per user (ARPU) to reach $66.63
India	Online Video Advertising to reach US $1 billion by 2021
Japan	User Penetration to hit 14.23% in 2021
South-East Asia	SVOD revenues are expected to grow to more than $200 million in 2021
OTT Video Revenues to reach $18,396 million in 2021	
OTT Advertising to remain main source of revenue $8,745 million by 2021	

Table 3. List of OTT Platforms available in India.

S. No.	Name of the OTT	Launch Date	Owned By
1	Netflix	6 Jan 2016	Morgan Stanley, Reed Hastings
2	Amazon Prime Video	6 July 2016	Jeef Bezos
3	SunNxt	June 2017	KalanithiMaran

(Table 3) cont.....

S. No.	Name of the OTT	Launch Date	Owned By
4	Aha	March 2020	Brian de Haff
5	Zee5	14 Feb 2018	TarunKatial
6	Disney+Hotstar	29 Mar 2020	Bob Iger
7	Sony LIV	22 Jan 2013	Sony Pictures networks(India)
8	Tentkotta	Feb 5	Varun Kumar
9	MX Player	20 Feb 2019	Karan Bedi
10	Jio Cinema	5 Sep 2016	MukeshAmbani
11	Airtel Xtream	2 Sep 2019	Sunil Bharti Mittal
12	Idea Movies and TV	4 Sep 2017	-
13	YouTube	14 Feb 2005	Google
14	Tata Sky	10 August 2006	HaritNagpal

3. TECHNOLOGICAL INNOVATIONS TO SOLVE CHALLENGES OF OTT

Challenges faced by OTT can be solved by the following technological innovations [15]:

1. Blockchain technology
2. 5G / 6G services
3. Local CDN networks.

4. DEFINING BLOCKCHAIN

A Blockchain is the data store that is distributed across a network consisting of many participants that rely on consensus based on the validity of the transactions without any central authority. In the blockchain, the transactions cannot be altered or modify as blockchain is a decentralized, distributed, and public ledger system. A blockchain is managed by anonymous users. Every user can check the data and verify or discard using consensus algorithms that cannot be altered [16]. For ensuring secure, transparent, and immutable transactions, a cryptocurrency uses blockchain technology, and securing data in IoT is successfully handled by blockchain technology [17, 18]. The working principle of blockchain is shown in Fig. (**1**). All the transactions happen *via.* smart contracts in blockchain (section 3.1). Working of blockchain and its attributes, applications can be found in [19]. Steps involved in blockchain are given below:

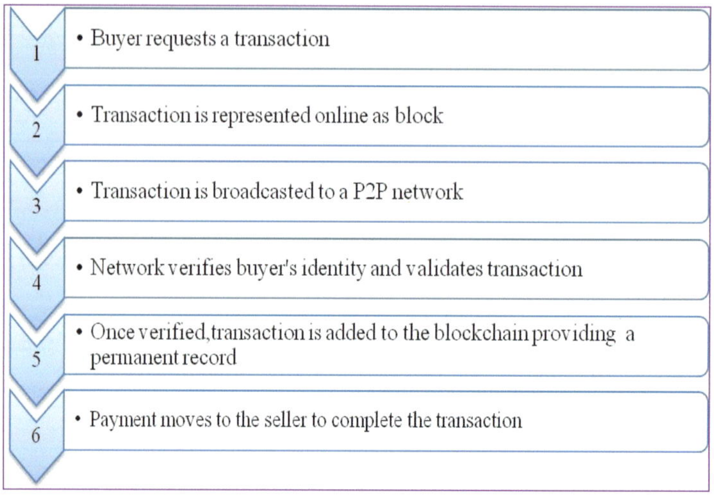

Fig. (1). Working of Blockchain.

1. A buyer buys a product online and makes a transaction.
2. Transactions in a blockchain are represented as blocks.
3. All the transactions in the blocks are broadcasted in the peer-peer network.
4. Blockchain network checks the buyer's identity and validates once verified.
5. All the verified transactions are added as a record and are added to the blockchain.
6. Finally, the transaction is completed as the payment moves to the seller.

COVID-19 has attracted many users to rely on OTT platforms. The country-wise growth of OTT applications (apps.) during 2018 and 2019 is shown in (Fig. **2**) and the percentage of OTT users in India during 2018-19 is shown in (Fig. **3**) and in fact, this has motivated us to work on OTT platforms and their implementation in the blockchain. Our proposed work provides a plethora of OTT applications, their implementation on blockchain technology, and the use-case scenarios in real-time. Blockchain technology provides many advantages to the entertainment industry and helps to prevent piracy. For better understanding, we have provided the applications of blockchain technology in the entertainment industry in sections 5 and 6. The benefits of adopting blockchain technology are highlighted in section 4.

Fig. (**2**) shows the country-wise growth of OTT apps. from 2018 to 2019. The graph shows that India has the highest number of users or subscribers of OTT contents during that period.

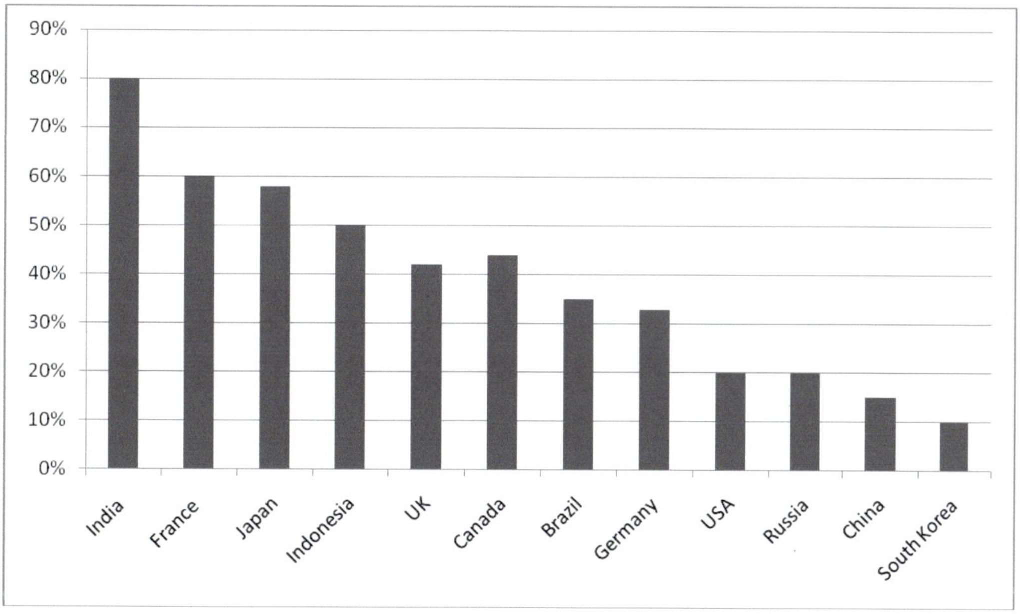

Fig. (2). Country-wise growth of OTT Apps during 2018-19.

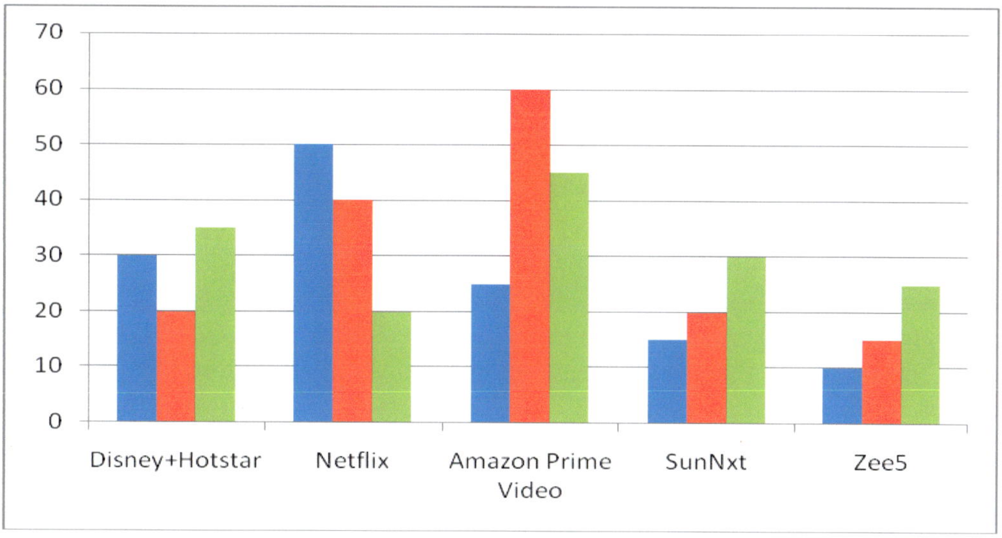

Fig. (3). Percentage of OTT users in India 2018-19.

Fig. (**3**) shows the percentage of OTT users in India from 2018-2019 (Apps.usage-wise).

4.1. Smart Contract

A smart contract is an agreement marked between two parties to do transactions. When the smart contract is signed, it cannot be void [20]. Traditionally, paper-based contracts were managed and validated by TTS. The issues with the conventional contracts as follows:

1. Traditional contracts are passive in nature.
2. Both the parties may not have the same data or information.
3. They need manual intervention from time to time.
4. They are costly.

5. PROPOSED BLOCKCHAIN BUSINESS MODELS, BENEFITS, AND CHALLENGES

A business model tries to build a model that can bring profits. A company spends more on advertising. Each organization will make plans of action which suit their business needs. For ensuring secure, transparent, and immutable transactions, a cryptocurrency uses blockchain technology. BC is a secure and distributed ledger that shares the copy of the ledger with each participating node [21]. Blockchain plans of action help improve organizations and advantage end clients.

A decent plan of action must concentrate on financial specialists and not business visionaries. Blockchain business thoughts must capacity successfully both at the large scale and smaller scale level, subsequently profiting the two workers and end-clients. For example, BloHosT (Blockchain-Enabled Smart Tourism and Hospitality Management) allows tourists to interact with various stakeholders through a single wallet identifier linked with a cryptocurrency server to initiate payments. BloHosT uses an immutable ledger, where no proofs are required during travelling, in this way it provides a hassle-free experience to tourists. A Tourism enabled Deep-Learning (TeDL) framework is used as a part of the BloHosT framework, which is trained on the experience of previously visited travelers. It provides rating scores to prospective travelers about the recently visited locations by previous travelers [22, 23]. The subsequent sections provide information on proposed business models, benefits, and their challenges. An example scenario is illustrated below.

The main role of a manufacturer is to create a product either from scratch or from any other natural source. Products can be created even by fabricating from many components viz., in the automobile industry. A manufacturing industry follows any of the two models: business–to–consumer that sells the products directly to the consumers. In business-to-business or B2B models, the product is outsourced to another company [24]. After that, the wholesalers purchase the item from the producer and then selling either to customers or to a retailer. Wholesalers act as middlemen between manufacturers to the retail stores. Retailers get products from manufacturers either directly or *via.* a distributor. Retailers may operate countrywide or they could operate independently. They make it easy for customers to buy the products of their choice. The franchise is a combination of all the above business models. A franchise incorporates all the business procedures and protocols in it. Blockchain business models are given below.

5.1. Blockchain- As- A Service (BaaS)

The most popular business model is the BaaS model. It helps a business system manage its blockchain system. This model allows companies for conducting research and testing processes *etc.* BaaS model allows companies to focus on their business development cycle. Bitcoin and Ethereum service like EBaaS (EthereumBlockchain as a Service) provides support to this model. Amazon Web Services, IBM BlueMix, and Microsoft Azure are examples of BaaS model.

5.2. Token Economy- Utility Token Business Model

Utility refers to the total satisfaction received from goods consumed. The utility business model works on the principle of tokens like Stellar and Ripple. Funds are transferred using XRP (Ripple) or XLM (Stellar) tokens.

5.3. Blockchain-Based Software Products

Companies expecting profits should buy blockchain solutions and should integrate it into their system. Blockchain supports the companies in payments and other aspects post-implementation. For example, Spotify bought MediaChainblockchain to solve their royalty issues and to solve issues regarding the talent hiring process.

5.4. P2P Blockchain Business Model

The Peer-Peer business model helps user to user directly. This business model uses BaaS, tokens, *etc.* Examples for P2P include Filecoin and IPFS used for storing and sharing data.

5.5. Blockchain Professional Services

Services provided to start-ups and other small companies to know and adopt the usage of blockchain. Blockchain provides auditing services *etc.* for the companies. For example, if a company has plans to assemble their custom business venture, they can go planning with companies like IBM, Deloitte, *etc.* to complete the task for them.

6. REVOLUTIONARY BENEFITS OF BLOCKCHAIN TECHNOLOGY

Blockchain Technology is a distributed ledger technology that has many benefits. Some of the benefits of Blockchain Technology are:

1. Provide faster transactions
2. Cost-effective
3. Hack proof
4. Transparency
5. Traceability
6. Tamper-proof data
7. Real-time data management
8. Secure record keeping
9. Easily auditable
10. Automation and many more.

7. CHALLENGES THAT CAN BE SOLVED BY BLOCKCHAIN IN MEDIA AND BROADCASTING INDUSTRY

Blockchain solves the problems faced by media and broadcasting and even the problems faced in OTT as mentioned in section 3.1. Table (**4**) shows the challenges faced by the media and broadcasting industry and the measures taken byblockchain in order to solve them [25].

Table 4. Industry challenges and steps that Blockchain tries to solve.

Challenges	Blockchain Implementation to Solve the Challenges
Piracy	Refrain content aggregators; provide tamper-proof copyrights of the owners. Payment of royalty to copyright owners.
Ineffective use of advertising	Depending on content usage, type of content being consumed, and AI-based agents can target only the relevant customers.
Pay per view beyond geography	Payment for each user is tracked in blockchain and payment for the specific user will be processed as per smart contracts.
Monetization of peer-peer entities	Blockchain monetizes each sharing through the automated real-time process.
Copyright and IPR issues	Blockchain provides micro-payments, cryptocurrencies so that users can pay only for the services they opt for.
Issues in distribution of dividends	Using smart contracts and micro-payments, transactions become transparent.

(Table 4) cont.....

Challenges	Blockchain Implementation to Solve the Challenges
Streaming music and royalty payments	Blockchains use "Hash" of the digital file that is associated with the original identities. Leveraging blockchain with AI ensures copyright owners are paid for their royalty.

8. TRANSFORMING OTT DIGITAL PLATFORM BUSINESS USING BLOCKCHAIN TECHNOLOGY

Blockchain technology provides advantages to OTT digital platform business in many ways. Some of the key features of blockchain for OTT digital platform business are listed below:

8.1. Providing Tokens for Audio and Video

With the adoption of blockchain, people can buy and sell assets using cryptocurrencies and so is copyright content too.

8.2. Provides Scope for New Artists and New Entrants

Blockchain creates new artists and fans in OTT platforms. It establishes direct communication between customers and artists.

8.3. Targeted Advertisements and Marketing

Blockchain helps in marketing by studying the current market situation and provide advertisements to the targeted customers easily. It provides transparency in marketing and advertising.

8.4. Royalty Payments and Smart Contracts

With the adoption of blockchain, royalty payments for artists will be transparent and hassle-free. Fig. (**4**) shows the royalty payment through blockchain.

8.5. The Decentralized Model of Content Delivery

Blockchain eliminates the centralized mode of authority for transactions, making them easier for peers to verify transactions directly.

8.6. Reduce Production Costs

Blockchain helps in making visual effects and rendering effects to movies at low cost and hence reducing the total production cost.

8.7. Micropayments

Blockchain promotes the use of digital currencies. By using the cryptocurrency wallet, the users can track their monthly expenses. Royalty payments can be directly paid to the copyright owners.

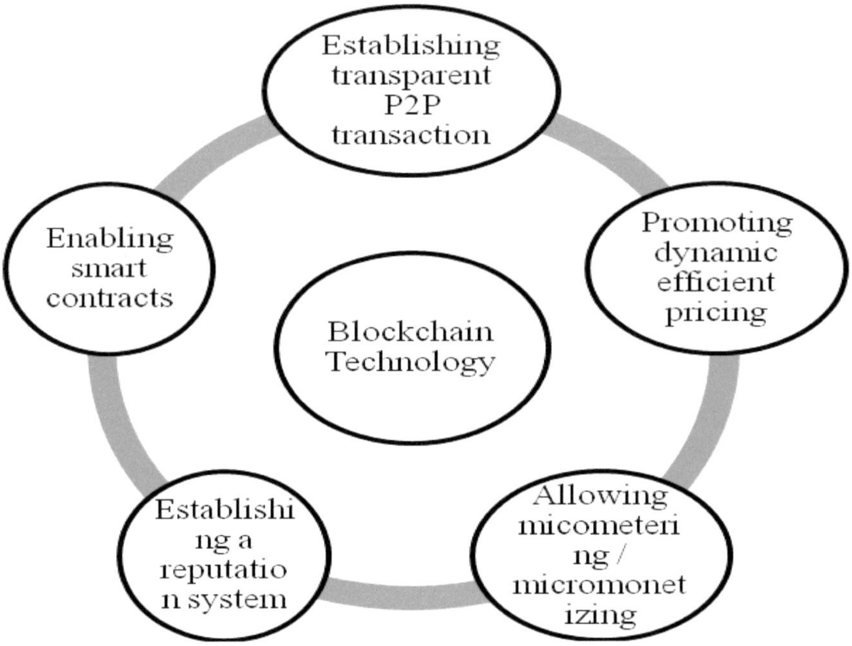

Fig. (4). Royalty payment through Blockchain.

8.8. Licensing and Monetization

Blockchain can provide a license to small and medium-range content creators who are unable to afford heavy amounts charged from the big production houses. It permits only authorized users to track their royalty payments.

8.9. Royalty Tracking and Payments

Blockchain ensures that all the participants get their royalty payments for the revenue generated with it. Blockchain provides digital watermarking against theft and unauthorized usage of the content. Blockchain provides effective transactions by decentralized and distributed networks and also enables peer network participants to verify their transactions.

8.10. Blockchain-Powered Cloud Space

Blockchain can be used as a decentralized system that provides space for decentralized apps. This space can be explored and used by the users for peer-peer cloud storage and data delivery network. Video advertisements are the special interests of blockchain applications. Leveraging blockchain will provide significant benefits to the advertising industry by identifying potential customers.

9. BLOCKCHAIN TECHNOLOGY - DISRUPTIONS AS A GAME-HANGER IN OTT PLATFORM BUSINESS AND REAL-TIME APPLICATIONS IN DIGITAL ADVERTISING

Blockchain has changed the phase of the music and entertainment industry. Recent reports state that Blockchain in the telecom and media market is expected to grow from USD 46.6 million in 2018 to USD 993.8 million by 2023 as per the Compound Annual Growth Rate (CAGR) of 84.4% [26]. Different versions of blockchain projects are in progress for video streaming. Some of the disruptions of blockchain technology in OTT include:

9.1. Opportunities for new channel dispatches

New channels for live occasions, sports, dreams, sci-fi, and news are probably going to be made. Blockchain will empower players to manufacture a stage that will step by step become an aggregator for content creators and the decentralized stage will encourage the situating of new shows. This will remove the need for a streaming device.

9.2. Advertising and free substance

Any plan of action in the M&E business is vulnerable to interruption by the free substance. Video ventures that are Blockchain-empowered are probably going to be exchanged through cryptographic forms of money that can be utilized by advertisers for channelizing advancements. Blockchain will guarantee that crypto-currencies are credited legitimately to the content creators without any intermediaries.

10. REAL-TIME APPLICATIONS OF BLOCKCHAIN TECHNOLOGY IN DIGITAL ADVERTISING AND OTT PLATFORM BUSINESS

There is a lot of focus on blockchain applications in digital advertising for OTT platforms. Premion, a leading OTT advertising platform, and Comcast

Multichannel Video Programming Distributor are examples of OTT advertising platforms. For transactions, Premion has partnered with MadHive that is built on blockchain technology. Premion, MadHive, and AdLedger as a blockchain consortium have started Campaign Reconciliation that is based on a proof-o--concept (POC).

10.1. Visual Content and Media

Ethereum based, FilmChain gathers, designates, and breaks down incomes in film, TV, and other digital media. FilmChain encourages transparency in the distribution process without third-party intervention. It also explores ways for global funding and promotes reaching global audiences. StreambedMedia is a Toronto-based company that is making content provenance mechanisms allowing creators to track content on social networking sites like YouTube, Instagram, *etc.* This platform allows for sharing information with other content creators and links the users to the creators for payments.

10.2. Block Graph TM

BlockGraphTM formerly known as FreeWheel deployed blockchain with premium content across digital and linear TV. BlockGraphTM will empower advertisers, developers, and administrators to plan, target, and report on promotion purchases across computerized, communicate, and streaming music utilizing blockchain technology. Using BlockGraphTM, advertisers can secretly coordinate their data set with developers, administrators, and others in the business to target or analyze buyers on any gadget without giving up sensitive client data [27].

10.3. Music

Backed by Sony and BMG, Vezt is a company that holds the copyrights of music. Fans can share the royalties of the songs. Vezt attempts to go over the music business by giving specialists, lyricists, and creators with sponsoring sourced really from fans. Royalties are encoded and are followed on-chain. Fans are offered to purchase music of their choice. Another player, Verifi handles the rights of the music creators. Verifi provides synchronize ownership across music companies. Audius, supported by Lightspeed Ventures, General Catalyst, and Kleiner Perkins, means to be the blockchain-based adversary to Soundcloud. Audius offers free encouragement for its artists, presents 90% of salaries back to the producer, and ensures extended discoverability and fan responsibility for top-tier authorities [28].

10.4. Engaging Audiences

After collaborating with Ripple's XSpring, Scooter Braun, and Warner Music Group, Audigent has gained popularity in fundraising for advertisers in entertainment, sports, and lifestyle space. YellowHeart is the first ticketing platform built on a blockchain. It allows event organizers to book a concert venue and set up rules for ticket management.

10.5. Current Scenario and Beyond

To transform the digital advertising supply chain, individual consumers also should be involved. Identity management is the core element of blockchain technology; therefore, consumers will play an important role in adopting the use of digital wallets. Many OTT platforms started direct-to-digital releases during the current pandemic situation in 2020; OTT platforms have started investing in upcoming films. Many digital premiers during COVID-19 were streamed by Amazon Prime Video. In June 2020, Disney+Hotstar announced digital releases of seven films on its platform worth Rs.100 crore. OTT platforms make money by focusing on direct-to-digital releases. New subscribers are the potential for the OTT platforms. To capture the Indian market, many OTT platforms have started investing huge amounts of money for providing digital content. Amazon Prime Video, Disney+Hotstar, and Netflix are some of the OTT players that have been aggressive in spending for content in India. Netflix has invested Rs.3,000 crore for original content during December 2019. Amazon Prime has doubled its investment as its viewership has grown six-fold in two years. Disney+Hotstar has more investment from its parent company Star India. The second big investment for Disney+Hotstar of Rs. 1,113 crore happened in April 2020. Star India and Star US property had invested Rs.1,066crore in the OTT platform for the 13th edition of the Indian Premier League (IPL) in March 2020 [29]. For example, myNK is a flagship product of MinersINC which is India's first blockchain-based entertainment ecosystem that connects content creators with consumers directly over a secured network [30].

11. MACHINE LEARNING (ML) ADOPTION IN BLOCKCHAIN (BC) – RESEARCH ISSUES AND CHALLENGES

There are many research challenges and issues in ML and BC that are yet to be addressed. The open issues and challenges of ML adoption in BC are shown in Fig. (**5**).

11.1. Suitability

In a distributed environment, for untrusted sources, blockchain is a viable solution. If performance is a major concern, then, a simple database is a better option. Therefore, the usability and architecture of blockchain must be clearly understood for any application before deployment.

11.2. Infrastructure

For blockchain-based applications, the hardware and network infrastructure designed exclusively try to improve the performance. However, research is going on for major usage in major companies for the adoption of blockchain for their applications.

11.3. Privacy

Privacy is the key issue in blockchain as the data stored in the blockchain is available to all the nodes in the network. Private Blockchains provide controlled access and encryption for securing the data. However, the ML model's adoption of these limited data imposed barriers for predictions and analytics.

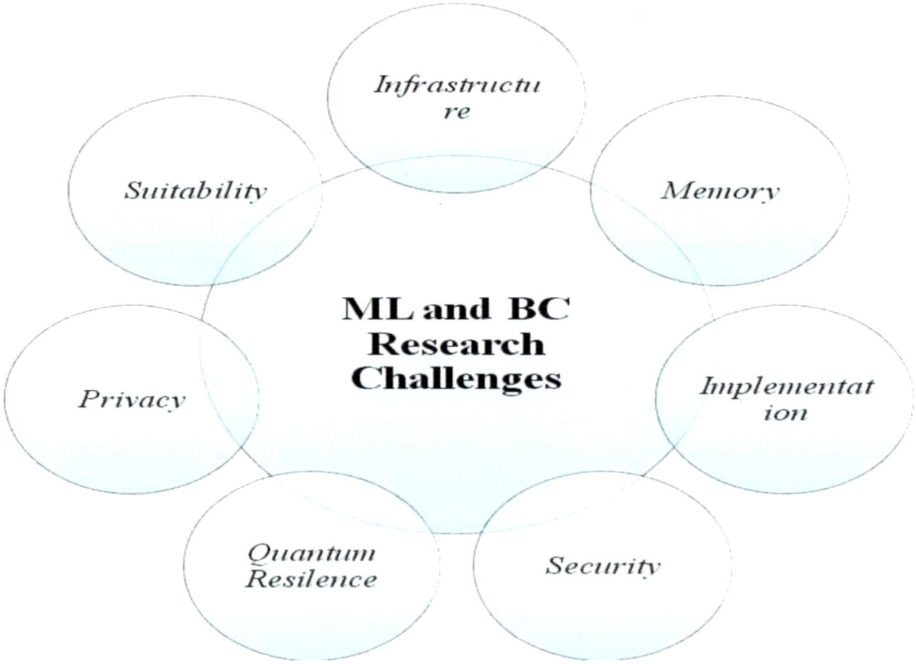

Fig. (5). ML adoption in BC – Research Challenges and Open issues.

11.4. Memory

The size of the data and the new blocks are constantly added to the blockchain network. Consequently, the performance of the blockchain is also affected by an increase in chain size which creates memory constraints. Blockchain is immutable, and storage of data is a major concern in most of the implementations.

11.5. Implementation

For larger applications, implementing blockchain requires high bandwidth of internet connection for a large number of transactions. Therefore, adding of blocks and transactions needs to be controlled.

11.6. Security

In a decentralized network, blockchains are prone to security issues and hence, the consensus protocol may be compromised (in public blockchains). In private blockchains, each node is identified, and an appropriate consensus protocol is placed.

11.7. Quantum Resilience

The hashing calculations utilized by blockchains could before long be broken with quantum PCs. Fortunately, quantum computing offers chances to support the exhibition and security of blockchains. Quantum cryptography can strengthen the security of the blockchain network as quantum correspondence is verified inalienably (clients can't copy another client). It can scramble whole P2P correspondences and supplant traditional advanced marks in the blockchain network. Research is going on to design blockchain with quantum computing [31]. Similarly, blockchain tries to solve security issues in smart cities [32, 33].

CONCLUSION

This paper discussed OTT platforms and their business in real-time. Over-the-top (OTT) has changed how individuals sit in front of the TV, and in some regions, it may overtake broadcast, cable, and satellite. With more audiences getting attracted to use OTT platforms, the OTT providers need to rely on the security of the users. Blockchain technology provides a suitable solution for providing security and preventing piracy. This chapter explores the benefits and advantages of using blockchain technology for OTT platforms. Royalty payments are paid securely using smart contracts without any third-party intervention. Distributed ledger technology provides security and privacy of the transactions in Ethereum. Blockchain technology protects the copyrights of the owners against any third-party attacks. This chapter is intended for the audiences who are interested to know about recent developments in OTT and blockchain technology. Blockchain technology will revolutionalize the future of the digital platform market and will expand its usability across many sectors in the coming years.

CONSENT FOR PUBLICATION

Not Applicable.

CONFLICT OF INTEREST

The author declares no conflict of interest, financial or otherwise.

ACKNOWLEDGEMENT

Declared none.

REFERENCES

[1] *Indian OTT Platforms - Report,* 2019.

[2] *The Wise Pivot, Accenture, Business Journal for India,* 2019.

[3] *The billion-dollar opportunity the Indian OTT industry is missing.*https://yourstory.com/ 2020/05/

[4] K.C. Yang, "A comparative study of internet regulatory policies in the greater China region: Emerging regulatory models and issues in China, Hong-Kong SAR, and Taiwan", *Telemat. Inform.,* vol. 24, no. 1, pp. 30-40, 2007. [http://dx.doi.org/10.1016/j.tele.2005.12.001]

[5] Phil Gomes, "Blockchain Technology: The Marketing Value of Digital Performanc", *SNCR 2020 Series Exploring New Communications Tools and Technologies,* pp. 1-20, 2020.

[6] W. Saad, M. Bennis, and M. Chen, "A Vision of 6G Wireless Systems: Applications, Trends, Technologies, and Open Research Problems", *arXiv,* 2019.

[7] F. Tariq, M. Khandaker, K-K. Wong, M. Imran, M. Bennis, and M. Debbah, "A Speculative Study on 6G", *arXiv,* 2019. http://arxiv.org/abs/1902.06700

[8] Z. Zhang, Y. Xiao, Z. Ma, M. Xiao, Z. Ding, X. Lei, G.K. Karagiannidis, and P. Fan, "6G wireless networks: Vision, requirements, architecture, and key technologies", *IEEE Veh. Technol. Mag.,* vol. 14, no. 3, pp. 28-41, 2019. [http://dx.doi.org/10.1109/MVT.2019.2921208]

[9] P. Yang, Y. Xiao, M. Xiao, and S. Li, "6G wireless communications: Vision and potential techniques", *IEEE Netw.,* vol. 33, no. 4, pp. 70-75, 2019. [http://dx.doi.org/10.1109/MNET.2019.1800418]

[10] N. Christin, B. Edelman, and T. Moore, "Bitcoin: Economics, technology, and governance", *J. Econ. Perspect.,* vol. 29, no. 2, pp. 213-238, 2015. [http://dx.doi.org/10.1257/jep.29.2.213]

[11] T. Bosona, and G. Gebresenbet, "Food traceability as an integral part of logistics management in food and agricultural supply chain", *Food Control,* vol. 33, no. 1, pp. 32-48, 2013. [http://dx.doi.org/10.1016/j.foodcont.2013.02.004]

[12] N. Chammem, M. Issaoui, A.I.D. De Almeida, and A.M. Delgado, "Food crises and food safety incidents in european union, United States, and maghreb area: Current risk communication strategies and new approaches", *J. AOAC Int.,* vol. 101, no. 4, pp. 923-938, 2018.

[http://dx.doi.org/10.5740/jaoacint.17-0446] [PMID: 29566775]

[13] S. Yadav, "Blockchain critical success factors for sustainable supply chain", *Resour. Conserv. Recycling,* vol. 104505, 2020. [http://dx.doi.org/10.1016/j.resconrec.2019.104505]

[14] Damilola Fowora, "Performance Evaluation of OTT Communication Services", *American Journal of Transportation and Logistics,* vol. 1, p. 2, 2018. [http://dx.doi.org/10.28933/AJTL]

[15] *Over the Top Platform in India.* https://www.drishtiias.com/daily-updates/daily-news-editorials/o-er-the-top-platform-in-india

[16] *Reinventing OTT with Blockchain.* www.muvi.com

[17] Lakshit Madaan, "Working principle, Application areas and Challenges for Blockchain Technology", In: *IEEE 9th International Conference on Communication Systems and Network Technologies (CSNT)*, 2020.

[18] B. Bhushan, C. Sahoo, and P. Sinha, "Unification of Blockchain and Internet of Things (BIoT): requirements, working model, challenges and future directions", *Wirel. Netw.,* 2020. [http://dx.doi.org/10.1007/s11276-020-02445-6]

[19] Aakash Biswal, "Blockchain for Internet of Things: Architecture, Consensus Advancements, Challenges and Application Areas", In: *5th International Conference on Computing, Communication, Control And Automation (ICCUBEA)*, 2019.

[20] R. Gupta, S. Tanwar, F. Al-Turjman, P. Italiya, A. Nauman, and S.W. Kim, "Smart Contract Privacy Protection using AI in Cyber-Physical Systems: Tools, Techniques and Challenges", *IEEE Access,* vol. 8, pp. 24746-24772, 2020. [http://dx.doi.org/10.1109/ACCESS.2020.2970576]

[21] M. Patel, S. Tanwar, R. Gupta, and N. Kumar, "A Deep Learning-based Cryptocurrency Price Prediction Scheme for Financial Institutions", *Journal of Information Security and Applications,* vol. 55, no. 102583, pp. 1-13, 2020. [http://dx.doi.org/10.1016/j.jisa.2020.102583]

[22] R. Gupta, A. Kumari, S. Tanwar, and N. Kumar, "Blockchain-envisioned Softwarized Multi-Swarming UAVs to Tackle COVID-19 Situations", *IEEE Netw.,* pp. 1-7, 2020.

[23] U. Bodkhe, P. Bhattacharya, S. Tanwar, S. Tyagi, N. Kumar, and M.S. Obaidat, "BloHosT: Blockchain Enabled Smart Tourism and Hospitality Management", In: *International Conference on Computer*. Information and Telecommunication Systems (IEEE CITS-2019): Beijing, China, 2019, pp. 237-241. https://blockgeeks.com/guides/understand-blockchain-business-models/

[25] Blockchain Council – accessed from https://www.blockchain-council.org/blockchain/the-be-t-blockchain-business-models/#:~:text=A%20blockchain%20business%20model%20is,depends%20on

[26] "Over the Top Video is Coming of Age", *Accenture Report,* 2018.

[27] Shubhangani Maheshwari, "OTT+: Industry Transformations and Innovations Ahead", *LTI – Let's Solve - L & T,* pp. 2-8, 2018.

[28] Interactive Advertising Bureau, *Blockchain for Video Advertising: A Market Snapshot of Publisher and Buyer Use Cases,* 2018.

[29] Forbes – https://www.forbes.com/sites/tatianakoffman/2020/02/26/how-blockchain-will-transf-rm-media--entertainment/#3659d1211d1b

[30] Money Control – https://www.moneycontrol.com/news/business/from-gulabo-sitabo-to-bhu--how-viable-are-digital-premieres-for-ott-players-5519641.html

[31] S. Tanwar, Q. Bhatia, P. Patel, A. Kumari, P. K. Singh, and W. C. Hong, "Machine Learning Adoption in Blockchain-Based Smart Applications: The Challenges, and a Way Forward", *IEEE Access,* vol. 8,

pp. 474-488, 2020.

[33] S. Gupta, S. Sinha, and B. Bhushan, "Emergence of Blockchain Technology: Fundamentals, Working and its Various Implementations (April 6, 2020)", In: *Proceedings of the International Conference on Innovative Computing & Communications (ICICC)*, 2020. [http://dx.doi.org/10.2139/ssrn.3569577]

CHAPTER 10

Blockchain-based Cultivating Ideas for Growth: A New Agronomics Perspective

Vishakha[1], **Nikhil Sharma**[2,*], **Bharat Bhushan**[2] and **Ila Kaushik**[3]

[1] *HMR Institute of Technology & Management, Delhi, India*

[2] *School of Engineering and Technology, Sharda University, Greater Noida, India*

[3] *Krishna Institute of Engineering & Technology, Ghaziabad, U.P., India*

Abstract: The development of nourishment and food is an essential requirement of nations for their affluence and welfare. Agriculture is the science and specialty of developing plants and livestock. In sedentary human civilization, agriculture plays a key role. The agribusiness needs to do a ton of work to keep up and fabricate the purchaser's trust with regards to the food quality check. A blockchain-based agricultural arrangement holds a guarantee for the agro-business with its capacity to acquire clarity and transparency in the framework. Minimal effort agrarian protection plans are progressively seen as instruments for giving social assurance to the individuals influenced by floods or dry seasons. In assisting with the diminishing effects, they endure because of such occasions. Therefore, this chapter introduces the idea of blockchain technology, extensive literature survey, including a review of blockchain development in the nourishment sector followed by the cases in the food supply chain. This chapter presented various opportunities and an ideal architecture of how blockchain will function in the farming sector. Finally, the chapter concludes by featuring open research difficulties in this field.

Keywords: Agribusiness, Agriculture, Blockchain, Farming Insurances, Food Safety, Internet business of Agri Products, IoT, Nourishment Supply network, Smart Agriculture, Smart Contracts, Supply Chain, Traceability, Transaction Costs, Underwater fishing industry.

* **Corresponding author Nikhil Sharma:** HMR Institute of Technology & Management, Delhi, India; E-mail: nikhilsharma1694@gmail.com

1. INTRODUCTION

Apart from cryptocurrencies, blockchain exhibit a wide variety of applications. The innovations in the field of blockchain are surely transforming numerous industries from banking to the healthcare sector and also the real estate business. Now research works are going on to implement the same in the agricultural sector. With the advancement in IoT applications, the technological domain, as well as financial sectors have acquired substantial growth in ecological observing applications to assess the quality of water, soil, and air. The world population is calculated to be 7.8 billion as of April 2020. With the continuous increase in population, there is a drastic increase in the demand for per-capita food.

Studies in 2014-15 showed that an adult has a 6.1 percent more calorie urge as compared to that of an adult in 1975-76. Increasing demand for food has remarkably affected the environment, which as a result has endangered many species. The destruction caused to the environment due to high food demand is in the form of deforestation, increased levels of carbon emission, *etc.* If the food supply chain is efficiently organized then there is a potential of reducing carbon footprint and environmental hazards which in turn will guarantee food safety [1]. In the current food supply chain, there are several stakeholders involved from production to consumption, making the situation difficult to retrieve actual step-by-step data for analysis. It is presented in the reports that in agricultural farming activities, a significant amount of carbon is produced in various processes. In the United States, it is estimated that among all the factors responsible for the generation of greenhouse gases, only transportation of food contributes 11% to the emission. It is observed that food production must be doubled by 2050 to meet the nutrients requirement of every individual [2].

Due to the increase in the cases of food consumption diseases, now the consumers want to know detailed information about their eatables and others. People show very little reliance on the existing food system. Blockchain has provided exciting solutions for these problems. It provides eternal evidence for each proceeding part which is then arranged into various blocks and no changes can be reflected there. It also helps in replacing those physical trackers and monitoring entities to prevent the imprecise impact of the traditional supply chain [3]. Tracking of the supply chain is the most important measure to protect the safety of eatables, securing them from malign vulnerabilities and encouraging food certification. LetsFarm is a start-up utilizing computerized reasoning with AI to enable ranchers over the globe. It utilizes transparent instruments and advancements to associate farmers so they can get the data they need from any place. Appropriate data can assist farmers with increasing their yield and to have a better salary from similar harvests that they are developing. LetsFarm likewise engages farmers with auxiliary salary by giving crucial data and expanding the pay of farmer's family units. After all, the overall growth of ranchers is the progress of the country all in all!. The Dutch Ministry of Agriculture, Nature, and Food Quality financed the main research venture, "Blockchain for Agri-food" which has been proposed to investigate blockchain suggestions for Agri-food. Pilot research shows that blockchain innovation empowered nourishment to be followed from farm to market in only a couple of seconds [4]. Blockchain additionally assists with watching bottomless items and diminish instances of illicit gathering and delivery cheats. The United Nations uncovers that nourishment fakes cost the worldwide economy around $40 billion every year because of unlawful exchanges. A ton of advancements originated from new businesses and the rural division isn't a special case. Ripe.io and Pavo Coin are two ongoing business models that use blockchain in the supply chain [5].

Ripe.io is a new business situated in SanFrancisco. Ripo.io centers around farming and offers clients an elevated level of straightforwardness. The framework created by Ripo.io can distinguish mugginess, readiness, and the temperature of the item. In this way, the rancher gets the data about the states of things. Blockchain achieving decentralization is not entirely technical in nature rather it's a combination of technical and smart engineering incentives. It began in 2008 with Satoshi Nakamoto, whose real identity is still not known to anyone, released a white paper that introduced a purely peer-to-peer version of crypto cash called bitcoin. There are four types of blockchain named as a private blockchain, public blockchain, federated blockchain, and the last one being hybrid. In private blockchain access is controlled, only a few users have the permission to view and verify the transaction. It is used in services where data security is a prime concern [6]. A public blockchain is one that has open access to all though transactions are anonymous. Transactions are transparent to those who have view access in the ledger. Federated blockchain is operated by a group or federation and only the members of the group have access. Hybrid refers to the system which uses public blockchain but also hosts private blockchain. Though data is stored on a public blockchain yet data privacy is not intruded. There is an incentive that is provided to the nodes for behaving honestly. There are two incentive mechanisms in the bitcoin named block reward and the other is transaction payment. In the service of creating a block in the blockchain, initially, the creator of the block includes the generation of special coin transactions in the block and then chooses the receiver address of this agreement. Block maker gets to the opportunity to gather the reward only if the block terminates up on long-term consensus branch. In the blockchain, the worth of block reward gets halved after every four years. Block reward is how new bitcoins are made and it is assessed that it will run out in 2140. There will be no new bitcoins if this standard remains unchanged. In transaction fees, the procedure creator of the transaction can decide to make the yield estimation of coin lesser than input esteem, and the rest of the amount will be the transaction expense to the creator of the block which is placed on the consensus branch [7]. There are many problems associated with these methods such as how to pick a random junction for each transaction or how to keep away every node from running the bitcoin node for collecting the reward. To improve upon this now bitcoins are generated by the process of consensus mechanism which includes various processes such as PoW, PoS, DPoS, and PBFT. In the Proof of Work (PoW) process, a bitcoin miner who finds the hash value first will be permitted to include another new block of exchange to the blockchain. In the Proof of Stake (PoS) mechanism, the more coins the stakeholder has, it is more likely that they will include a new block of exchange to the blockchain. In Delegated Proof of Stake (DPOS), coin holders can utilize their balance to choose a list of modes to be possibly permitted to add new transaction blocks to the blockchain. Practical Byzantine Fault Tolerance (PBFT) relies on no. of nodes to affirm trust. When enough feedbacks are obtained which in general is 51%, the transaction is declared as a valid transaction. There are mainly two important terminologies in the blockchain named as a consensus mechanism and smart contracts which need to be understood before studying the utility of it in the agricultural domain. Consensus Mechanism is a way to guarantee a mutual agreement on a data point. Each vertex in the system grid has a duplicate of a similar record(ledger). It is secured in nature and an economic framework of the cryptographic protocol. Objectives of a consensus mechanism include agreement seeking, collaboration, cooperation, inclusive property, and participation. There are three basic steps of consensus, the first one being endorsement which determines whether to accept a transaction or not. Then comes ordering, which sorts all the transactions into a series in a specified period. The last one is the validation which verifies the endorsement policy. Smart contracts, also known as a self-executing contract, is a computer convention that digitally facilitates, checks, or upholds the presentation of an agreement by avoiding middlemen interaction and validates it over a decentralized platform by all peers who stores the blockchain. It is used for the exchange of money, shares, *etc*. It is self-verifying, self-executing in nature, and has resistance to any change. It turns legal obligations into automated processes. It is cheaper as there are no third-party fees involved. It guarantees a greater degree of security.

The other sections of the chapter are standardized as follows, Section 2 presents a literature review, Section 3 describes different opportunities of blockchain technology in the agriculture field, Section 4 discusses the application of blockchain in agriculture, Section 5 illustrates use cases, Section 6 explains Blockchain-Based Architecture in Agriculture and challenges followed by the conclusion in Section 7.

2. LITERATURE SURVEY

In a traditional system, the seed company produces the seed which is identified according to global standards and updates the local record. The farmer buys the seed, harvests the crops, and sends it to the grain elevator which stores the produced crop in various warehouses. Various grain processors buy the grains from warehouses and refine them to make the end product. Then distributors take those end products and sell them to retailers who further sell the product in small identifiable quantities to the customer [8]. Agriculture in India can be categorized into various phases such as production, supply chain, processing, and marketing. Fig. (**1**) represents the various phases in the chain that lead to credit risk and limit the flow of credit due to poor supply of inputs and outdated farming policies in the production phase, high wastage, and poor transportation facility along with many intermediaries in supplying phase.

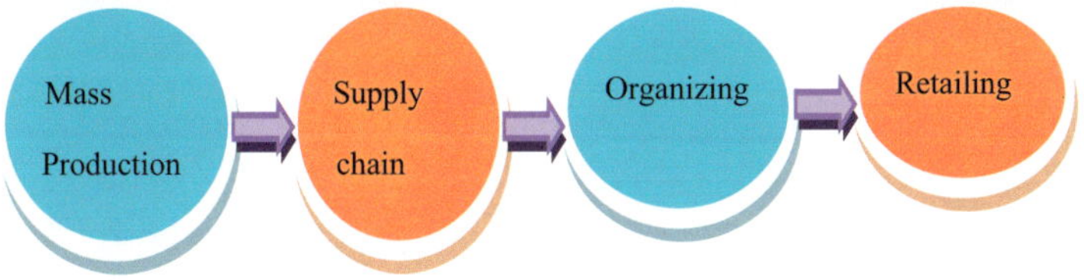

Fig. (1). Phases of supply chain.

Buyers need to know the starting point of nourishment and they even can pay moreover to discover all essential data about the eatables. They can see food accreditation but regular confirmation can be misrepresented as seen in the present system. However, blockchain being immutable in nature will make it difficult to change any record subtly like date, and substance which will stay unaltered. A single scanning of a QR code will give a shopper all data about nourishment –*i.e.* which type of seeds are used for the production purpose, what pesticides are used in the process, how much time it is put in the shop *etc.* Similarly, it can be used for poultry purposes to know the exact time, what conditions it lived in, what infections it had, *etc.* Just with a single click, all the necessary information will reach the consumer [9].

The worldwide workforce is estimated to be 46%, out of which only the farming sector presents 8.4% of the whole world's monetary, and its overall creation is 9,084,800 million. Blockchain gives secure information trade and a carefully designed vault for these reports and delivery events which will save billions of dollars wasted due to the misinterpretation of data. Maersk and IBM are utilizing blockchain technology to make a worldwide carefully designed framework for digitizing the exchange work process and following shipments end-to-end, eliminating grindings including expensive point-to-point correspondences [10]. In the case of agriculture, India is one of the largest nations which constitute majorly for production purposes. Among all sectors, the primary sector of India contributes significantly to the economy though it is decreased down to 15% due to the continuous evolvement of industries and other commercial sectors. Fig. (**2**) shows the division of available land in India. India is the second biggest natural product maker on the planet, the assessed measure of cultivation creation is 314.7 million tonnes. Total horticulture sends out from India is evaluated to be US $38.54 billion [11].

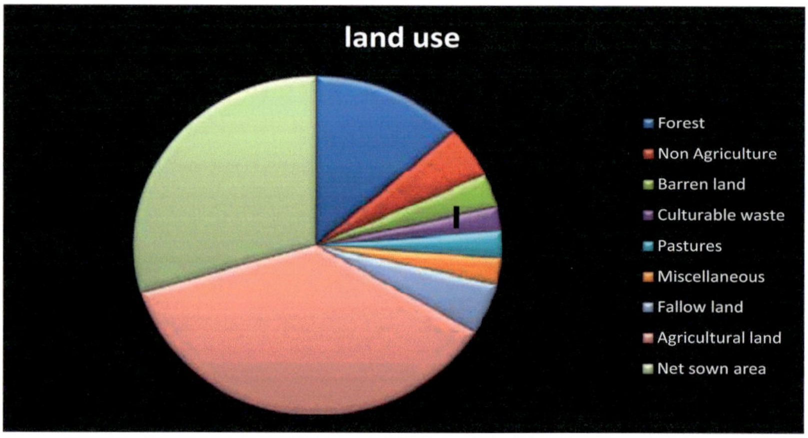

Fig. (2). Land distribution in India.

During the 2017-18 yield year, food grain creation is evaluated at a record of 284.83 million tonnes. The Indian government is focusing on the creation of 287.2 million tonnes by 2021. Fig. (**3**) shows the crop distribution in some of the states of India and it is clear that wheat, cotton, paddy, groundnut, and mustard are some of the major crops. A combination of machine learning concepts with blockchain innovation will boost up the economy in approaching years [12].

As clearly depicted from Fig. (**4**), sugarcane crop has the highest yield among all crops in India. The import or export of a particular crop mainly depends on the cultivation process and yield of a particular area. As a large amount of finance is lost in the farming practices due to the middleware, it's now high time to integrate the blockchain technology with that of the agriculture sector [13].

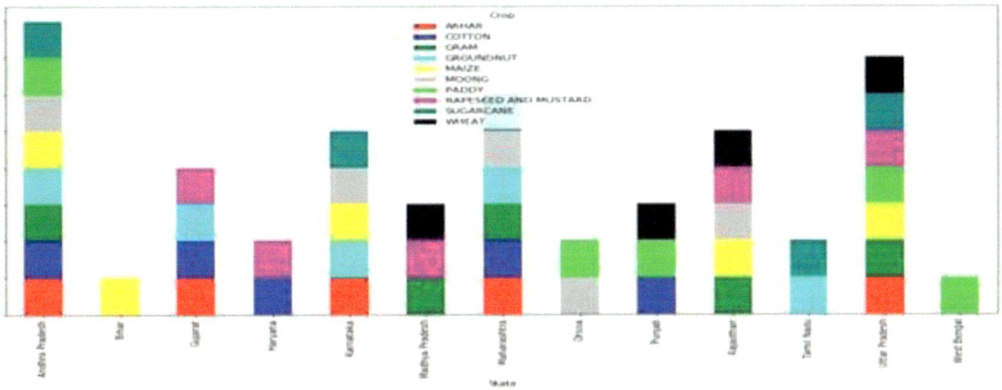

Fig. (3). Crop distribution of few states of India.

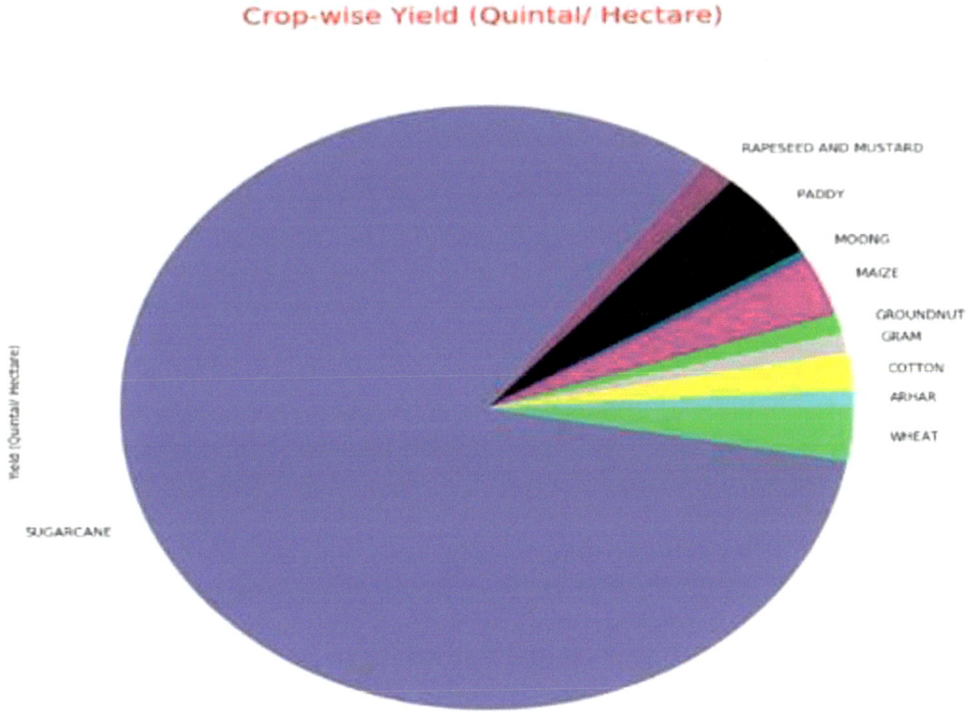

Fig. (4). Crop wise yield in India.

The utilization of blockchain innovation to accomplish multifaceted administration of the nourishment advertise is the government's interest, through the arrangement of administrative records of the nourishment showcases the exchanged data. This can successfully take care of the issue of the nourishment administrative procedure. As indicated by the comprehension of the significant government divisions, there are a few necessities of government administrative experts on the nourishment production network. The first one being precisely gathering the data on all parts of the nourishment store network and then recovering Information about social events and capacity of the nourishment production network from planting (rearing) to the entire procedure of utilization. These necessities coordinate with the mechanical qualities of the blockchain which stores data on every exchange. Tian in [14] examined the beneficiaries and drawbacks of blockchain and RFID for the traceability of the farming supply chain. Tian *et al.* [15] proposed a nourishment production network dependent on inspection of risk and control of critical sites that utilizes IoT and blockchain. Caro *et al.* [16] represent Agri Block IoT which is a blockchain-based detectability arrangement incorporating information from various connected IoT gadgets along the supply chain. They built up a utilization case for tracing the produce from farm to the state of consumption and present execution comparisons through both Hyperledger and Ethereum. Tse *et al.* [17] reviewed how to apply blockchain technology to the nourishment inventory network and contrasted the blockchain-based arrangement and traditional supply arrangements at a high conceptual level. He also emphasized the key elements concerning integrity, security, and trust Tripoli and Schmidhuber *et al.* [18] talk about the utilization of various technologies of distributed ledger and brilliant consensus for expanding efficiency, give detectability in the horticulture. They recognized both specialized difficulties and obstacles to the reception to presume that distributed ledger technologies have remarkable potential in accomplishing manageable improvement objectives. Mao and Dianhui *et al* [19]. present a blockchain-based credit evaluation framework through crypto contracts for enhancing the efficiency of the executives in the nourishment production network. Lin *et al.* [20] surveyed blockchain ideas for the model of Agri-ICT arrangement and introduces an ICT system prototype for agriculture implementing blockchain innovation. Galves *et al.* [21] audited difficulties and future utilization of blockchain for guaranteeing recognizability and genuineness in the food stock chains. Mao *et al.* [22] proposed an associated blockchain way to deal with a systematic and nourishment exchanging framework. They proposed a streamlined improved viable byzantine adaptation to internal failure calculation called iPBFT to enhance the exchanging arrangement of purchasers in the nourishment store network. Mao *et al.* [23] approve their suggested nourishment exchanging framework utilizing fraternity-based blockchain using a contextual analysis applied to Shandong locality in China. Schneider *et al.* [24] structured a model blockchain framework to improve clarity and self-operated forms in the agricultural sector. Lucena *et al.* [25] presented a methodology for grain standard estimation utilizing blockchain and brilliant agreements. They present usage answer for a genuine instance that brought about 15% included valuation for hereditarily altered free for soy grain trades from grain shipper commerce in Brazil. Holmberg and Aquist *et al.* [26] analyzed the obstacles in executing a blockchain-based recognizability arrangement in the pasteurizing business. Some ongoing instances of blockchain pilot application in the agricultural supply chain consist of wheat supply in Australia facilitated with the help of blockchain technology through Agri digital platform using Ethereum and food traceability initiative by Walmart through IBM (International Business Machines) Hyperledger [27]. Chinaka *et al.* [28] concentrated on how executing blockchain-based arrangements can encourage worth move by interpreting rancher's assets in Africa, for example, arable lands, animals, and produce implemented to small scale agriculture. Louis Dreyfus, an enormous item merchant, effectively finished the first ever blockchain-based ware exchange of soybeans to the Shandong Bohi Industry of China [29] from the US. As it is noticed from these related works that there is a growing pattern in embracing blockchain innovation for transparency, upgraded data safety, confirmation of different standards in nourishment, and farming stockpile chains. Zhao *et al.* [30], presented a stage for constant information checking in horticultural-related applications dependent on remote sensors through M2M. The framework thinks about information assortment, the executives, and appropriation under the extent of nursery control. A remarkable part of the use cases examines the theoretical utilization of blockchain in horticultural supply chains missing the mark regarding specific usage structure or approach.

3. OPPORTUNITIES

There are numerous opportunities for blockchain technology in the nourishment sector [31, 32] such as procurement tracking, crop, and food production management, management of agricultural finances and insurances, increasing transparency, economic observation, and covering green bonds, *etc.*

3.1. Procurement Tracking

The major obstacle in the farming sector is to track the delivery and payout for the conveyance of food. These days, the procedure relies upon an outsider for planning the merchandise conveyance. The vendors as in the traditional supply system have an operator who guarantees that the products are conveyed securely and purchasers have a specialist to suggest settlement and review the conveyance. The participation of various operators adds significant expenses to the framework and makes the whole procedure tedious. With the help of blockchain technology, the entire procedure can be improved to a solitary distributed record.

3.2. Land Registry

In India, the United Nations Development Program is working with many associates and companions to make land vault increasingly solid there. At an elevated level, this venture will catch and invariably record every exchange all through the offer of a property. The Swedish government's territory proprietorship authority known as Lantmäteriet has directed land roster and property exchange on the blockchain. They believed that this project gives a secure approach to have digitalized authenticity and that it could diminish a huge number of dollars of costs for the administration. The Republic of Georgia is probing the utilization of the bitcoin system to approve property-related government exchanges.

3.3. Underwater Fishing Industry

The other use case is present in the underwater Fishing or Angling Industry where blockchain technology can be utilized to follow and stop illicit, uncontrolled, and unregistered fishing which represents the prominent danger to marine environments. In New Zealand, the World Wildlife Fund is dealing with a pilot venture to get rid of illicit angling and the maltreatment of human rights in the fish industry of the Pacific Islands.

3.4. Crop and Food Production Management

With the assistance of smart cultivation, IoT sensors could bring significant data like the water level, soil temperature, compost, and fertilizer particulars, *etc*., and direct it to the blockchain. It will support upgrading the nature of the cultivation procedure just as the quality of produced crops.

3.5. Climate Emergency Control

Farmers need to confront the issues concerning climate emergency control such as eccentric climatic conditions consistently. Because of excessive rainfalls, it gets hard for developed harvests to endure flooding. Purchasers are never informed of when did the harvests endure awful climatic conditions and for what reasons the market comes to terms with the high up surging prices. As it is feasible for the included individuals in the blockchain arrangement to detect the climate conditions, farmers can rapidly ask for and get protection guarantees with the help of smart agreements.

3.6. Management of Agricultural Finances and Insurances

Another use case lies with the management of agricultural finances and insurances. Lack of clarity in records and credit history poses significant among smallholders and financial institutions. Today, budgetary administrations don't just permit the small farmers to put resources into cultivation yet also help them in settling liquidity limitations. By using blockchain, the farming fund process turns out to be progressively transparent and reasonable and empowers shared control convenience.

3.7. Increasing the Transparency

The opportunity is consistently expanding. Transparency in farming is also considered as one of the important use cases. Barilla, Italian pasta, and pesto sauce maker have collaborated with IBM to handle detectability and transparency in its pesto creation cycle. Starting from the development stage, going through treatment and collecting in the field to transportation, stockpiling, quality control to the creation and afterward to the consumers, all particulars and features are followed and made accessible on a blockchain framework so that the client can check by scanning QR code of the pesto.

3.8. Economic Observation and Covering Green Bonds

This consists of economic observing, checking, and covering green bonds, which were made to finance the schemes and projects that will benefit the ecosystem. It is important to have credible trailing, recognizability, and confirmation components to help in improving the trust of financial investors in atmosphere smart activities. Carbon credits and exchanging them could make a profit by the belief that blockchain presents. There are numerous opportunities for blockchain technology in the nourishment sector such as procurement tracking, crop and food production management, management of agricultural finances and insurances, increasing transparency, economic observation and covering green bonds, *etc.*

4. APPLICATIONS

This segment consists of four classes of utilizations in agrarian and nourishment areas, namely smart cultivation, agricultural insurance, exchanges of agricultural items, and food supply network.

4.1. Smart Agriculture

Basics of the Agri-nourishment frameworks are the fundamental information and data on the natural assets that help all types of cultivation. Various stakeholders and actors produce and oversee information and data according to their requirements and limits. Smart agribusiness is highlighted by the use of IoT, ICT, and different present-day information assortment and examination techniques including sensors, unmanned flying vehicles, and AI. A key issue of setting up smart cultivation is building up a far-reaching security framework that encourages the utilization and the executives of information [33]. The blockchain innovation serves to store information and data that different stakeholders and farmers create all through the whole worth-added procedure, from seed sowing to trade, of delivering a farming item. It guarantees that the information and data are clear and unambiguous to the included stakeholders and farmers and every single registered information is changeless. Conventional ways control information in a centralized manner and are inclined to improper information, information mutilation, and abuse the same as a digital rack. For instance, ecological observing information is largely controlled by centralized administration substances that have their advantage [34]. They can control the conclusion related to information. Many smart cultivation models are presented and executed dependent on the joint use of blockchain and IoT innovations. Patil *et al.* suggest "a blockchain-dependent prototype which is lightweight for brilliant conservatory greenhouse farms", where IoT sensors go about as a private blockchain that is controlled centrally by the proprietor.

4.2. Nourishment Supply Network

With expanded development and serious rivalry in the market, nourishment supply networks have become longer and more composite than any time in recent times. There are some regular issues in nourishment supply networks, for example, food quality and security, food tracing, nourishment trust, and inefficiency of the store network, which includes extra danger to the whole economy, society, and human health. From the makers' point of view, the utilization of blockchain innovation sets up a trusted association with customers and develop the notoriety of their items, by clearly giving data of individual item in the blockchain [35]. This would make it hard for providers of misrepresentation and low-quality items to remain in business sectors and enforces all providers to improve the nature of their products in the entire farming and nourishment parts. Undertakings can accomplish the estimation of their items and in this manner increment their competition in the market. It helps to address the purchasers' anxiety about the quality, security, and ecological accessibility of nourishment.

The utilization of blockchain makes it possible for the producers and purchasers to associate with each other since customers can comprehend the nourishment creation process easily and in a more characteristic way. The current blockchain innovation in the food store network is still in the beginning phase of improvement. All stakeholders, including makers, purchasers, and government administrative bodies, would thus be able to be profited [36]. For instance, the DNA of domesticated animals, pesticide build-ups of vegetables, or grain can be checked and confirmed by any stakeholder engagement with the supply network of the item. In the current time, the gathering of such information for all items can lead to higher costs, yet for the testing phase, it tends to be done on the sample test. Alibaba, JD.com, and Wal-Mart are effectively executing blockchain detectability ventures and utilizing it to follow the whole procedure of foodstuff creation, preparation, and deals.

4.3. Internet Business of Agri Products

The internet business and exchange of rural items face some vital issues to explain. On-spot cash on conveyance along with management administration are the most vital difficulties looked at by internet business organizations, particularly in developing nations like India. But this difficulty is not creating hindrances anymore due to the setups of e-commerce organizations like Grofers, big basket, *etc*. Moreover, internet business retailers likewise need to deal with small orders including various diversified items that require more time which causes high working expenses for web-based business organizations. A business venture of Hubei locality in India, Old Farmers' Shopping Mall which is a web-based business organization, can be followed back to the source and all the creation data is a questionable asset by customers. Before the products are placed in the stores, various detailed data such as seed sowing, irrigation information, preparation, and fertilizing are recorded. They additionally give fundamental information on makers, transportation coordinators, stockpiling days, and stock-keeping temperature [37]. Clients just need to filter the QR code on the products and all the data will be accessible to them. This strategy can successfully keep away from the phony of illicit traders, middlemen, and remake customer's trust in farm items from online businesses and their providers. Blockchain innovation may give appropriate answers for some parts of these issues such as data security. It gives private key encryption which is an incredible asset that gives the confirmation prerequisites. It would thus be able to connect the information of all parts of sowing and collection of rural items securely and unchangeably. The blockchain furnishes a computerized payment arrangement with zero rates. Besides, the utilization of digital currency in the exchange of agricultural items will lessen exchange costs more significantly. It also reduces the expenses of cultivators.

Numerous rural items are delivered by family units but due to the low exchange volume and little scope, customary internet businesses are not willing to offer assistance for them, accordingly barring these members from the market. Blockchain can significantly lessen exchange costs and consolidate them into the market once more.

4.4. Farming Insurances

Climate limits endanger agrarian creation, putting nourishment security in danger where both the harvest and animals' creation are influenced, and environmental change is required to additionally worsen climatic conditions in the future. Agrarian protection plans are generally an all-around perceived approach to predict and perceive the climate-related dangers in advance. Here, ranchers pay protection fees before the crop season starts and get protection pay if they experience a misfortune on their farmland. In this way, the safety net provider bears all the safeguarded hazards and cultivators can deal with their budgetary presentations to climatic conditions. Besides, complete insurance inclusion with no deducible amounts is conceivable and installments can be made convenient and automated soon after an unfavorable climate occasion is estimated. Errors among pay-out and on-farm misfortune can happen which is indicated as premise chance. Three sources of premise hazard can happen named spatial premise hazard, temporal basis hazard, and plan premised hazard. The spatial premise hazard denotes any contrasts among estimated and the on-farm climate through spatial separation technique. Temporal or fleeting premise hazard defines that an uncertain time window is picked for list assurance as depicted that instead of evaluating developing season precipitation procedure calculates entire year precipitation. Plan premise hazard abridges every other remaining single residual source such as missing climatic factors or one-sided specialized applications [38].

Cultivation protections contrast with how misfortunes are evaluated and thusly how payments are activated. Protections that get reimbursed to the ranchers dependent on a destruction appraisal that was made by a specialist on the farmland are signified as repayment-based protections. Repayment-based protections can cover misfortunes, but in some cases, they are inclined to issues emerging from deviated data issues. Ranchers are needed to be better educated about both unfavorable choices and moralized hazard issues. A Swiss-based organization Etherisc gives decentralized harvest protection dependent on blockchain innovation that gives pay-outs dependent on climatic information in decentralized insurance protocol token mechanism as local cash. Another protection supplier is situated in New York City, World Cover, which gives index protection agreements to small cultivators in Ghana, recreated the utilization of an

Ethereum blockchain-based keen agreement in which pay-outs would be made in the digitalized currency Ether. Another brilliant harvest protection supplier is Arbol where a rancher can suggest an agreement that incorporates the excellent installment, a pay-out, and a climate occasion that triggers the pay-out, and then a financial specialist, as counterparty can consent to that proposed agreement.

Installments can be made convenient and machine-dependent on climate information that triggers the pay-out as characterized in a smart agreement. Secondly, climate data and other information sources such as plant development data or information gathered by farm apparatus can be naturally incorporated using a brilliant oracle improving premise chance reduction which makes the recorded assurance and pay-out process progressively effective. The utilization of blockchain innovation in web-based business and exchange of agricultural items is still in its earliest stages and the present case isn't just great as how to guarantee the legitimacy of the transferring procedure of information into blockchain is as yet an issue and a question to the blockchain developers. Later on, a prospective alternative might be IoT [39]. Also, blockchain's qualities of conveyed, distributed, non-tamper-able, recognizable needs to be more generally and profoundly investigated to improve the profitability proficiency and productivity of farming creation and exchange.

5. USE CASES

With the emergence of the various prospectus in the field of blockchain, a variety of applications have been studied and implemented side by side [40]. Various use cases of agriculture include food safety, supply chain traceability, transaction cost, opening new markets, and logistics.

5.1. Food Safety

It is by all accounts the territory where the most work has just been done because there is a clear personal stake from both maker and shopper. IBM alongside organizations like Walmart has begun driving the charge in this limit. Carrying transparency or clarity to the food supply chain will permit us to distinguish and expel awful entertainers and poor procedures. This guarantees perfect conditions from farming land to market, and we can pinpoint the source rapidly in case of a food sanitation breakout. This could spare time, cash, and lives.

5.2. Traceability

The advantage of purchasing localized food is constantly depicted as "you most likely are aware of where your food originates from and who developed it and it's fresh". Imagine a scenario where we could get this going at scale. This means, regardless of the place where you purchased your food, you knew where it originated from, however when it was reaped and prepared, and even who delivered it. Organizations like Ripe.io are attempting to take care of this very issue. This could likewise go far to forestall food extortion, erroneous marking, and repetitive agents.

5.3. Transaction Costs

It is both divided and reliant on specifically knowing a counter-party before you could confide in them to work together. Organizations like AgriDigital are making progress in making transparent and productive stock and supply chains using blockchain innovation. They are applying the innovation legitimately to the grain exchange and plan to venture into other horticultural wares, for example, cotton.

5.4. Opening New Markets

It is another use case in this field. In a future digital recording scene, Agri Ledgeris opening new markets to farmers in the ongoing developing world utilizing blockchain. The reason here is that on the off chance that we can make trust and responsibility among advertising players, there is a decreased need to assess every individual separately on their reliability and capacity to execute. This implies advertise players that couldn't set up a trust before in any way, shape, or form as they didn't reside near one another, they didn't have a convention for if things self-destructed, an opportunity to build up another relationship didn't legitimize the worth, and so on. They presently could work together without somebody expecting to handle trust (and take an edge) in the center. This additionally implies that impeded market members can have a kind of "seat at the table" through this innovation.

5.5. Logistics

Any individual who has worked in the horticultural supplying chain knows the difficulties faced due to lack of coordination. Managing items in large quantities that frequently have a short period of usability is questionable with a ton of dollars on the line. Additionally, the supply network can be unsettled. Organizations like UPS are joining the Blockchain in transport alliance to assume a primary job in the keen coordination system of things to come, based on blockchain innovation. As this is already emerging in various other industries, the cultivation industry is going to be the next in this chain. Due to extensive research, many applications have been implemented in this domain, and further, a lot of researches is being continuously made for improving the existing limitations. Many start-ups in this domain such as FARMS, Agri-Digital, Ag-Unity, TE-Foods, Hi Tractor, Agri-ledger, Shamba, *etc.* are doing well in this field. FARMS stands for Financial and Agricultural Risk Management for Smallholders. Along with increasing a farmer's economical literacy, it also teaches the various ways of risk management.

The FARMS idea is empowered by a blockchain-based virtual cash stage incorporated with satellite information and versatile cash arrangements, which guarantees straightforward secure exchanges and "reserving" of assets, mechanized installments, and data dashboards. Farmers deal with the virtual money known as "dry spell coins" that are kept in their own COIN22 versatile wallet account. All the exchanges are now only a click away and can be checked at any random time through SMS. Agri-Digital is a blockchain for the food supply chain. For global-based industries, it provides cloud-based products and solutions for their management. It creates a link between grain producers, purchasers, financers through a solitary stage, permitting them to contract, convey, and make installments safely and progressively.

In Kenya, IBM in partnership with a Nigerian start-up Hello Tractor has started blockchain cultivating applications. It is a rural innovation organization that associates tractor proprietors to smallholder farmers who needs tractor benefits through an Internet of Things innovation. Their innovation makes a successful win circumstance for both the tractor proprietor and farmers as tractor owners can productively spread their tractor employing business and farmers can conveniently access tractor services for cultivation.

AgUnity has built up an infrastructure that is giving a pathway to monetary incorporation for the world's underprivileged farmers. It is straightforward portable assistance that enables little farmers to plan, exchange, and track regular exchanges. This is a path for ranchers to collaborate, earn, save money for the future, and effectively purchase items and services. The application guarantees that whenever small-scale farmers give their crops to other farmers or lend farming tools, everyone involved in the process gets fairly paid.

TE-FOOD is the world's biggest openly available, farm-to-table nourishment traceability arrangement. It serves 400,000 business exchanges and handles 6000+ business clients every day. It introduces nourishment history to the purchasers. The blockchain record contains the evidence of the data entered by the distinctive production network members and information can't be distorted by a nourishment organization. Shamba Records is a Kenya-based Agri-tech start-up. It has manufactured a blockchain-based stage that utilizes artificial intelligence and enormous information to gather farmers harvesting records, process installments, *etc.* It provides many features to the users such as information assortment and mapping, smart agreements, *etc.* making farms progressively proficient and gathering data that can permit them to get to money-related administrations.

6. BLOCKCHAIN-BASED ARCHITECTURE IN AGRICULTURE AND CHALLENGES

Smart contract plays an effective role in agricultural assurance, food traceability, and green bonds. The architecture of blockchain implemented agricultural activities can be studied in two phases. The first phase shows the collection and cleaning of data and storing it in the smart contracts as shown in Fig. (**5**). The various stages of agriculture include soil and crop monitoring, storage, and distribution system of eatables and marketing as shown in Fig. (**5**). A lot of data is required to be collected to maintain the quality of the supply chain and to establish the faith of customers in blockchain technology. In the soil monitoring system, data such as pH, temperature, and amount of other minerals of soil should be stored. The number of pesticides, fertilizers used and the water used for the irrigation purpose needs to be stored which is now possible using the sensors such as IoT devices. Various weather controls need to be noted down such as wind speed, moisture content, barometric pressure, precipitation, ultraviolet radiation, *etc.* In terms of storage and distribution of entities data such as quality control labels, transportation information using sensors, and data related to the security of food during the inspection of warehouses need to be entered [41]. In the marketing procedure, the bill of the data including the taxes according to the renowned norms should be there in the system. At this point, the way toward cleaning and advancement of the gathered information will happen to guarantee that it is organized and reasonable, before saving it on the blockchain. Data identified with timestamp, demography, and type will be added to the information for making it increasingly organized [42]. Meeting consistent guarantees that the recognizable data related to the information gathered from IoT gadgets is ensured and follows safety efforts. When the information is advanced, it is placed into the AI-prepared format. Data will be made increasingly quickly with AI calculations. After the data processing step, they are going to be processed using a smart contract and get stored there to avoid any turbulence and changes.

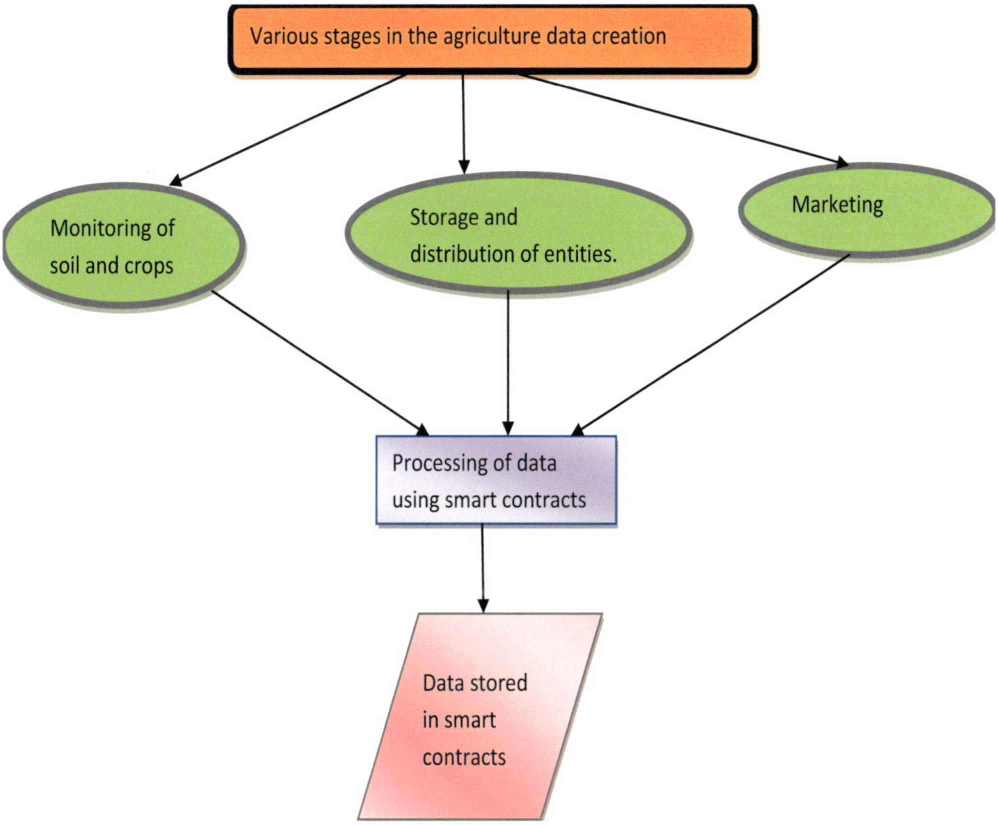

Fig. (5). Phase 1 of blockchain-based architecture in agriculture.

The second phase of the architecture involves the hashing and utilization of various algorithms to further identify the utilization of blockchain in agriculture as shown in Fig. (**6**). After the storing of data in smart contracts, it will divide into blocks so that hashing of the data block takes place. Now the data is stored in various blocks with their respective hash functions. This data is now become immutable and secured, and it can be utilized to track down the supply chain, calculate acquired land for production purposes, reduce the amount of resource wastage in natural disasters such as floods and drought, *etc*. It will also help the financial system and customers to keep an audit on the recorded prices. The people who want to invest their money in agricultural land will be benefitted as they will know the quality of soil and other factors beforehand and can make decisions [43]. Customers who are buying food from the market can ensure the quality and nutrients well in advance and if there is a defect in eatables, a systematic investigation can be easily achieved in considerably less amount of time as data is present in the blockchain and it can't be modified.

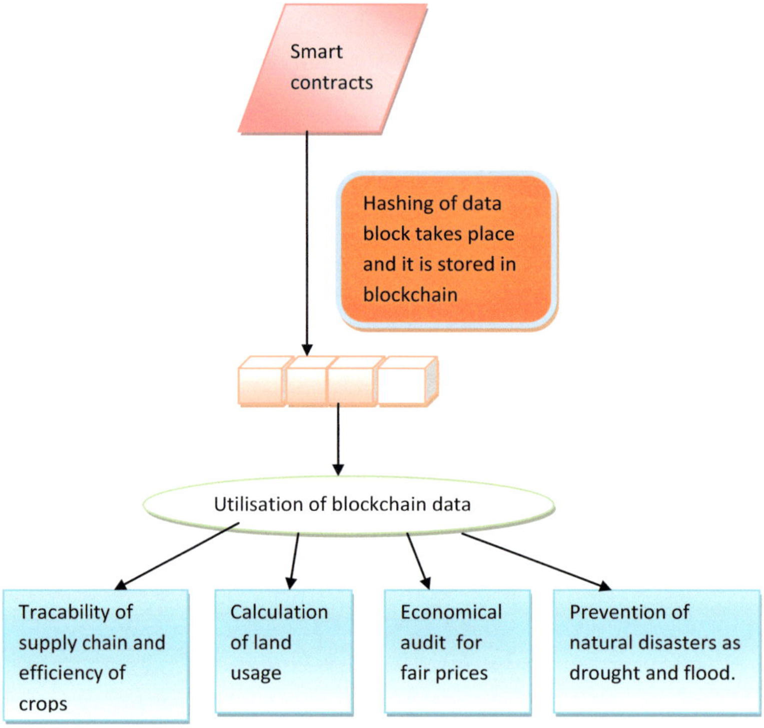

Fig. (6). Phase 2 of blockchain-based architecture in agriculture.

Blockchain technology will secure the farmers from crop failure situations by predicting in advance the trends of weather and other climatic conditions. Linking of sensors with the distributed ledger will result in the continuous updating of the records in real-time. It will result in the increased efficiency and a fair payment system for the farmers. After the implementation of blockchain, the agriculture sector too will become transparent and can detect fraud to prevent the situation of black marketing. It will also attain the attraction of investors. It will also result in the exchange of stocks between the farmers and in the future can introduce cryptocurrency in the agricultural domain.

Regardless of a large number of potential favorable benefits, some key restrictions stay for applying blockchain innovation in farming and nourishment sectors [44].

- First, a lot of further research is required to give authentic and exact data to the blockchain record. This may be particularly significant on account of smallholder cultivation. The data produced in the cultivation procedure is dispersed and claimed by individual farmers. Blockchain innovations' advantages for farmers are highly reliant on the size of the farming land.

- Second, transferring information on the blockchain can be expensive, which will be an obstruction to the appropriation of blockchain innovation in the area. The introduction of blockchain technology should be step by step, starting from the resource planning corporate, storage house management, and manufacturing industries.
- Third, blockchain doesn't incorporate existing inheritance frameworks directly. To be effectively actualized, the innovation should be connected to a current database and heritage frameworks. For example, industry asset planning and assembling execution frameworks.
- Building an establishment to use blockchain development is routinely tedious.
- The arrangement of administrative structure around blockchain is in its earliest stages and thus involves high danger. Various blockchain ventures, particularly those managing money or cross-fringe exchanges, requires KYC/AML consistency and it is critical to comprehend the national structure before digging into these activities. The regular changes in the cost of bitcoin and news regarding the hacking of digital currency have brought expanded regulations and guidelines by various nations involving the banning of cryptocurrency in some countries.
- The other disadvantages include high energy requirement as the data can be of size 100-200 gigabytes which require a large amount of energy for processing. Less speed of transactions is also a major drawback.

CONCLUSION & FUTURE SCOPE

Food well-being is a significant duty of the legislature and administrative specialists. In this manner, the administration needs to make a cross-industry or interdepartmental expert framework to successfully control the nourishment production network. The food supply chain based on blockchain technology can be traced from the farms to the retailer's shop or groceries within a second. Blockchain has immense potential to transform agriculture, which is a massive industry though it won't be seen as glamorous as in the healthcare sector or finance system. In this work, we overviewed the different perspectives of blockchain technology, advancement in the farming sector with the utilization of blockchain, and introduced a perfect model of how blockchain will work in the cultivation division. Different recent research work in this area has been surveyed, which gives tremendous opportunities for blockchain innovation in agriculture. A remarkable part of the use cases examines the theoretical utilization of blockchain in horticultural supply chains missing the mark regarding specific usage structure or approach. Despite the advantages of blockchain technology, there are still some challenges in advancing the blockchain innovation for helping the administrations track, screen, and review the food chain and helping producers to record the exchanges authentically and transparently. Blockchain and man-made reasoning are set to assume endlessly noteworthy jobs in the food supply business, remembering for nourishment security and broadening, state industry, and innovation specialists. It is of extraordinary essentiality to improve the administrative guidelines of the nourishment production network, to improve administration level and proficiency, to forestall lease chasing, and to breed defilement. Implementation of blockchain in agriculture involves many benefits as it will ensure the improved quality of the supply chain. It increases traceability as the consumers know the exact location where their eatables are produced. PavoCoin is an IoT-based software platform that is built on the PavoCoin framework, based on Ethereum that helps ranchers in the procedure of harvest development. Besides, this arrangement can likewise gather information about social occasions, handling, and dissemination of the item. Because of the usage of blockchain innovation, the procedures can be effectively checked and the data is put away. Blockchain innovation carries plenty of creative answers for farming. Blockchain-based programming let farmers improve regular procedures and increase the income of the current business.

CONSENT FOR PUBLICATION

Not applicable.

CONFLICT OF INTEREST

The author declares no conflict of interest, financial or otherwise.

ACKNOWLEDGEMENTS

Declared none.

REFERENCES

[1] H. Watanabe, S. Fujimura, A. Nakadaira, Y. Miyazaki, and A. Akutsu, "Blockchain contract: Securing a blockchain applied to smart contracts", In: *2016 IEEE International Conference on Consumer Electronics (ICCE)*, 2016. [http://dx.doi.org/10.1109/ICCE.2016.7430693]

[2] F. Dabbene, "Food traceability systems: Performance evaluation and optimization", *Comput. Electron. Agric.*, vol. 75, no. 1, pp. 139-146, 2011. [http://dx.doi.org/10.1016/j.compag.2010.10.009]

[3] M. A. Khan, "IoT security: Review, blockchain solutions, and open challenges", *Future Gener. Comput. Syst.*, vol. 82, pp. 395-411, 2018. [http://dx.doi.org/10.1016/j.future.2017.11.022]

[4] L. Lucas, "(2018). From Farm to Plate, Blockchain Dishes Up Simple Food Tracking. Accessed: Jun. 12, 2018. [Online]. Available: ", https://www.ft.com/content/225d32bc-4dfa-11e8-97e4-13afc22d86d4

[5] A. Bogner, and M. Chanson, "A Decentralised Sharing App running a Smart Contract on the Ethereum Blockchain", In: *Proceedings of the 6th International Conference on the Internet of Things - IoT'16.*

[http://dx.doi.org/10.1145/2991561.2998465]

[6] K. Salah, M. H. Rehman, and N. Nizamuddin, "Blockchain for AI: Review and Open Research Challenges", *IEEE Access,* vol. 7, pp. 10127-10149, 2019. [http://dx.doi.org/10.1109/ACCESS.2018.2890507]

[7] H. R. Hasan, "Combating Deepfake Videos Using Blockchain and Smart Contracts", *IEEE Access,* vol. 7, pp. 41596-41606, 2019. [http://dx.doi.org/10.1109/ACCESS.2019.2905689]

[8] K. Toyoda, P. T. Mathiopoulos, and I. Sasase, "A Novel Blockchain-Based Product Ownership Management System (POMS) for Anti-Counterfeits in the Post Supply Chain", *IEEE Access,* vol. 5, pp. 17465-17477, 2017. [http://dx.doi.org/10.1109/ACCESS.2017.2720760]

[9] D. Folinas, and I. Manikas, "Traceability data management for food chains", *Br. Food J.,* vol. 108, no. 8, pp. 622-633, 2006. [http://dx.doi.org/10.1108/00070700610682319]

[10] C. H. Bazoni, E. I. Ida, and D. F. Barbin, "Near-infrared spectroscopy as a rapid method for evaluation physicochemical changes of stored soybeans", *J. Stored Prod. Res.,* vol. 73, pp. 1-6, 2017. [http://dx.doi.org/10.1016/j.jspr.2017.05.003]

[11] https://www.dhyeyaias.com/current-affairs/perfect-7-magazine/changing-land-use-patt-rn-and-climate-change

[12] J.C. Smith, A. Ghosh, and R.J. Hijmans, "Agricultural intensification was associated with crop diversification in India (1947-2014)", *PLoS One,* vol. 14, no. 12, 2019. [http://dx.doi.org/10.1371/journal.pone.0225555] [PMID: 31826001]

[13] (n.d.). Retrieved September 25, 2020. http://www.yieldgap.org/india

[14] F. Tian, "An agri-food supply chain traceability system for China based on RFID & blockchain technology", In: *2016 13th International Conference on Service Systems and Service Management (ICSSSM)*, 2016. [http://dx.doi.org/10.1109/icsssm.2016.7538424]

[15] F. Tian, "A supply chain traceability system for food safety based on HACCP, blockchain & Internet of things", In: *2017 International Conference on Service Systems and Service Management*, 2017. [http://dx.doi.org/10.1109/ICSSSM.2017.7996119]

[16] M. P. Caro, M. S. Ali, and M. Vecchio, "Blockchain-based traceability in Agri-Food supply chain management: A practical implementation", *2018 IoT Vertical and Topical Summit on Agriculture - Tuscany (IOT Tuscany),* 2018. [http://dx.doi.org/10.1109/iot-tuscany.2018.8373021]

[17] D. Tse, B. Zhang, Y. Yang, C. Cheng, and H. Mu, "Blockchain application in food supply information security", In: *2017 IEEE International Conference on Industrial Engineering and Engineering Management (IEEM)*, Singapores, 2017. [http://dx.doi.org/10.1109/IEEM.2017.8290114]

[18] M. Tripoli, and J. Schmidhuber, *Emerging Opportunities for the Application of Blockchain in the Agri–Food Industry.,* 2018. [Online]. Available: https://FAO.org

[19] D. Mao, F. Wang, Z. Hao, and H. Li, "Credit Evaluation System Based on Blockchain for Multiple Stakeholders in the Food Supply Chain", *Int. J. Environ. Res. Public Health,* vol. 15, no. 8, p. 1627, 2018. [http://dx.doi.org/10.3390/ijerph15081627] [PMID: 30071695]

[20] Y. Lin, J. Petway, J. Anthony, H. Mukhtar, S. Liao, and C. Chou, "Blockchain: The Evolutionary Next Step for ICT E-", *Agric. Environ.,* vol. 4, no. 3, p. 50, 2017. [http://dx.doi.org/10.3390/environments4030050]

[21] J. F. Galvez, and J. Mejuto, "Future challenges on the use of blockchain for food traceability analysis", *Trends Analyt. Chem.*, vol. 107, pp. 222-232, 2018. [http://dx.doi.org/10.1016/j.trac.2018.08.011]

[22] D. Mao, Z. Hao, and F. Wang, "Novel Automatic Food Trading System Using Consortium Blockchain", *Arab. J. Sci. Eng.*, vol. 44, no. 4, pp. 3439-3455, 2018. [http://dx.doi.org/10.1007/s13369-018-3537-z]

[23] D. Mao, Z. Hao, and F. Wang, "Innovative Blockchain-Based Approach for Sustainable and Credible Environment in Food Trade: A Case Study in Shandong Province, China", *Sustainability,* vol. 10, no. 9, p. 3149, 2018. [http://dx.doi.org/10.3390/su10093149]

[24] M. Schneider, Design and prototypical implementation of a blockchain based system for the agriculture sector, 2017.

[25] P. Lucena, A.P. Binotto, F. da Silva Momo, and H. Kim, *A case study for grain quality assurance tracking based on a blockchain business network,* 2018. https:// arxiv.org/abs/1803.07877

[26] A. Holmberg, and R. Åquist, *Blockchain technology in food supply chains: A case study of the possibilities and challenges with an implementation of a blockchain technology supported framework for traceability.,* 2018.

[27] R. Kamath, "Food Traceability on Blockchain: Walmart's Pork and Mango Pilots with IBM", *Journal of the British Blockchain Association,* vol. 1, no. 1, pp. 1-12, 2018. [http://dx.doi.org/10.31585/jbba-1-1-(10)2018]

[28] M. Chinaka, Blockchain technology—Applications in improving financial inclusion in developing economies: Case study for small scale agriculture in Africa, 2016.

[29] (2018). Bloomberg. [Online]. Available:, https://www.bloomberg.com/news/articles/2018-0--22/dreyfus-teams-with-banks-for-firs tagriculture-blockchain-trade

[30] J. Zhao, J. Zhang, and Y. Feng, "The study and application of the IOT technology in agriculture", In: *2010 3rd International Conference on Computer Science and Information Technology*, 2010. [http://dx.doi.org/10.1109/iccsit.2010.5565120]

[31] M. Roopaei, and P. Rad, "Cloud of Things in Smart Agriculture: Intelligent Irrigation Monitoring by Thermal Imaging", *IEEE Cloud Computing,* vol. 4, no. 1, pp. 10-15, 2017. [http://dx.doi.org/10.1109/mcc.2017.5]

[32] Y. Voutos, P. Mylonas, and E. Spyrou, "An IoT-Based Insular Monitoring Architecture for Smart Viticulture", In: *2018 9th International Conference on Information, Intelligence, Systems and Applications (IISA)*, 2018. [http://dx.doi.org/10.1109/iisa.2018.8633630]

[33] C. Manchanda, N. Sharma, R. Rathi, B. Bhushan, and M. Grover, "Neoteric Security and Privacy Sanctuary Technologies in Smart Cities", *2020 IEEE 9th International Conference on Communication Systems and Network Technologies (CSNT),* 2020. [http://dx.doi.org/10.1109/csnt48778.2020.9115780]

[34] A. Grogan, "Smart farming. Engineering &", *Technology,* vol. 7, no. 6, p. 38, 2012. [http://dx.doi.org/10.1049/et.2012.0601]

[35] P.P. Jayaraman, A. Yavari, D. Georgakopoulos, A. Morshed, and A. Zaslavsky, "Internet of Things Platform for Smart Farming: Experiences and Lessons Learnt", *Sensors (Basel),* vol. 16, no. 11, p. 1884, 2016. [http://dx.doi.org/10.3390/s16111884] [PMID: 27834862]

[36] A. K. Saha, J. Saha, R. Ray, S. Sircar, S. Dutta, and S. P. Chattopadhyay, "IOT-based drone for improvement of crop quality in agricultural field", *2018 IEEE 8th Annual Computing and Communication Workshop and Conference (CCWC).*

[http://dx.doi.org/10.1109/ccwc.2018.8301662]

[37] T. Moribe, H. Okada, K. Kobayashl, and M. Katayama, *Combination of a wireless sensor network and drone using infrared thermometers for smart agriculture. 2018 15th IEEE Annual Consumer Communications & Networking Conference.* CCNC, 2018.

[38] Delmolino K., Arnett M., Kosba A., Miller A., and Shi E., *(2016, February 22). Step by Step Towards Creating a Safe Smart Contract: Lessons and Insights from a Cryptocurrency Lab.,* 2016. Retrieved September 25, 2020, from https://link.springer.com/chapter/10.1007/978-3-662-53357-4_6

[39] A. Kosba, A. Miller, E. Shi, and Z. Wen, "Hawk: The Blockchain Model of Cryptography and Privacy-Preserving Smart Contracts", In: *IEEE Symposium on Security and Privacy (SP)*, 2016. [http://dx.doi.org/10.1109/SP.2016.55]

[40] T. Hammerich, *(2018, January 04). 5 Potential Use Cases for Blockchain in Agriculture.,* 2020. Retrieved September 25, 2020. https://futureofag.com/5-potential-use-cases-for-blockch-in-in-agriculture-c88d4d2207e8

[41] B. Bhushan, "Transaction Privacy Preservations for Blockchain Technology", *Advances in Intelligent Systems and Computing International Conference on Innovative Computing and Communications,* pp. 377-393, 2020. [http://dx.doi.org/10.1007/978-981-15-5148-2_34]

[42] F. Zhang, E. Cecchetti, K. Croman, and A. Juels, "Town Crier", In: *Proceedings of the 2016 ACM SIGSAC Conference on Computer and Communications Security*, 2016. [http://dx.doi.org/10.1145/2976749.2978326]

[43] T. Varshney, N. Sharma, I. Kaushik, and B. Bhushan, "Authentication & Encryption Based Security Services in Blockchain Technology", In: *2019 International Conference on Computing, Communication, and Intelligent Systems (ICCCIS)*, 2019. [http://dx.doi.org/10.1109/ICCCIS48478.2019.8974500]

[44] K. Inria, and K. Bhargavan, "Research, M., Authors: Karthikeyan BhargavanInria. (2016, October 01). Formal Verification of Smart Contracts: Short Paper. ", Retrieved September 25, 2020, from https://dl.acm.org/doi/10.1145/2993600.2993611

CHAPTER 11

Blockchain Solutions for Big Data Management

Deepak Kumar Sharma[1,*], **Saakshi Bhargava**[2], **Aashna Jha**[3] and **Sudhir K. Sharma**[4]

[1] *Department of Information Technology, Netaji Subhas University of Technology, Dwarka, Delhi 110078, India*

[2] *Department of Physical Sciences and Engineering, Banasthali Vidyapith, Tonk, Rajasthan, India*

[3] *Department of Electronics and Communication, Netaji Subhas University of Technology, Dwarka, Delhi 110078, India*

[4] *Department of Computer Science, Institute of Information Technology & Management, New Delhi, India*

Abstract: The managing of unprecedented growth of data in the growing world is an important task. Knowing that the world is facing development in the numerical aspects and multiplicity of digital data that are normally produced by both consumers and technologies, dealing with this huge amount of data and finding the finest way to store, process, and organize it is necessary. This is the point where blockchain comes into the picture by providing significant inputs as it is the decentralized system for private data. Certainly, several industry experts are considering blockchain and its welfare for many improvements in different fields. Big Data is the recklessly rising sector in the ecosphere as every industry wants to get an understanding of the customs arrangements of their customers, where Big Data mentions huge datasets that are examined to divulge fundamental outlines using progressive statistical representations and data mining. The data produced is of petabytes range and when we are dealing with such a large range of datasets, problems related to it arise and not only collection of data is focused but security measures are also given extra importance, and proper care of produced data is taken so that no malicious action takes place.

Keywords: Big Data, BIot, Bitcoins, Blockchain, Consensus Algorithm, Cryptocurrency, Cryptography, Data mining, Decentralization, Distributed ledger, Electronic Health Record, Immutable network, IoT, Peer to Peer Network, Private Blockchain, Proof of Stake, Proof of Work, Public Blockchain, Public Key, Smart Contracts.

* **Corresponding author Deepak Kumar Sharma:** Department of Information Technology, Netaji Subhas University of Technology, Dwarka, Delhi 110078, India; Tel: 9868861080; E-mail:dk.sharma1982@yahoo.com

Sudhir K. Sharma, Bharat Bhushan, Parma N. Astya and Narayan C. Debnath (Eds.)

1. INTRODUCTION

Blockchain and Big Data are two technologies that continue to expand at a phenomenal rate. Both have been developed separately and have largely been applied in various industries independently from each other. Blockchain applications have been centric towards cryptocurrency and bitcoins with their distributed ledger technology (DLT) attracting both tech enthusiasts and potential investors in this new area of business. It has further expanded into other fields such as banking and supply chain management, finding use in all spheres of life. Blockchain technology truly can disrupt the current economic system of the world by its decentralized structure and removal of the third party. Big Data has become a buzzword in recent years with data multiplying like never before. Its applications cannot be limited to just one field as data is utilized and generated everywhere. From sensors to social media websites, big data is everywhere around us. Challenges arise when it comes to utilization and analysis as it holds the key to vital information. This information invariably proves to be valuable to businesses and governments alike, studying the performance of their products and services.

The major contribution of the following chapter will be highlighting the:

- linking up of the two powerful technologies Blockchain and big data.
- focusing on how Blockchain technology can change the way we deal with big data and make it a much more efficient process.
- highlighting the variety of benefits such as ensuring data security and performing data analysis, - Blockchain's advent and its integration with big data can serve a variety of industries ranging from finance to medicine.

The paper is organized as follows. The introduction includes Mechanism, Contemporaneous advancements in blockchains, and the challenges it must face, it also includes the basics of big data, its types, and characterization which are focused on in the second part of the same section. Section 2 comprises how big data and blockchain can together make a difference. Section 3 highlights the applications when the two technologies are used together. The final two sections are completely dedicated to further advancements and the conclusion.

2. INTRODUCTION TO BLOCKCHAIN

Blockchain technology [1] has revolutionized the world in more than one way. It is safe to say that it has covered multiple and a variety of spheres ranging from the economy [2] to healthcare. The history of how blockchain came to be can be credited to Satoshi Nakamoto, who outlined the basic workings of the technology and since then it has continued being developed for a variety of applications. Ethereum took things a step further and developed the concept of smart contracts. Blockchain is often referred to as Distributed Ledger Technology (DLT). A simple way to look at it would be to take the example of a Google Doc or a Wikipedia Page. Here, our document is distributed amongst many and every person can make a change in real-time and any updates are visible and transparent to all. Since blockchain is based upon DLT and everyone has access to the ledger, the information is transparent thus increasing accountability [3].

A major advantage that blockchain [4] has over existing systems is that there are no transaction costs involved. Infrastructural costs to maintain the system exist but any user making any trade will not face any additional costs. This happens because blockchain cuts off any third parties owing to its decentralized system. This will have serious consequences in the future economic system considering that many businesses currently make a profit by being the third party connecting the consumer to the product. For example, a yearly subscription to any magazine will stop being popular as the user can just pay a very small amount per article considering no additional transaction costs will be levied.

Blockchain is quite literally what its name implies - a chain of 'blocks.' Here 'blocks' are digital pieces of information stored in a public database 'the chain.' Despite its growing significance in today's world, blockchain is not a new technology. It is in fact an amalgamation of three proven and existing technologies [5], explained in Fig. (**1**).

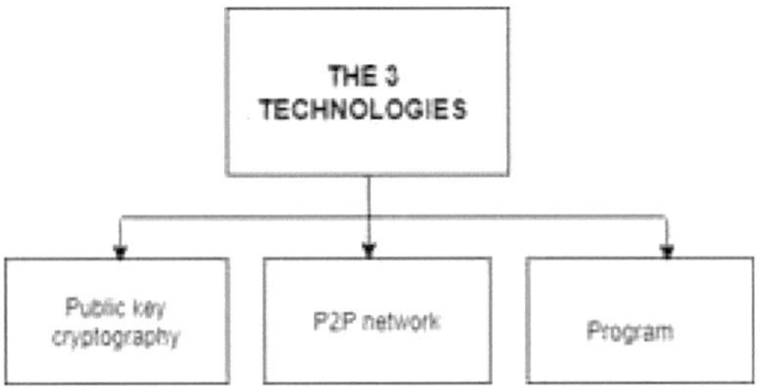

Fig. (1). 3 technologies.

The Peer to Peer Network is the defining feature of blockchain technology. The network is nothing, but a system of nodes connected and interconnected with each other. Each node is a computer network that can either take any input or perform functions and send its output. There is no hierarchy among different nodes and there is a uniform topology with the work being divided equally.

Public Key Cryptography [6] uses the concept of two keys, one public and one private. The public keys are as the name suggests public and distributed amongst the members while the private key is possessed by a few. A public key can encrypt the message in a manner that only the person holding the private key can read it. The person possessing the private key can create a digital signature so that anyone with the relevant public key can validate the information.

The program refers to the protocol which is essentially a set of rules governing the p2p nature of the ledger. It covers aspects such as validation trade and listing down the mechanism for the blockchain to work. The protocol is run by a digital asset which creates an element of self-interest to keep the blockchain going. These digital assets are essentially rewarding in return for computing power used to mine. These can either be coins or tokens depending upon the scenario.

2.1. Mechanism

Just as three technologies form blockchain technology, three pillars are holding up the blockchain mechanism. These three pillars are immutability, decentralization, and transparency. Immutability refers to the non-tamper able nature of blockchain owing to its hash function. Decentralization speeds up the transaction process and provides better security and accountability. Transparency is an obvious consequence of the decentralized system. While it protects the private information of the users, the transactions are still made public making it a very safe system to work with. The basic mechanism behind the working of a blockchain can be broken down into three steps [7]:

a. Once someone requests a trade/transaction, the same is recorded. This block stores information such as the timestamp, trade details, and each party's digital signature.
b. The transaction is verified. This job is done by a network of computers (called nodes)
c. This is stored in the form of a block among many other similar transactions. Each block has a unique code called 'hash'. Despite the similarity of any two trades, every block has a unique hash. Each block is also given the hash of the previous block, thus forming a blockchain.

All the steps are shown in the Fig. (**2**), making it clear with every step:

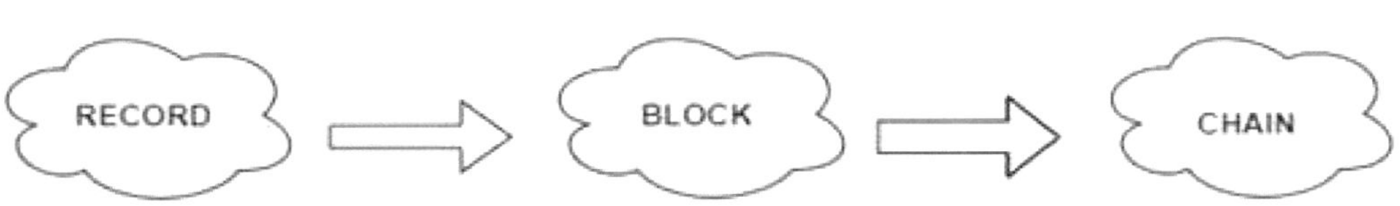

Fig. (2). Blockchain formation.

Since blockchain is completely decentralized, trust becomes a problem. Blockchain [8, 9] is open to everyone and each node remains anonymous thereby making it difficult to validate the information passed. Therefore, consensus models are developed to ensure trust in the newly decentralized system of nodes. There are two types of consensus models [10]:

2.2.1. Proof of Work

To add any block to the chain, the nodes must perform mining to validate the information and record the transaction. This involved solving a difficult computation puzzle that consumes a lot of power. In return, they receive rewards such as tokens or coins.

2.1.2. Proof of Stake

This was created as an alternative to the Proof of Work model. It provides more security and less risk. According to this concept, users can buy tokens that allow them to mine or validate transactions. More coins or tokens lead to more mining power.

2.2. Types

The Distributed Ledger Technology (DLT) that blockchain works with is a boon to the modern world. It increases security [11], improves accountability, and leads to greater transparency. It even cuts down the need for a third party hence reducing transaction costs. There are certain limits to it. DLT needs to be customized and worked upon according to the needs of the users leading to a need for categorizing different types of blockchains. There are four types of blockchains depending upon their use of Distributed Ledger Technology (DLT) [12]:

2.2.1. Public Blockchain

These blockchains are non-restrictive and permission-less. Anyone can be a part of the blockchain as a user or miner and transactions are completely transparent. Starting with public blockchain which is completely an open foundation. Public blockchain permits every user to participate in the system. These are created so that they are completely decentralized in nature, no user/miner has the right to control the recorded data in the chain formed. It is resilient to censorship as everyone is permitted to join the system irrespective of the location they are in, the network they want to fetch, *etc.* hence it makes it extremely difficult for the ruling classes to lock them down.

2.2.2. Private Blockchain

These blockchains are restrictive in nature and are also referred to as permissioned blockchains. Consent is required to join the network and the transactions are visible to only the members of the blockchain. They are centralized in nature and authorization and accessibility controls are handled by an organization. An authenticated consent is needed for joining the network, only the participants that are associated with the network can access the data. These are comparatively more centralized. This type is highly used in cases where the data is a sensitive issue for the organization. There may be the involvement of a token in the system which will help in easy management of the entities fetching the data.

2.2.3. Consortium Blockchain

These have semi-decentralized systems wherein instead of a single entity, a group of organizations governs the blockchain. It has a similar approach to that of a private blockchain and can be considered as a sub-type of the same.

2.2.4. Hybrid Blockchain

A hybrid blockchain uses features of both private and public blockchains. Users are given the option of deciding which data goes up on a public platform and which data remains private. The transactions can either be verified within the network or on a public network, which increases the number of nodes for hashing thereby increasing the security of the system. The features of hybrid systems provide tractability at a significant amount and help in enabling easy connections with the protocols present in blockchain systems. Effectively used in various business aspects where the focus is on security and flexibility.

2.3. Contemporary Advancements in Blockchain

With Blockchain technology continuously blooming and growing, it continues to grow and expand in terms of applications and implementations. Blockchain has become a buzzword in the world of tech and all enthusiasts are in some way or the other part of it. After seeing more than 40 percent growth since 2018, the future of blockchain looks even more promising. The statistics are highly encouraging with job offers on LinkedIn tripling from 2017 to 2018. The cryptocurrency [1] market was sized to be around 600 billion dollars and global spending on blockchain solutions estimated to be around 2.1 billion dollars in 2018. There has been a sharp increase in global interest related to blockchain since 2016 showing immense potential for further growth through raising awareness [8, 9, 13, 14].

While most players in the tech world already have their hands on blockchain technology, it is not without risks. Since it is a new and largely untested technology, introducing it to the already functional system in place might lead to breaches and security issues. Cloud providers with large and established customer bases seem to be at the forefront of including blockchain technology [13 - 16] into their business model. Microsoft Azure is one of the frontrunners in incorporating the technology by focusing on services such as Ethereum and Hyperledger Fabric methods. It has also built up the Azure Blockchain Service and Workbench. Amazon Web Services has also released Managed Blockchain to its public. IBM Cloud and Oracle blockchain platform are also basing their solutions on Hyperledger Fabrics, shown in Fig. (**3**).

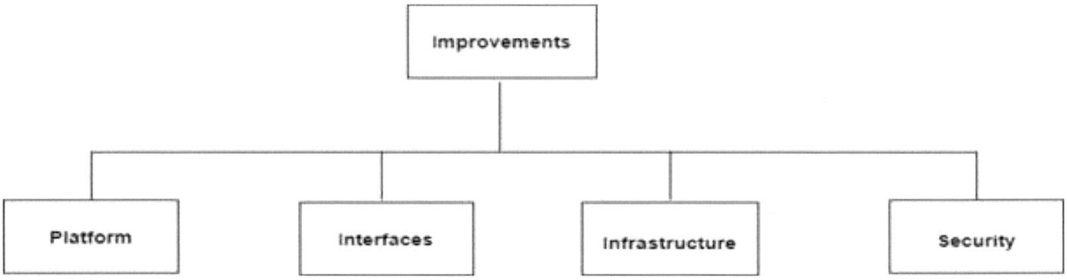

Fig. (3). Advancements made in sectors *via* blockchain.

There are four major areas where contemporary advancements in blockchain technology are taking place [17]. Platform advancements include the ability to sustain operations despite component failures, a support system for storing encrypted data, and smooth switching between the two consensus mechanisms. Interface developments comprise many changes such as developing a mechanism to authenticate using established identity providers and privacy and permission features for transactions. There is a need to develop an infrastructure that supports cross-network interoperability and a network capable of handling many nodes. As expected, most modern contemporary advances in blockchain technology are still targeted towards improving security and carrying out smooth analytics.

2.4. Challenges

Despite its innumerable benefits listed in section 2.3, blockchain technology is not without its challenges. While having features such as a decentralized system and data security [18] which are the need of the hour, implementing these is a hard task. Since it is still a newly developed technology, some drawbacks need to be countered to develop a technology suitable for use in all spheres. Steps such as countering existing performance issues, improving privacy, and developing an easy-to-use platform are crucial before integrating blockchain into various applications. There are majorly four problems plaguing blockchain development [19]:

2.4.1. Increased Performance

While blockchain certainly has its advantages in carrying out transactions it still cannot compete with the existing systems. The key aspect turns out to be speed which is usually only 5-7 transactions per second in comparison to tens of thousands of transactions carried out by established systems. This rules out blockchain's applicability [20] in large-scale models. To tackle privacy issues consensus models are developed which again increase the transaction duration.

2.4.2. Interoperability

Interoperability is probably the most important issue that needs to be tackled. Different blockchain platforms require translations to communicate [21] with each other which proves to be a very cumbersome task. There is a need to develop a system of standardization to improve interconnectivity and facilitate communication.

2.4.3. High Cost and Complexity

Another challenge faced by blockchain technology is its need for intensive computing. It consumes high electrical power leading to high costs. A recent study published by Elite Fixtures calculated the costs of mining one bitcoin in South Korea to be around 26000 dollars. Besides, there is the cost of developing and maintaining blockchain servers and networks.

2.4.4. Lack of Supportive Regulation

The absence of supportive regulation certainly remains to be an issue. With cryptocurrency prices spiking recently and phenomena such as Initial Coin Offering (ICO) taking place, the speculative nature of the market is quite scary. In addition to that newly developed technologies relying on a blockchain, such as smart contracts don't have any regulatory system in place. This inhibits both the developers and the users and discourages investments.

3. INTRODUCTION OF BIG DATA

Big Data is the latest buzzword in technology taking tech enthusiasts and multinational companies by storm. It is no surprise that the world we live in is a data-driven and statistical analysis of this data is key to good governance, increased revenues, and overall a more productive society. With such a variety of applications and promising results, understanding big data has become more crucial.

First and foremost, it is imperative to understand what data is. Data is nothing but a set of characters, symbols, or quantities upon which a variety of operations are carried out and that can be transmitted in various formats. Big Data is essentially just data but a very large magnitude of it. It's usually a humongous dataset that continues to grow exponentially over time. This makes the data very hard to work with as the normal operations we used to perform on normal data cease to work.

Big Data has become such an essential part of today's world not only because of its applications but also because of its sheer growth. Around 90 percent of the world's total data has been produced in the past two years alone showing its massive growth over the recent period. IBM estimates that 2.5 quintillion bytes of data are produced daily globally [22]. These statistics effectively prove the need for big data analysis in contemporary times and the requirement for cost-effective yet efficient solutions for managing such data. Big Data includes not just the data but also its frameworks and tools required to work with it. Data mining, storage, scrapping, visualization, and all such operations come under the same heading.

The importance of big data in various industries cannot be ignored. The utilization of big data leads to the formation of effective business plans, thus giving companies a competitive advantage. It also helps give fruitful insights into customer activities leading to efficient marketing campaigns. This provides better customer service, improves products, and leads to higher conversion rates. This data can come from a variety of sources such as social networking sites, real-time data sensors, medical records, and more. This includes raw data which might be operated upon using tools such as data mining to make it more usable for analytics.

3.1. Types of Big Data

With big data being such an expansive field covering a multitude of operations, it comes as no surprise that there are a variety of datasets to be dealt with. Often, we can classify most of them into three categories [23]:

3.1.1. Structured

This refers to data that can be stored, retrieved, and processed in a fixed and specific format. This data is stored in an easy-to-read format which makes it easy to operate upon and derive information from the same. It is highly organized making basic operations such as storing and searching an easy task. With data growing exponentially converting data to this form proves to be a hard task. An example of such a data set would be an employee's table in a company with predefined and organized rows and columns describing various attributes such as name, age, designation, and more [24].

3.1.2. Unstructured

Unstructured data refers to data lacking any specific form. It is raw data and because of its huge size and unstructured format, it is very hard to work with it. Deriving information, processing, and performing basic operations on this data is a difficult job despite the data being readily available to most companies. Email is a basic example of such a dataset.

3.1.3. Semi-structured

This type of data contains components from both structured and unstructured data. Despite not being classified under a specific repository, it has some sort of tags to distinguish elements from each other. The data represented by an XML file is an example of the same.

3.2. Characterization of Big Data

Considering the popularity of Big Data in modern times, it was necessary to have certain defining characteristics. The characteristics help identify and categorize the data sets as required by the user. In 2001 Doug Laney, an analyst at Gartner identified the 3 V's of big data, namely volume, variety, and velocity with the volume being the key characterizing component. Further studies and research lead to the listing of three more V's namely variability, veracity, and value [25] shown in Fig. (**4**).

3.2.1. Volume

The volume of data is what classifies any data as big data. An enormous volume of data signifies that the dataset is big data. This huge volume of data can come from any source such as business, machines, humans, and a myriad of other sources.

3.2.2. Variety

Variety refers to the variety of sources and the types of data being processed. This could be structured, unstructured, or semi-structured data. Earlier data was generally available in clean spreadsheets and databases but now data is extracted in various forms such as PDFs, emails, photos, and more. This makes analysis, mining, cleaning, and other operations on such data a tedious task.

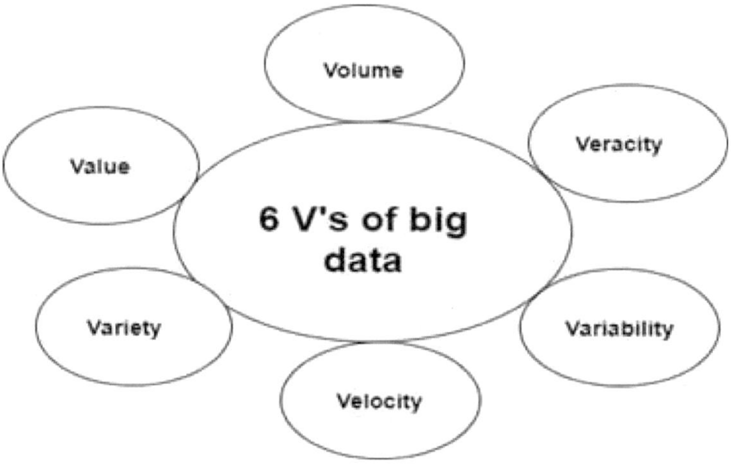

Fig. (4). 6 V's of big data.

3.2.3. Velocity

Velocity is the characteristic that tells us how fast the data is being generated in real-time. It comprises the rate at which the data is changing and linking different data sets. This velocity signifies the true capabilities of data depending on how fast the data is being processed.

Besides the three main V's described we have three more V's listed down recently. Veracity determines how much the data can be trusted. Value is nothing but the business value of the data and variability determines the different ways of formatting the data.

4. USE OF BLOCKCHAIN IN BIG DATA

The technology called Blockchain [26] has been ruling for the last two decades, but it gained importance after the introduction of Bitcoins in the world. Blockchain completely focuses on distributed ledger systems, this decentralized network topology gives priority to the security systems on a higher level. Every transaction that is made *via* the consumer is stored in individual blocks. These blocks are created for storing the information and whenever a new transaction is made a new block is formed slowly this results in a chain of blocks and hence the technology is named BLOCKCHAIN. The transactions related information that is stored in the blocks must be validated by the user every time for maintaining the proper network and enabling efficient functioning. Not only the information related to the transactions but also the timestamp recording is done in a tamper-proof way. A single change that is made in the data is recorded with the proper timestamp, which is then unalterable, thereby increasing the transparency of the system. That is why blockchain is a secured system that helps in the proper preservation of data uprightness. Smart contracts [27, 28] are a feature of Blockchain technology, this functionality is greatly important in spontaneous resolving of the transactions in a network.

Developers concentrate on updating the information regarding each block by coding about the specifics such as payments that are present in the wallet, information about the bank accounts, and all the other details about the specifics. Once the transaction gets implemented, validation can be taken from the user who is connected to the network.

Big data is the collection of big sets of data, every data that is collected from different devices may be from sensors, networks, *etc.* Data compiled is tremendously huge and multifaceted and the processing of the traditional data. The data extracted is used for the estimation of patterns and trends that the market follows. The mechanism that big data follows is in high demand nowadays and this is because of the real-world application this technology covers underneath it. Big data is the collection of big sets of data, every data that is collected from different devices may be from sensors, networks, *etc.* Data compiled is tremendously huge and multifaceted and the processing of the traditional data. Whenever a transaction is made, it is stored in the form of ledgers also cloud services are used for recording and storing purposes but involving cloud services is a bit expensive to handle for organizations and companies. Market reactions are analyzed and calculated so that the prediction for the future market can be made easily and this is one of the major starring roles of Big data where Blockchain [29] provides big support and acts as an aid.

Blockchain is an effective method for operational data storage. Not only this but the network it creates *i.e.* decentralized network is efficient in permitting admittance to multiple operators. Several parties performing transactions normally accumulate the transactional info in diverse ledgers. The parties that are involved in the transactions can be made to work on one sole network *via* Blockchain. Transactions that are taking place are recorded inside the network which is operational for the same and can be easily validated by the users of the party. As all the information is stored in the blocks formed from the blockchain hence it will help in easy access to the details stored within them. The design of the blockchain is done in such a way that it can help users to sight past transactions smoothly and can examine the trajectory of the transaction that is made.

Employing blockchain technology, Big data can be made cost-effective for corporations, as Blockchain upholds a lot of capability of storing large quantities of data and for a longer time. Corporations can elect for storage of data on a decentralized network arrangement with the usage of Blockchain. In arrears to these technologies, initiatives that will be taking place won't be incurring costs for data storing display place. The supplementary advantage of consuming the Blockchain to grip Big Data is the solicitation of Smart Contracts. Once the essential material is collected smart contracts can accomplish transactions inevitably, thereby reducing the cost of a transaction.

The actual world example where both blockchain and big data are used simultaneously is in the banking sector in Japan. Around 50 Banks [26, 30] made an association and prepared an agreement with "Ripple" [31]. Here, Ripple is an open tracked network that is constructed based on the technology named Blockchain. Internationally, Ripple ranked third in marketplace capitalization. This coalition arrived with the commitment to practice blockchain with big data for the menace-free and lower price transactions. It was made promising by refurbishing the outmoded Banking archetypal. The conventional archetypal had several parties that are involved and had further risk features in them. To plug in the menace and contrivance control themes, banks had to suffer by paying supplementary costs. The cost incurred because of this could have been saved by using networks of blockchain. The partnership of the Banks is also responsible for reducing the transaction time ominously.

Big Data can have a supplementary coating of security if executed on a network of blockchain. The primary layer of security can be endorsed to the network building of blockchain. Unlike the outdated approaches, the material or the content that is found in the network is protected and is not replicated. Furthermore, using Blockchain, Big Data can be easily secured, and the information can be easily organized and can be treasured. Execution and analysis of data then become more resourceful and easier. Blockchain technology is also used for fraud recognition.

4.1. The Motivation for use of Blockchain in Big Data

Technologies like blockchain and big data are harmonizing technologies and can completely transform the technology by introducing better storing and data exploration. Blockchain is the ruling technology of recent years, it is a database that simplifies database management and provides transparency about each record that is maintained. Blockchain makes it highly secure database technology, every record that is created in the database is known as a block and each block has details of the transaction *i.e.* made by the user. This decentralized network helps in managing and analyzing the data effectively. The record that is created includes the date of the transaction and the link that is associated with the preceding block.

Decentralization in blockchain technology is the main advantage, as no one gets the right to control the entered data, hence the integrity of the system is maintained. Continuous checks are made when the system is on any network. Every machine on the network has the same data on it, the data that is corrupted cannot come in the chain that is built. For instance let us assume the healthcare sector, wherein a hospital the data of the patients are maintained and it is ensured that the data which is collected is secured, not only this healthcare sector has to focus on updating the data related to each customer so that single detail about the health condition of the patient is missed. Now if the healthcare databases are placed on the network of blockchain then any employee can access the network easily and can update the information regarding the patient, it is also focused that the data source is kept unchangeable. Due to poor supervision of the data in the healthcare sector the risk increases, as this can lead to mishandling or poor diagnosis for the patient also if the proper track of the details related to the patient is not taken then the information related to tests can get misplaced. All sorts of risks can be easily avoided with the help of blockchain, the Fig. (**5**) shown explains the areas that are covered to keep records.

Fig. (5). Places and fields, responsible for data tracking.

The real motivation for using blockchain and big data together is due to the following reasons:

1. **Better data analysis**: Data analysis is also counterparty by blockchain technology, its real-life example was seen in 2017 when 27 Japanese banks [32] decided to sign up for the startup Ripple [31], which simplified the money transference between the bank financial records with the assistance of blockchain. Normally the transfers take place on a real-time basis and these transfers are expensive, this is because the risk factor [27, 33] increases if the transactions use the identical asset. The blockchain forms a chain that helps in the easy elimination of the risk factors involved with each transaction. Real-time fraud detection can be easily made using blockchain as it will help in tracking every transaction made by the user present on the network, also permitting banks to reconnoiter data in an exploration of arrangements in actual time. Hence both the technologies together can help in strengthening the security systems in banks.
2. **Better security:** Big data and blockchain together are also helpful in preventing data leaks in the system. When the information gets stockpiled on the system, the highest posted employee of the corporation will have to go through layers of permission from every point of the network. Thereby protects the system from every criminal interference with the data. By extension lead, the technology named Blockchain permits allotment of data with extra tranquility.
3. **Fulfilling privacy concerns [15, 16, 34]:** With the increased use of blockchain, there are several issues related to the confidentiality of the system, and this was the main reason why this technology became popular in the market. Quite a few specialists are apprehensive about the transaction accounts that may be subjugated to shape customer outlines or further misapplications. And on the involvement of blockchain, the transparency of the data gets enhanced. Just in case if the entry of data is not proved, the system will completely reject it. Hence the technology is known for data transparency.

4.2. Architectures of Blockchain

In the simplest form, blockchain technology is a series of timestamps [22, 31] creating incontrovertible registers which are then copied by the number of computers owned by different users present in the network. Each block that is created is protected and is forced to maintain cryptographic [35] ideologies. The main reasons for the popularity of blockchain are:

·A solitary object does not own the data stockpiled within the blockchain
·Cryptographical [35] data storage is done
·Chains of blocks created are incontrovertible, hence any interference within the data is not at all allowed.
·Transparency of the system is highly maintained

Blockchain was established for the manipulation and distribution of data all around the network very efficiently. A public blockchain is the famous type and Bitcoin is the part of the public blockchain. Now while the execution or implementation of a bitcoin 3 point needs to be followed:

- Who is making the transaction and from where?
- To whom the transaction must be sent?
- The money information

The block-1 of the blockchain is known as the genesis block and the previous hash block has the value 0. Fig. (**6**) elaborates how a data block looks like.

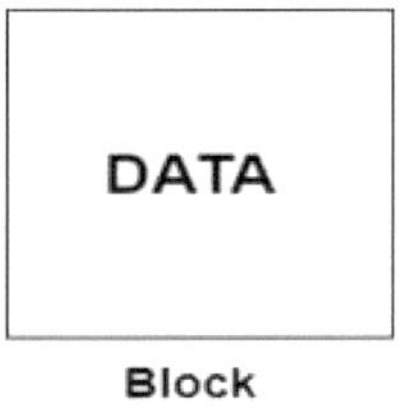

Fig. (6). Data block.

Every time a transaction is made or data storage has to take place a block is created and as the data keeps on increasing the number of blocks also increases concerning it hence there is a requirement of a Block header in a case like this. As data keeps on increasing the chain is formed, and for creating the chain and linking each block there is a great need for block headers. These block headers help in recognizing the sequence of each data block, also every block will have a hash of the previous block so that the linkage of each block can be easily done. The advantage of having hashes in the system is to provide immutability, *i.e.* once a block is created it cannot be changed. How the data blocks are linked to each other in the system is shown in the figure below. Each block contains data in it followed by a hash and the block number. Hash is the address of the next block, provided to maintain the linkage of each block in the system, explained in Fig. (**7**) through the diagram.

Fig. (7). Data blocks resulting in a blockchain.

Now block header is something that holds everything important for a data block to have, every time a transaction is made or data is stored a proper stamping of time is needed, hence the first element of a block header is a “time-stamp”. Next, a block header must include the information regarding the “version” which is the second most important thing included in a header. The third element or information is regarding the “mekle root”, which includes all the transaction history that took place. Then there is a nonce and difficulty target and a previous hash, as shown in Fig. (**8**).

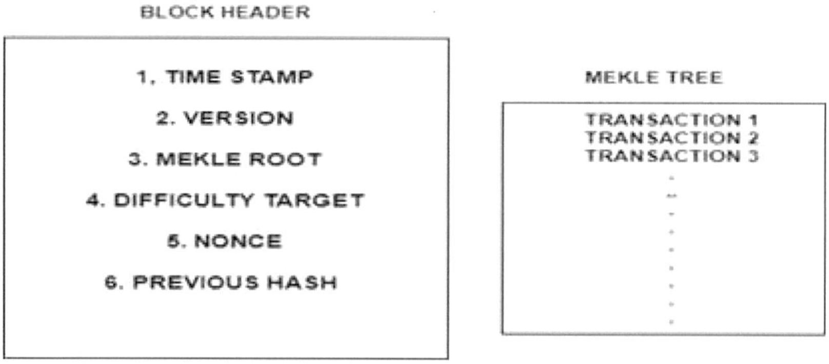

Fig. (8). Block header and mekle tree architecture.

To make this system work efficiently, there is a requirement of a concept like “PROOF OF WORK” and the terms difficulty target and nonce are a part of this concept. Although blockchain is known for its feature of immutability what if there is a great need to add or subtract data or a block from the chain, for changing the data there will be a need to change the hash address of the block. If the data of any block is changed, it will affect the data in the next block and so on the chain formed will get disturbed. Hence, the regeneration of hashes for each block must be done which will create a problem. But as the system is created in such a way that everything is connected through a network and we are living in an age of supercomputers, hence it is not possible but how does this system become secure now, so whenever there is a change in the blockchain the concept of “PROOF OF WORK” comes into play. Now focusing on the concept of “PROOF OF WORK”, here there is a need to do some processing whenever a block must be added, and this concept includes some points such as:

- Before a change must be made, the block must be validated
- To add the block in a blockchain, at least 10 minutes are needed for each block
- Blockchain must be stored in multiple machines

Every machine in a blockchain network will have a copy of the blockchain. "Consensus Algorithm" is also used to make the changes whenever the addition of data must be made in the blockchain. For making the changes in the blockchain we need a few things like a supercomputer and a 50% network of the blockchain, which is not possible because the concept discussed in section 2.1 called "proof of work", a large amount of CPU's and GPU's and affording all of this is not at all possible. Hence due to these reasons, the blockchains are kept secured. This is how the architecture of the blockchain can support data management on a larger scale.

4.3. Comparative Study

Big data works on three V's are volume, velocity, and variety, which signifies that the data collected must be measured with the following terms. The data size must be defined, and it is included in the term called volume. The speed with which the data changes is defined under velocity and the data sources from where the data is collected or sent are defined by the term variety of data. Big companies like Amazon, Flipkart, *etc.* acquire millions and millions of data in a minute hence handling such a vast amount of data with frequent changes is a big challenge that is handled by big data through various platforms. Each day this technology called big data is reaching new heights and is becoming popular, it is an important tool for effective analysis of data that is currently on demand. Handling data has always been challenging for big corporations and companies hence according to their applications they developed different data platforms such as yahoo developed Zookeeper, Cassandra was developed by Facebook and many more developments like these were made. Storing big data was a challenge, hence storing and accessing the data lead to a few questions like:

· When there are multiple copies of data then how to find which data is an authenticated one?
· How to handle if the data gets crashed?
· How to monetize the data, how to know about the third-party with whom we wish to share the data?

With all these questions, the focus was to manipulate and distribute the data effectively without compromising on its security, this is when blockchain came into the picture, blockchain provided us with the platform where a secured database can be created which is immutable in nature. A block of data that is created is sequentially arranged and the database is so maintained that nobody can change the existing data. The problem of multiple copies can be easily solved by this technology as only one block is assigned for one type of data, there is no chance of data to get lost in the system as the hashes follow the data blocks very strictly and the block header helps in a systematic arrangement of the processing that will take place with each transaction.

On noticing the later technology of blockchain [13 - 16], researchers thought of adding the former and the latter together for building the better system and this new technology was named "BIGCHAINDB". The advantages of this technology are that the infrastructure can easily be spread across various locations and the properties of the database, such as integrity and consistency, are also maintained simultaneously.

Blockchain DB works on the data pipeline which includes every step from data collection to data management. The steps are as follows:

· Data is collected *via* IOT sensors
· kinesis/event hub
· Stream analysis
· HFDS storage
· Spark data cleaning
· Spark normalization
· MongoDB storage
· Tableau analysis

Before the data pipeline step, time stamping of the input data is done which is as follows:

· Create a transaction (a hash of the data and metadata)
· Cryptographically sign the transaction
· Write the transaction to the blockchain database, this will automatically timestamp the transaction.

BigchainDB [36, 37] has features like decentralization, immutability, low latency, customizable, rich per missioning.

Blockchain and big data when combined work on three key parts:

· A computer networks
· A network protocols
· Consensus mechanism

Each computer in the system copies the ledger and single changes are made in the algorithm to ensure that the changes made are valid. Whatever gets approved is added to the chain data. Many companies are creating their private blockchain because this will help them eliminate the chances of interference, saving both time and money, thereby increasing the safety and credibility of the network.

4.4. Challenges and Solutions

As per the title, the main target is to find how blockchain can help in the efficient management of big data which is the fastest rising segment. In every single business model, the collection of accurate insights is the most important point, collecting insights and then analyzing the use patterns according to the customers' demand. While talking about big data, data sets become complementary. Big data [38] is a technology that deals with the huge set of datasets that are analyzed and the patterns are revealed accordingly using progressive statistical representations and data mining. But at the same time, this technology has some challenges to work upon, which are discussed as follows:

4.4.1. Data Management

Due to the production of massive amounts of the day each minute in every possible sector, data management is the biggest challenge for companies. They find it difficult to manage the huge amount of data as a large volume of data is present and organizing this data properly and then finally concluding from the organized data is a tedious task. Not only management of the data is focused but retaining the data fetched is also necessary. The collected data is highly versatile in nature, it can be unstructured as well as structured data, hence classifying each type and drawing conclusions will allow corporations to collect insights from the market demands and then they can effectively make changes in their respective products. Hence, overcoming this challenge is extremely important for which blockchain can be used, as blockchain [39] provides well-defined blocks that can not only retain data but every input data is timestamped and is completely immutable.

4.4.2. Risks

When a corporation has a large amount of data to analyze and if in case it mistakenly misinterprets the data fetched then this can create risks for different levels because a flawed result can lead to a great loss which can affect both the company and the market. Hence, understanding the data efficiently is very important. To build efficient models for better prediction, corporations must understand data and how it follows the complex relationship [40] with the system. Blockchain can also help in reducing the risk factor as it is the systematic technology focusing on how to easily analyze the data and store it in the system, hence blockchain solutions can increase the efficacy when combined with big data.

4.4.3. Data Security

Data stealing is an increasing region of misconduct, and according to the recent surveys it has been seen that the more data a system has, there will be more chances of hackers attacking it. And as each company deals with its customers and must provide security for the information shared, threats like these should be completely prevented. For data protection, the use of blockchain can be made, being a decentralized network, it will allow data to seep in but is highly secured and immutable, hence will protect data from all kinds of threats and will ensure data privacy.

5. APPLICATIONS

The various applications are discussed in this section.

5.1. Healthcare

When discussing blockchain and its applications, most people tend to think about bitcoins and other financial applications. Strangely, some of the most promising future applications for blockchain are presented in more than two fields. Healthcare is one such field presenting varied and useful blockchain applications that can potentially change the field. The applications vary widely from relief efforts to tracking pharmaceutical trials but blockchains decentralizing and the democratic principles remain key to the efforts, as elaborated in Fig. (**9**). There are ten major blockchain applications in healthcare [41].

Despite offering many areas of improvement in the field of healthcare, the most promising application is perhaps Electronic Health Records/Electronic Medical Records (EMR) [42]. EMR is a medical record maintained by the health provider containing information such as diagnosis, prognosis, and lab test results. Maintaining the integrity of this data is of the utmost importance while maintaining the patient's privacy. Blockchain provides an elegant solution for the same using its distributed ledger technology. Using blockchain will enhance security while at the same time provide easy access to medical records.

5.2. Education

Blockchain has the potential to systematically transform the education system with its technology. Its applications are extensive, ranging from infrastructural improvements to smart contracts. Blockchains used in educational institutions cannot be underestimated considering that this sector deals with big data in a variety of formats. Blockchain technology can also successfully link up validators, educators, students, and employers all in one system, thereby making all actions seamless and more efficient. Verifying transcripts and other important documents is usually a labor-heavy task involving a lot of documentation. With the advent of blockchain technology verification of these transcripts can be made a click process. The technology can also be used to store student directories and will provide a lot of added benefits considering its distributed ledger technology. Transportation issues can also be solved by employing blockchain-based startups such as 'Arcade City' [43]. Cloud storage is also a potential area of improvement using technology.

Fig. (9). Blockchain applications in healthcare.

Smart contracts can revolutionize many industries in the world, including education [44]. Once certain conditions are met, it can affect educational institutions and make them more efficient by reducing documentation and executing agreements. Scholarships and funding transactions will become hassle-free if smart contracts are implemented. Financial aid will only be received by the student in case the required coursework is complete.

5.3. Finance

The financial industry is probably the largest and most data-intensive industry in the market. It is giant, deals with tremendous amounts of data, and has speed as a necessity in all transactions. When it comes to big data, blockchain, AI is one of the first adopters and experimenters of possibilities in the financial industry. Efficiency is a critical matter, and blockchain allows the way for the transaction of these funds globally. Ledgers have changed the financial industry that's one of the reasons that this sector is taken up by the blockchain. Consumer expectations are changing, they want a better experience, they want their needs to be matched, that's when AI is also used. This helps in offering better services and it can be done at a much faster pace. The financial industry is producing lots and lots of data every single second with the transaction that is made. Several factors play an important role when it comes to the financial industry. Our financial lives are changing the acceleration of digital transformation, customer and data-driven financial services are key to these changes transforming financial services with blockchain and big data. When the customer's integrated authentication information is registered with the digital identity, it is lately propagated throughout blockchain enabling convenient and secure user authentication for a wide variety of services. Using blockchain-based digital points, users can make app-to-app payments, can transfer these points overseas in real-time, and can collect those points *via* ATM, because all these transactions are enabled through blockchain with increased limits and safety. Integration of scattered customer financial information such as spending, investments, and assets can now be shown in an app and financial information for analysis is de-identified and is managed securely through Blockchain. It also has AI virtual assistant which can recommend the virtual product and customers can register their recommended product at once. Next, the digitalization of finance also changes the financial environment, AI virtual assistant allows financial institutions to provide faster customer services. It also makes it easy for customers to submit documents, and while making insurance claims customers can authenticate themselves easily, and the data gets directly transferred from one place to another through blockchain.

5.4. IoT

As we move into the world of connectivity and networks, a new feature in technology is introduced. The technology present at the time of the industrial age was machined, people at that time were trying to put their hands into the mechanization of systems so that the information from the environment can be recorded efficiently by slowly moving towards how to efficiently manage every single connection between the machines. Presently, almost every device is connected through the network.

The emphasis is on cooperating IoT [45] and blockchain [46, 47] and fusing them to form a new technology named BioT. This technology will help the customer by providing a decentralized network that collaborates with IoT and can help in resolving the issues by adopting peer to peer network. Millions of data are generated and are shared between the devices which lower down the cost and assign computational and storage requirements crossways several diplomacies, thereby, preventing the network from failure.

When peer to peer network becomes customary, several defies are introduced related to the security of the system, IoT when focuses the aspect of security [48], does not only focuses on protecting the sensitive data but includes many other things in it. When blockchain and IoT get combined, they lead to a solution that can easily maintain the privacy of the network, this is done by asking for validation each time the data is accessed by an individual, the agreement has to pass for processing each transaction, this can help in avoiding deceiving and robbery.

CONCLUSION

Blockchain is in its emerging phase and has got hyped in a very short time. When the technology will develop further, more tangible use cases can be acknowledged and discovered, and big data management will become easier with the involvement of blockchain in it. Large amounts of data with massive datasets must be handled properly as storing this data, its manipulation, and its distribution are the major challenges for handling such large amounts of data. All these problems related to big data can be solved using blockchain.

The only apprehension is that blockchain presentation in this respect will be exclusive to chase, which is due to data storing *i.e.* done on the block. Blocks present in blockchain deal with comparatively minor quantities of data equated to the huge capacities of data composed every second for the technologies like big data. But it is dealt with intuitively by creating a chain of blocks containing the actual data, blockchain thereby provides the platform for handling such large amounts of data efficiently.

CONSENT FOR PUBLICATION

Not applicable.

CONFLICT OF INTEREST

The author declares no conflict of interest, financial or otherwise.

ACKNOWLEDGEMENTS

Declared none.

REFERENCES

[1] "Block chain Technology report to the US Federal Advisory Committee on Insurance", Available online: (Accessed on 10 April 2018) https://www.treasury.gov/initiatives/

[2] M. Swan, *Block chain: blueprint for a new economy* 1st ed. O'Reilly Media, 2015.

[3] M. Pratp, *Blockchain, introduction and application,* 2018. Last visited 15 March 2020 https://hackernoon.com/blockchain-technology-explained-introduction-meaning-and-applications-edbd6759a2b2

[4] "Bitcoin could be here for 100 years but it's more likely to 'totally collapse',Nobel laureate says, 2018. Available online: (Accessed 1 February 2018). ", https://www.cnbc.com/2018/01/19/bitcoin-likely--o-totally-collapse-nobel-laureate-robert-shiller-says.html

[5] N. Bauerle, "Nolan Bauerle. 2017. Blockchain Technology. Last visited15 March 2020", https://www.coindesk.com/learn/blockchain-101/how-does-blockchain-technology-work

[6] J. Bonneau, A. Narayanan, A. Miller, J. Clark, J.A. Kroll, and E.W. Felten, "Mixcoin: anonymity for bitcoin with accountable mixes", In: *International Conference on Financial Cryptography and Data Security*. Springer: San Juan, Puerto Rico, 2014, pp. 486-504. [http://dx.doi.org/10.1007/978-3-662-45472-5_31]

[7] M. Murray, "Blockchain mechanisms and implementation Last visited 15 March 2020", http://graphics.reuters.com/TECHNOLOGY-BLOCKCHAIN/010070P11GN/index.html

[8] D.K. Sharma, A.K. Kaushik, A. Goel, and S. Bhargava, Internet of Things and Blockchain: Integration, Need, Challenges, Applications, and Future Scope.*Handbook of Research on Blockchain Technology.* Academic Press, Elsevier, 2020, pp. 271-294. [http://dx.doi.org/10.1016/B978-0-12-819816-2.00011-3]

[9] A. Chhabra, V. Vashishth, and D.K. Sharma, "A game theory based secure model against Black hole attacks in Opportunistic Networks", In: *proceedings of 51st Annual Conference on Information Sciences and Systems (CISS)*, 2017, pp. 1-6. [http://dx.doi.org/10.1109/CISS.2017.7926114]

[10] S. Kumar, *Consensus Mechanism in Blockchain Technology,* 2019. Last visited 15 March 2020 https://www.capgemini.com/2019/02/why-there-is-so-much-fuss-aroundconsensus-model-in-block chain/

[11] D. Arora, S. Gautham, H. Gupta, and B. Bhushan, "Blockchain-based Security Solutions to Preserve Data Privacy And Integrity", In: *2019 International Conference on Computing, Communication, and Intelligent Systems (ICCCIS)*, 2019, pp. 468-472. [http://dx.doi.org/10.1109/ICCCIS48478.2019.8974503]

[12] *Types of blockchain,* 2019. Last visited 15 March 2020. https://dragonchain.com/blog/differences-between-public private-blockchains/

[13] V. Vashishth, A. Chhabra, and D.K. Sharma, "GMMR: A Gaussian mixture model based unsupervised machine learning approach for optimal routing in opportunistic IoT networks", *Computer Communications, Elsevier,* vol. 134, no. 15, pp. 138-148, 2019. [http://dx.doi.org/10.1016/j.comcom.2018.12.001]

[14] A. Chhabra, V. Vashishth, and D. K. Sharma, "A fuzzy logic and game theory based adaptive approach for securing opportunistic networks against black hole attacks", *International Journal of Communication Systems,* 2017. [http://dx.doi.org/10.1002/dac.3487]

[15] V. Vashishth, A. Chhabra, and D.K. Sharma, "A Machine Learning Approach Using Classifier Cascades for Optimal Routing in Opportunistic Internet of Things Networks", In: *16th IEEE International Conference on Sensing, Communication, and Networking (SECON)*, Boston, MA, USA, 2019. [http://dx.doi.org/10.1109/SAHCN.2019.8824952]

[16] A. Khanna, S. Arora, A. Chhabra, K.K. Bhardwaj, and D.K. Sharma, Iot Architecture for Preventive Energy Conservation of Smart Buildings.*Energy Conservation for IoT Devices. Studies in Systems, Decision and Control.,* M. Mittal, S. Tanwar, B. Agarwal, L. Goyal, Eds., vol. 206. Springer: Singaporepp. 179-208. [http://dx.doi.org/10.1007/978-981-13-7399-2_8]

[17] K.K. Bhardwaj, A. Khanna, D.K. Sharma, and A. Chhabra, Designing Energy-Efficient IoT-Based Intelligent Transport System: Need, Architecture, Characteristics, Challenges, and Applications.*Energy Conservation for IoT Devices. Studies in Systems, Decision and Control.,* M. Mittal, S. Tanwar, B. Agarwal, L. Goyal, Eds., vol. 206. Springer: Singapore, 2019, pp. 209-233. [http://dx.doi.org/10.1007/978-981-13-7399-2_9]

[18] H. Arora, "Major areas of blockchain influencing it", Last visited 15 March 2020. madesimple.com/introduction-to-blockchain-technology-and-what-it-means-to-big-data/

[19] S. Wang, L. Ouyang, Y. Yuan, X. Ni, X. Han, and F. Wang, "Blockchain-Enabled Smart Contracts: Architecture, Applications, and Future Trends", *IEEE Transactions on Systems, Man, and Cybernetics: Systems,* vol. 49, no. 11, pp. 2266-2277, 2019. [http://dx.doi.org/10.1109/TSMC.2019.2895123]

[20] N. Miskelly, "Problems in blockchain development", Last visited 15 March 2020., https://www.bobsguide.com/guide/news/2015/Jul/21/big-data-challenges-risks-and-solutions/

[21] S. Soni, and B. Bhushan, "A Comprehensive survey on Blockchain: Working, security analysis, privacy threats and potential applications", In: *2019 2nd International Conference on Intelligent Computing, Instrumentation and Control Technologies (ICICICT)*, 2019, pp. 922-926. [http://dx.doi.org/10.1109/ICICICT46008.2019.8993210]

[22] H. Saini, B. Bhushan, A. Arora, and A. Kaur, "Security vulnerabilities in Information communication technology: Blockchain to the rescue (A survey on Blockchain Technology)", In: *2019 2nd International Conference on Intelligent Computing, Instrumentation and Control Technologies (ICICICT)*, 2019, pp. 1680-1684. [http://dx.doi.org/10.1109/ICICICT46008.2019.8993229]

[23] IBM news, Last visited 15 March 2020. https://www.newgenapps.com/blog/future-of-blockcha-n-technology-applications

[24] M. Thibodeau, Distributed Ledger Technology, Last visited 15 March https://hedgetrade.com/3-type--of-blockchain-explained/

[25] Mohammed Zuhair, and Al Taie, *Structured Distributed Ledger,* 2016. Last visited 15 March 2020 http://blog.agroknow.com/?p=4690

[26] *Big data introduction* . Last visited 15 March 2020. https://www.guru99.com/what-is-big-data.htm

[27] P. Danzi, A. E. Kalør, Č. Stefanović, and P. Popovski, "Delay and Communication Tradeoffs for

Blockchain Systems With Lightweight IoT Clients", *IEEE Internet of Things Journal,* vol. 6, no. 2, pp. 2354-2365, 2019.
[http://dx.doi.org/10.1109/JIOT.2019.2906615]

[28] J. Libkind, *Smart Contracts,* 2019. Last visited 15 March 2020. https://www.investopedia.com/news/are-smart-contracts-best-blockchain/

[29] K. Christidis, and M. Devetsikiotis, "Block chains and Smart Contracts for the Internet of Things", *IEEE Access,* vol. 4, pp. 2292-2303, 2016.
[http://dx.doi.org/10.1109/ACCESS.2016.2566339]

[30] T. T. A. Dinh, R. Liu, M. Zhang, G. Chen, B. C. Ooi, and J. Wang, "Untangling Blockchain: A Data Processing View of Blockchain Systems", *IEEE Transactions on Knowledge and Data Engineering,* vol. 30, no. 7, pp. 1366-1395, 2018.
[http://dx.doi.org/10.1109/TKDE.2017.2781227]

[31] A. Webb, *Ripple Blockchain,* 2020. Last visited 15 March 2020. https://ripplecoinnews.com/ripple-blockchain

[32] E. Cheng, *Japanese Bank News,* 2017. Last visited 15 March 2020. https://www.cnbc.com/2017/12/27/ripple-jumps-after-news-of-link-to-some-japanese-credit-card -companies.html

[33] Mark van Rijmenam, *Risk factors in Blockchain and big data,* 2019. https://medium.com/dataseries/7-blockchain-challenges-to-be-solved-before-large-scale Last visited 15 March 2020.

[34] *Privacy Concerns,* 2020. Last visited 15 March 2020. https://thesphere.io/2018/10/20/caution-bi--data-privacy-concerns-ahead/

[35] *Cryptographic Ideologies,* 2020. Last visited 15 March 2020. https://economictimes.indiatimes.com /definition/cryptography

[36] *BigchainDB.* Last visted 15 March 2020. https://www.bigchaindb.com/whitepaper/bigchaindb-whitepaper.pdf.Last

[37] C. Thomas, "ascribe announces scalable blockchain database BigchainDB", *Coin Report.* February 2016 https://coinreport.net/ascribe-announces-scalable-blockchain-database-bigchaindb/

[38] A. Rai, *Improvements in big data,* 2019. Last visited 15 March 2020. https://www.upgrad.com/blog/what-is-big-data-types-characteristics-benefits-and-examples /#Advantages_of_Big_Data_Features

[39] T. Ali Syed, A. Alzahrani, S. Jan, M. S. Siddiqui, A. Nadeem, and T. Alghamdi, "A Comparative Analysis of Blockchain Architecture and its Applications: Problems and Recommendations", *IEEE Access,* vol. 7, pp. 176838-176889, 2019.
[http://dx.doi.org/10.1109/ACCESS.2019.2957660.]

[40] A. Sharma, *Relationships of Big data and Blockchain.,* 2019. Last visited 15 March 2020. https://hackernoon.com/how-blockchain-and-big-data-complement-each-other-92a1b9f8b38d

[41] B. Weinberg, *Blockchain in Healthcare,* 2019. Last visited 15 March 2020. https://openledger.info/insights/blockchain-healthcare-use-cases/

[42] B. Dimitrov, *Healthcare in Blockchain and Big data,* 2019. Last visited 15 March 2020. https://www.forbes.com/sites/biserdimitrov/2019/07/08/major-improvements-are-coming-to-block chain-in-2020/#608bb01b55b6

[43] D. Malets, *Blockchain News,* 2019. Last visited 15 March 2020. https://technorely.com/blog/emr-using-blockchain/

[44] Jake Frankenfield, *Smart Contracts,* 2019. Last visited 15 March 2020. https://www.investopedia.com/terms/s/smart-contracts.asp.Last

[45] T. Sharma, S. Satija, and B. Bhushan, "Unifying Blockchian and IoT:Security Requirements, Challenges, Applications and Future Trends", In: *2019 International Conference on Computing, Communication, and Intelligent Systems (ICCCIS)*, 2019, pp. 341-346. [http://dx.doi.org/10.1109/ICCCIS48478.2019.8974552]

[46] A. Dorri, *Block chain in internet of things: challenges and solutions. arXiv preprint arXiv:1608.05187,* 2016.

[47] I. Makhdoom, M. Abolhasan, H.r Abbas, and W. Ni, "Blockchain's adoption in IoT: The challenges, and a way forward", *Journal of Network and Computer Applications,* vol. 125, pp. 251-279, 2019. [http://dx.doi.org/10.1016/j.jnca.2018.10.019.]

[48] W. Zhou, "Reviewing IoT Security via Logic Bugs in IoT Platforms and Systems", *in IEEE Internet of Things Journal.* [http://dx.doi.org/10.1109/JIOT.2021.3059457]

CHAPTER 12

Blockchain Security Solutions for IoT and Big Data

H. Abhijith[1,*], **Deepti Gupta**[1] and **Shilpi Sharma**[1]

[1] *Amity School of Engineering and Technology, Amity University, Noida, U.P., India*

Abstract: Technologies shaping the future, Internet of Things (IoT) and Big Data, are the leading research topics in the computer science department. Every field like this is prone to attacks from hackers and adversaries, which is why there is a need for proper security method implementations. The current nature of the Internet of Things uses centralized servers for data collection and analysis requirements, which invites many security concerns. Similarly, big data deals with a huge amount of data that is processed and analyzed every day. The blockchain network can fill this need for a better security solution. Even though it is in its infancy but due to the features, such as Decentralization, Persistency, Anonymity, and Auditability, it is able to strengthen the security of the various IoT and big data applications. This paper discusses the security flaws in the existing centralized infrastructure used by the above technologies and presents the security solution to solve the flaws.

Keywords: Big data, Blockchain, Internet of Things, Security solution.

1. INTRODUCTION

The Internet of Things (IoT) is a collection of interconnected computing devices, mechanical and digital computers, objects, animals, or unique identifiers (UIDs) that can transmit information over a network from one person or without the need for human-computer interaction. However, it comes with many security issues that have many similarities with the security of IT [1]. Many current IoT networks rely on centralized networking modes for connecting to servers or cloud services for data processing and storage. The fear is that the server will become a bottleneck and a new target for cyber-attack, as well as a failure point that will disrupt the whole network and harm the consistency of the tests. Consequently, it remains complicated how to create a fully reliable and interconnected ecosystem to support such embedded devices and computer resources for data transmission [1].

* **Corresponding author H. Abhijith:** Amity School of Engineering and Technology, Amity University, Noida, U.P., India; E-mail: abhijithrajihari@gmail.com

Sudhir K. Sharma, Bharat Bhushan, Parma N. Astya and Narayan C. Debnath (Eds.)

Big data is a concept describing the vast amount of data that inundates an enterprise on a regular basis- both organized and unstructured.

However, what is relevant is not the volume of information but what the organizations do with the said critical information. Some users use this info for their own gain and do selfish mining or share private information with companies. So, to overcome these issues with IoT and Big data, blockchain is implemented [2]. Blockchain is a decentralized system, which removes the use of a third party in a transaction thereby creating a peer-to-peer connection. It is based on functionalities like encryption, decentralization, immutability, and transparency. All the data stored in a blockchain is coupled in blocks like a database. All the transactions are connected with nodes. When a new transaction appears, the sender via a peer-to-peer network communicates it to all the different nodes. As the transactions are being validated, it is stored in the transactional pool. When the transactions are being validated in the pool, miners create a new block and store all the transactions thereafter which the block is mined [2].

This paper discusses the security flaws associated with IoT and Big data. It also tells about the possible security problems that are associated while implementing blockchain. This paper also gives some possible solutions to these problems. There are various examples to elaborate the idea of implementing and its various outcomes in this paper. We review some of the alternatives given by other papers like cloud-based drone systems for data collection [3] and Fair Access [4]. The paper focuses on the security solutions based on blockchain designed for an IoT network. These approaches include the security maintenance of IoT computers, safe firmware upgrades, and trust verification of a trustworthy computer base, authentication of IoT device identity, and secure data store access to control information systems. The paper also focuses on a Blockchain-based IoT Device Security Architecture in Smart Homes where the architecture consists of three levels, namely local smart home networks, an overlay network, and cloud storage [1]. Entities use blockchain transfers for coordination between themselves in each stage. This paper reflects on the IoT blockchain platform by analyzing future data interruptions and security issues during the interaction with IoT components. These security issues include confidentiality of data, lack of resources for design practices, inadequate information on upgrade and maintenance [5].

The paper is organized as follows:

Section II presents the literature related to the topic. Section III analyzes and discusses various security issues faced by IoT and big data, followed by a review of the proposed and implemented security solution of blockchain. Section IV discusses the growth of the security issues discussed in the previous section and how there is a need for a blockchain solution. Section V summarizes the related work. Section VI concludes the paper with an outline of open issues and future work.

2. LITERATURE REVIEW

In this section, we will discuss the various conclusion derived from the papers read as part of the background study.

A study conducted by [6], Zheng *et al.* raises various privacy issues and security threats like lack of optimally controlled role in communication between the devices in the IoT to prevent hijacking and cyberattacks, fairness in data collection and use, and identification in IoT. These challenges can be solved by blockchain as it enables a decentralized or a distributed network. However, it also brings out challenges like a proper ledger storage facility, severe inadequacy of appropriate legal standards, and limited research in the technology. Karafiloski *et al.* [7] discuss some major characteristics that build up a blockchain network such as auditability, anonymity, persistency, and decentralization. These characteristics help to build a secure network, which can be used for Big Data and IoT. A proper consensus algorithm is key to a successful blockchain network. An efficient consensus algorithm provides safety and convenience. There are also the same challenges that occur while using a blockchain network some of which are scalability and privacy leakage (Table **1**).

Table 1. Summary of Literature Review.

S. No.	Title	Conclusion	Gap Identified
1	Blockchain Solutions for Big Data Challenges	Blockchain gives the user control of all their data and transactions. This concept can influence Big Data to find a solution for storing and managing data in a distributed manner on a P2P network.	The paper mentions the use of healthcare without considering the heavy computational cost of using a blockchain network in time-critical events.
2	Making Big Data Open in Edges: A Resource-Efficient Blockchain-Based Approach	The key concept of Proof-o--Collaboration is that participants contribute to the big data sharing so that they can also benefit from other participants' collaboration.	The mentioned PoC mechanism model considers the blockchain as an entity, which is an extreme case.
3	A Survey on the Security of Blockchain Systems	Blockchain 2.0, where the use of smart contracts is enabled, have problems like Criminal smart contracts, Vulnerabilities in a smart contract, Under-optimized smart contract, Under-priced operations.	A major advantage of a smart pool is its ability to prevent pool hopping which could have been mentioned.

(Table 1) cont.....

S. No.	Title	Conclusion	Gap Identified
4	Blockchain: A Distributed Solution to Automotive Security and Privacy	The privacy of the proposed novel automotive security architecture method is inherited from the BC where each node uses a unique PK to communicate with other overlay nodes.	An architecture like this requires an efficient way to store keys as each vehicle owns multiple keys for communication with SPs or users, which may change during the vehicle's lifetime.
5	IoTChain: A blockchain security architecture for the Internet of Things	For efficient multicasting of IoT resources, a self-healing group key distribution scheme is used for enabling large and dynamic groups of users to create group keys for secure multicast communication over unreliable networks.	The third phase of the authorization flow states that only a legitimate client that triggered the smart contract can solve the challenge. However, there is no way to verify he/she is the legitimate client.
6	The Blockchain as a Decentralized Security Framework [Future Directions]	The blockchain is an effective solution for the century's old consensus problem. At the same time, the blockchain is not a universal solution to any problem having to do with transaction verification and security.	An actual implementation of the security framework could have added more to the research paper.
7	Decentralizing Privacy: Using Blockchain to Protect Personal Data	This paper combines off-blockchain storage to construct a personal data management platform focused on privacy, and how blockchains could become a vital resource in trusted computing.	In this paper, the solution proposed queries for raw data. However, a better approach might never let a service observe the raw data, but instead, to allow it to run computations directly on the network and obtain the final results.
8	Can Blockchain Strengthen the Internet of Things?	There is no single point of failure or vulnerability in blockchain, except with the clock needed for time stamping.	The paper does not have a real-life implementation differentiating on how secure the blockchain can be as compared to the decentralized blockchain network.
9	Blockchain-Based Security Solutions for IoT Systems	The paper focuses on the security solutions that cover the secure management of IoT devices, secure firmware updates, trust evaluation of a trusted computing base, IoT device identity validation, secure data storage system for access control information.	More research should have been done on lightweight cryptographic algorithms for the medical field as they are needed for the practical implementation of blockchain-based security solutions.

According to Thakore *et al.* [8], blockchain is a distributed ledger accessible to the public that stores all the executed transactions in the system. The way forward in big data using blockchain is combining blockchain with smart contracts.

Blockchain combined with smart contracts can contribute to inventing the next era of application with a more established security and verification system. When users build and post data, they will also remain primary data owners. With respect to the surveillance that is achieved by recording the behavior and desires of users, users should at least have knowledge of it and any advantages. The Blockchain can be a proxy for privacy control rights or a completely autonomous social network can be introduced. Blockchain provides user control of all data and transactions they make. While preventing any checks from third parties. This definition may affect Big Data in seeking a solution for the distributed storage and management of data on a P2P network.

Xu *et al.*concluded [9] that blockchain overcomes the need for a third-party arbitrator on a centralized network for coordinating transactions among entities (Table **1**). Blockchain bases its implementation on four main ideas; mining, distributed public ledger, ledger copies Synchronization, and a peer-to-peer network. Merging blockchain and IoT helps support peer-to-peer communication enabling autonomy and thus removing all the bottlenecks that would have occurred otherwise. IoT and blockchain mergers can be viable solutions for both economic efficiency and business needs. Blockchain is always not a good idea for an architecture base it depends on the type of application, which demands the use of features of the blockchain.

A blockchain network is as good as its consensus algorithm; according to Reyna *et al.*, [10], we see a green proof of collaboration consensus mechanism. The key concept of proof of collaboration is that participants contribute to the sharing of big data so that they can also benefit from the collaboration of other participants. While blockchain brings so many exciting features such as decentralization and immutability, the restricted computing resources, network, and computer storage resources present challenges to the blockchain architecture.

Li *et al.* [11] suggested (Table **1**) that in an IoT network, any non-trustworthy part of the network can tamper with the information provided in line with their own interests, thus feeding unreliable information in the system. To solve this, we have to implement a distributed network using blockchain, which is trusted by all its participants that guarantees the immutability of the data. Blockchain provides the decentralization and security required for a secure IoT. Integration of blockchain improves the following; Decentralization, Market of services, Identity, Autonomy, scalability, Reliability, Security, and Secure code deployment. Even though Blockchain is a good alternative to the centralized cloud-based data collection network, there are still some challenges like Scalability, Storage capacity, Legal issues, *etc.*

Dorri *et al.* [12] concentrated (Table **1**) on the vulnerability in the security of the blockchain technology by researching the existing blockchain systems like Ethereum, Bitcoin, *etc.* They discuss the 51% vulnerability where the consensus mechanism itself has 51% vulnerability, and then the adversaries exploit this vulnerability to take control of the blockchain network and other problems like double spending, transaction privacy leakage, and private key security. All these problems existed in blockchain 1.0, there are some problems specific to blockchain 2.0 where the use of smart contracts (A smart contract can be considered as a lightweight dAPP (decentralized application) are enabled, like Vulnerabilities in a smart contract, Criminal smart contracts, Under-optimized smart contract, Under-priced operations. The paper also discusses enhancements to be made on the blockchain network; one of the enhancements is the implementation of a smart pool.

In a study [13], Alphand *et al.* suggested (Table **1**) a new, blockchain-based vehicle safety architecture. BC inherits the anonymity of the current system, where each node uses a special private key that communicates with other overlay nodes. So, an overlay node protects overlay nodes from being registered. To store data that is subject to the privacy, each vehicle is fitted with in-vehicle storage. The architecture supports evolving automotive technologies by offering a safe way to exchange data while offering end-user security. The focus of the proposed architecture called Lightweight Scalable Blockchain is to create a decentralized privacy-preserving and secure blockchain-based architecture for the smart vehicles, which have a low overhead. The paper also discussed various applications pertaining to the proposed architecture from car-sharing services to smart charging services.

Puthal *et al.* [14] suggested (Table **1**) an IoTChain architecture that combines the elements of OSCAR (Object Protection Infrastructure for the Internet of Things) and the ACE authorization system. IoTChain architecture uses a single ACE authorization server blockchain. The said blockchain handles demands for authorization by smart contracts. In addition, a primary distributing scheme for the self-healing community is used for the effective multicasting of IoT resources. The self-healing group key distribution allows the creation of group keys for dynamic groups of large numbers of users to secure multicast communication over an unreliable network.

Banerjee *et al.* [15] indicates that the blockchain network can only be introduced if it is relevant and allows for improved benefit protection. The agreement is confirmed by the participants by means of predefined processes of authentication and consensus, without any intervention from a central third-party program. Owing to its heavily secure nature achieved with sophisticated cryptography, the information contained in the global public ledger is resistant to any tampering. And the system seeks cybersecurity uses. As centralized systems are getting rid of in the IoT, so mobile devices can upgrade applications, fix glitches, and talk directly. The blockchain can be a successful answer for the century's old consensus problem. However, blockchain cannot be expected to solve everything related to verification.

Kshetri *et al.* [16] classify (Table **1**) the different intrusion prevention and detection techniques by approaches, network structures, applications, *etc.* It also delves into different collaborative security techniques. The paper also focuses on the need for publicly accessible datasets, as the position of real-world datasets in evaluating the proposed protection strategy cannot be overestimated, especially predictive. The need for safe storage of publicly accessible IoT databases in order to establish a specification for these databases using blockchain technology in order to maintain transparency of shared data. The future of the blockchain can be seen in both civilian and military contexts, including the drone internet, the Battlefield internet, and the Military things internet. Therefore, Blockchain becomes all the more important for providing a secure decentralized network architecture.

Pulkkis *et al.* suggested that [17] (Table **1**) IoT devices have the ability to use smart contracts to execute autonomous transactions. IoT computers are vulnerable to malware, DDoS attacks, remote hijacking, and data theft attacks. When any of the systems connecting to the IoT network was infected, the whole network and the associated system may also be affected. In the blockchain, it is impossible to alter a transaction that has already been accepted to make untrustworthy devices connected to the network by feeding fake signatures into a framework. There's no single point of failure or weakness in blockchain except for the time-stamping clock necessary.

Zheng *et al.* [18] focuses on the already existing and proposed security solutions based on blockchain designed for an IoT network. Security solutions include secure management of IoT devices, secure firmware updates, trust assessment of a trusted computing base, validation of IoT device identity, secure data storage system for access control information. This also focuses on a Blockchain-based IoT System Protection Infrastructure in Smart Homes in which the system has three layers, including local smart home networks, an overlay network, and cloud storage. Entities use blockchain transfers for coordination between themselves in each stage. The categories of transactions include genesis transactions, storage transactions, control transactions, and transaction tracking. They also put emphasis on the use of IoT devices in the field of medicine where a proposed plan is reviewed.

Dorri *et al.* suggested that [19] Blockchain can transform the traditional industry by its various characteristics namely anonymity, decentralization, *etc.* This technology can be applied to several fields other than bitcoin too but right now, it is guarded by it. Many smart contract applications have been designed to overcome the difficulties and problems faced by Blockchain. However, this paper does not give any solution for problems like selfish mining. There is no way proposed to detect the trading patterns of the users so that it can be used to suggest feasible partners, according to their pattern. Smart contract languages have many limits and defects in them.

Khan *et al.* [20] suggested that blockchain is known for its privacy and security. An optimized blockchain is introduced here so that the overhead present in the typical blockchain can be eliminated while retaining its benefits. This blockchain constitutes a hierarchical architecture that uses a centralized private Immutable Ledger at the local end so that overhead can be eliminated and uses a decentralized public blockchain at higher-end devices for the trust of the users. Although, the example used in this paper *i.e.* the scenario of a smart home has application agnostic architecture for diverse IoT use cases. No extensive evaluation on the impact of design on security and overhead generated in the overlay. No comprehensive analysis on security and consensus of the framework.

In a study [21], Minoli *et al.* addressed security issues of IoT, and possible solutions have been given including implementing Blockchain. These issues are created because of the immature standards of IoT and also due to the resources that are constrained. IoT does not have secure hardware and software deployment, design, and development. This paper summarizes many open challenges like single points of failure, blockchain vulnerabilities but does not provide any solution for the same. The paper does not give any survey results or graphs to evaluate the solutions.

Atlam *et al.* [22] conclude that blockchain is used in the application layer and at the lower layer, which makes it more convenient to use across the layers and enables the synergetic use of the mechanism. Blockchains are embedded with various security mechanisms like encryption, firewalling, *etc.* to facilitate IoT integrity. However, not all the problems can be resolved using blockchain mechanisms because it is not practical. Those systems entail nodes with the appropriate capabilities to support the P2P functionality.

According to Ouaddah *et al.*, [23], IoT is nowadays used everywhere in our day-to- day life. However, the client/server model associated has many issues like security and scalability. To overcome these issues blockchain is implemented as it provides distributed peer-to-peer interaction where no involvement of a third party is required and trust is not breached. This paper also shows that although with the implementation of blockchain many issues have already been resolved, new challenges are continuously emerging that need to be addressed.

Casino *et al.* [24] has introduced a new blockchain applicability area, which is access control by access control framework Fair Access. Bitcoin-like blockchain-based cryptocurrency offers consistency and this framework leverages it to provide a transparent and stronger access control tool. This paper has used UML to provide us with a dynamic and static description of the framework. A detailed technical application is mentioned along with the initial execution and implementation using Raspberry Pi and a typical IoT use case.

Rabah *et al.* [25] highlight all the features of blockchain and shows how it is ideal for many applications. Blockchain should not replace every database system there is as there are some places where the traditional methods should be used instead of blockchain, as it is more beneficial. There is a survey conducted to show many of the industries and domains using blockchains. Individual characteristics of blockchain are shown so that appropriate blockchain can be selected for the required purpose.

Liang *et al.* [26] provide detailed information about big data, IoT, blockchain, and AI. Big data can facilitate services for both public and private services. It carefully assembles data and tells which data should be shared and which data to be kept private. This can benefit many organizations and industries. This paper shows a similarity between big data, IoT, blockchain, and AI and how they are dependent on each other. This mutual relationship makes them the ideal alternative to every problem.

The deduction derived from the paper by Liang *et al.* [27] is that there are many areas of cyber-attacks increasing day by day in IoT applications. The advancement of this technology gives rise to many threats. This paper focuses on removing those threats using blockchain. To exemplify this idea, they have given a cloud-based drone system for the collection of data. This paper proposes a general architecture of a drone data collection system using blockchain. This system ensures reliability and reduces the number of data loss and risks for real-time data collection using a drone system. A prototype has been evaluated for the drone system to contemplate its performance.

Yue *et al.* [28] discuss ProvChain, a data provenance infrastructure for ensuring data operations in a cloud storage environment while improving security and availability at the same time. ProvChain stores the project history as provenance data to be hashed into the nodes of the Merkle tree. Blockchain-based data provenance can have credibility and reliability by exploiting the blockchain network 's global computational capacity. The hashed identity of users is retained in the given architecture in order to protect their anonymity from the rest of the nodes in a blockchain network.

In the paper by Zamora *et al.* [29], blockchain technologies are incorporated to address some of the important issues like exploitation of personal data and storage, incorporating blockchain and smart contracts to create a decentralized model of data exchange without intrusive third parties, splitting the existing "island" network, and increasing data reputation. For the data supplier, the decentralized architecture eliminates the threats to data protection posed by over-centralization to data storage; as for customers, the blockchain operating model guarantees consistency in the knowledge collection phase and protects the privacy of users and the right to learn.

3. METHODOLOGY

In this section, the methodology of investigating the rising threat of two of the major problems namely ransomware and botnet faced by IoT and big data is introduced. After discussing the security risks, security solutions are also being introduced.

The data source for both ransomware and botnet detection were collected over the year 2019, *i.e.* from January 1 through December 31. Data collected for ransomware particularly ransomware ryuk was from the customers of Malwarebytes [30] from the accounts that are active so as to reduce any irregularities in the data. After the collection of the data, we plot a graph showing the detection of the ransomware ryuk by each month. Data of botnets detected were collected using the "follow the spam" [31] method and then a graph was plotted showing the detected botnets by nine countries that had the greatest number of botnets detected over the year 2019.

3.1. Security Challenges

3.1.1. Security Challenges in IoT

Botnet Attacks A botnet is a network of multiple internets connected devices, where every device is running one or more than one bot and are in control by the attacker. They are used to perform various types of illicit attacks, one of the main being Distributed Denial-of-Service (DDoS) attacks as the adversary has full access to the affected devices [32]. It becomes more dangerous as a user may be unknown if their device is part of a botnet. Botnets are made by attacking the weak point of a device in the IoT network and exposing its vulnerability. After the vulnerability is exposed, the attacker gains access to the device and continues to affect the other devices in the network as they are in a centralized network creating a botnet. One of the most famous and known examples of a botnet is the Mirai botnet. Mirai is a malware that has infiltrated IoT devices and co-opted them into a botnet for DDoS. By continuously propagating to weakly designed IoT devices [33], Mirai triggers a DDoS against a group of target servers at its height, Mirai corrupted and co-opted nearly 600k devices [34]. The botnet is also evolving as most of them have a distributed architecture which makes it difficult to trace the attackers down [35].

Ransomware Attacks Ransomware is the most common type of attack performed on any platform. It is a subset of malware and only has a single purpose to encrypt the user's data to lock them out of their own files, and then the attacker demands a ransom for the removal of the said malware [36]. In terms of IoT, the ransomware attack could be more than just locking out the victim but could jeopardize confidentiality, integrity, and availability [37]. The Internet Crime Complaint Center (IC3) reported a loss of around $8.9 million in the year 2019 alone. One example is the WannaCry / WannaDecryptor; it is a form of ransomware called crypto-ransomware that applies encryption and decryption algorithms to computer data, and it is riskier if it targets back-end application servers because IoT devices at the forefront do not contain a significant amount of data [37].

Data Integrity IoT in this new era is everywhere and some estimates show that by 2025, the world will have approximately 21 billion IoT devices [38]. This leads to a huge level of sensitive data collected by the sensors and actuators embedded or connected with these devices. Hence, it is important the integrity of this data is protected and authentic. This is where the challenges arise *i.e.* to maintain the data integrity. It becomes all the more important as some of the sensors in the IoT network have high data collection rates for bandwidth and low latency (real-time). Suitable techniques for data integrity such as encryption and watermarking are therefore required [39].

Authentication Whenever a device is used, it always performs an authentication check in order to verify the user trying to access the device has the appropriate permission to do so. An IoT network consists of sensors, actuators, internet gateways, Edge IT, and a data center each having its unique functionalities to perform certain operations. In an IoT network, each of these components has to be properly authenticated to make the network safe to implement. There is already existing infrastructure for this purpose in IoT acknowledged as Public Key Infrastructure (PKI) where digital certificates are used to provide the authenticity proof of the IoT device but the use of blockchain's use of distributed ledger could enhance PKI and ensure digital certificate management is auditable and any changes made are irreversible [40].

3.1.2. Security Challenges in Big Data

Data Growth. Big data deals with an enormous amount of data and it keeps increasing every day. Today, everybody uses a centralized data center for this flow of data. By the end of 2020, the total amount will be sufficient to fill a stack of tablets that reach 6.6 times from Earth to Moon [41]. YouTube the media-sharing platform single-handedly generates so much data that they have a server with the capacity of one Exabyte (one billion gigabytes) as every minute 300 hours of video is uploaded on the platform [42]. This ever-growing scale of data with much of the data being data unstructured needs to be put in check so that the centralized data center does not overflow.

Ownership and Monetization. Digital Proprietary deals with the ownership of digital data that can be an artwork in the form of audio, video, or text. It is very important that the author or creator of an artwork receive proper credit for their work. Currently, if a creator puts their artwork onto a platform there is no way to protect the authenticity of that artwork as people can impose as the original creator of the artwork and take credit for it. Creators do not even have a proper channel to be fairly paid for their work [7].

Data Modification. The authenticity of the data is of utmost importance as it is analyzed and processed and correct data means correct analytical results. Data modification makes this process difficult as the data could be modified and generate incorrect insights. Similar to data modification, data validation is also a challenge. Sometimes organizations doing the analytical research receive the same fragment of data from different systems, which does not always agree with the records on those different systems. For example, an electronic health record (EHR) program in a hospital might have a prescription of medication separate from that of its partner pharmacy [41].

Data Security. The most crucial challenge is protecting the data from adversaries who may try to mine sensitive information. Data security not only means to secure the data from stealing but also means to secure the data from possibly being false. Cybercriminals may try to do so by generating fake sensor data and thus the report will be incorrect. Organizations using big data research to sell their products aggregate their data in a single central data server, storing both structured and unstructured data. It becomes a valuable target for attackers by centralizing data in one place, which can potentially leave huge amounts of information exposed, which could undermine organizational trust and damage its reputation [43].

3.2. Blockchain Solutions

3.2.1. Security Solutions for IoT

AutoBotCatcher- Gokhan *et al.* [5] proposed a blockchain solution to catch the malicious botnets incurring illicit activities. They proposed an Auto Bot Catcher, which uses a Byzantine Fault Tolerance (BFT) blockchain in a permissioned setting that detects the bots by processing the network flow data. The use of BFT is explained by its characteristics of assigning the role of generating block to a small set of actors. Using the blockchain in a permitted setting helps to keep adversaries' stored network data confidential, as only a certain set of pre-identified block generators can access the above data. BFT approach follows the two-thirds consensus protocol, *i.e.* to reach consensus on the current set of rules introduced by one of the block generators, which at least two-thirds of the pre-identified block generators have to decide upon. The set of rules is the same mutual contact graph, set of blocks processed, and community mapping of IoT devices within this proposed mechanism. The AutoBotCatcher is comprised of two entities Agents, who monitor the network traffic flow, and block generators who as the name suggests, are part of the consensus and block generation process.

As shown in Fig. (**1**), AutoBotCatcher processes the safely stored network flow data of IoT devices and then generates a mutual contact graph after the pre-processing of determining whether the IP address belongs to the *blacklist* and *whitelist* maintained by agents. If a blacklisted IP address is detected, then agents sever the network connection or force it to shut down essentially quarantining it. After the generation of the mutual contact graph, it is analyzed by performing Dynamic Community Discovery (DCD) using the Louvain method [22] but by giving it, the community set of IoT devices from the previous state. Then it performs two checks perturbation check and botnet check for old and new communities respectively. A perturbation check is performed to add or remove the IP addresses from the blacklist based on them being a part of a botnet managed by the block manager. Whereas, botnet check classifies the new communities either as a botnet community or as a safe community also managed by the block manager. The last stage consists of the block manager updating the blacklist from the identified bots and simultaneously updating the blacklist of all IoT devices using a smart contract.

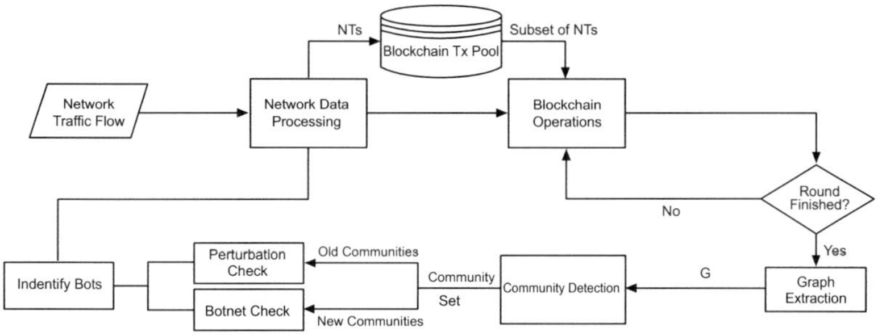

Fig. (1). System Flow of AutoBotCatcher.

Framework for Prevention of Ransomware Attack. Kaur *et al.* in a study [44] proposed a framework to prevent ransomware attacks by using the blockchains smart contract feature. In the framework, there are regular gateway checks for malicious ports or IP addresses. However, if any advanced malware breaks through then the blockchain smart contract check three main things: System Calls; Authenticity; Access Control. If the software behaves normally like read/write file or query a file then it is deemed as a normal user behavior but the access of sensitive information like network information or kernel level information, the user is alerted of malicious software in the system. The user then gives it appropriate permission to execute if it is non-malicious software. The flagged aforementioned software may try to make malicious system calls to encrypt or gain control of the desktop then the blockchain will stop the process in all the devices except both the honeypot devices if it safely runs on those devices and no ransom calls are made the software is deemed as non-malicious. However, if a ransom call is made then it is flagged as malicious software, and the software is uninstalled from the device, and honeypot devices are updated with new rules. This framework also supports a backup feature, which uses the blockchain cloud infrastructure.

Sensing data integrity. In 2019, Hang *et al.* [45] implemented blockchain to make an IoT-based Blockchain Platform. Similar to the previously discussed solutions, this is also heavily based on the use of smart contracts. The smart contracts mentioned in the paper contains five fields: Device owner registration function; Device registration function; Sensor reading function; Actuator Writing Function; Event Notification. This smart contract is connected to the ledger, which receives ledger updates and sends back update results. The ledger and the smart contract make the IoT-Blockchain network and is connected to the application client, which executes the smart contract and receives ledger updates. When a new device is added to the network, the client registers the device invoking the device registration transaction mentioned in the aforementioned smart contract. After that consensus, a process is held and each peer updates his or her blockchain with this new transaction followed by the client being informed of the transaction's execution. When the device is successfully registered, the device owner can deploy a task to be done by a particular device. The targeted device after executing the task sends the result to both the server and blockchain. The blockchain then updates the distributed ledger of each peer and sends the result to the device. In addition, alerting the device owner if the pre-defined conditions are satisfied, for example, humidity level of the air reaches an unsatisfactory level for crops to grow in an agriculture-based IoT network.

Bubbles of Trust. In 2018, Hammi *et al.* [46] proposed an authentication method where several encapsulated regions containing a number of IoT devices are made. In these regions, the IoT device can trust each other but IoT devices in two different regions cannot access each other. This region is called a bubble in the proposed architecture. All of this is achieved by the use of public blockchain-enabled smart contracts. This bubble comprises two major components, Master and Follower. Master is appointed in the initialization phase (it can be any device) and has a public/private key. Whereas, followers create an elliptic curve private/public key and have a ticket in the form of structure data type detailing the follower's group ID, Object ID, Public Address, and a Signature created using master's private key. In summary, in the initialization phase master selects a group ID and provides the object with its signed tickets. Master then relays a transaction, which consists of the master's identifier (Object ID) and group identifier (Group ID) of the group to be created, and upon the verification of the uniqueness of both the aforementioned identifiers, the bubble is created. After the master creates the bubble, followers relay their transaction to join their desired bubbles. Here, the uniqueness of the follower's identifier (Object ID) is verified by the smart contract along with the verification of its ticket, which is done by using the master's public key. Upon successful first transaction of a follower, the authenticity of the follower is established and a ticket is not needed for authentication.

3.2.2. Security Solutions for Big Data

Ownership Management. There have been many attempts to do ownership management right and there have been some successful cases and unsuccessful ones. The protocol generated by Ascribe called Secure Public Online Ownership Ledger (SPOOL) is listed in [7] authors. SPOOL is a protocol, which is used to record the rightful ownership of public digital content. They also allow the creator to make certain rules regarding their content like a fixed number of editions. These editions are kept in BigchainDB [47] as one and hashed for the blockchain. Now, when the creator sells one of their editions a transaction is initiated with the information of hash value, edition, and new ownership. The transaction is then signed by the creator and relayed. In addition, the work can be tracked if the inquirer knows the content's hash value using a blockchain explorer. However, due to some underlying infrastructure problems, Ascribe had to create a new protocol called as Ocean protocol in 2017. It is a decentralized data exchange protocol, which uses smart contracts, blockchain technology, tokens and unlocks data for AI [48]. It empowers the creator with more control over their content.

Monegraph is another implementation using blockchain that creates a platform for the artist to trade their work with correct ownership management. It allows the artists to make a customized license certificate, which includes the usage requirements of the art. History of the ownership of the said art is stored in the blockchain and other essential data about the art is stored in document databases.

Decentralization, Distributed, and Immutable. The main issues of big data like data growth, security, and validity can be solved by implementing blockchain. Blockchain has key characteristics of data immutability, which helps confirm that data was not modified ensuring data validity [49]. Data security is provided by the blockchain network as every transaction is recorded and a possible data breach happening is close to null, as there is no single point of failure due to its decentralization. The distributed nature of a blockchain ensures efficient handling of data. One of the solutions offered for proper authentication is decentralized authentication, which uses keys generated by elliptic curve cryptography replacing the traditional method of username and passwords. The only password used by the user is for him/her to access the private key provided that the user could only use that in their own device. The protocol used for identification is based on irrefutable identity verification using public-key-based digital signatures [49].

4. RESULTS

In this section, an evaluation of the veracity of the security threats to IoT and Big Data is done. The two cases that taken here are ransomware and botnets. Ransomware has become more of a threat to enterprises rather than the consumer. As we can see in Fig. (**2**), a particular case of ransomware ryuk has run rampant in the year 2019.

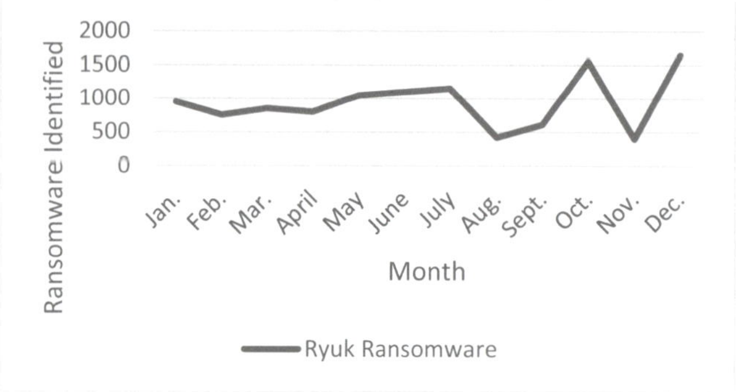

Fig. (2). Ransomware detected for the year 2019.

Overall, there has been a decrease in the ransomware attacks on consumer networks, but the financial damages incurred are still heavy as there has been a 29% increase from Q2 of 2019 to Q3 of 2019 in ransom paid.

The number of suspected botnets was on the rise too in 2019. As seen in (Fig. **3**), for the year 2019 the number of suspected botnet IP's in the most affected country china increased 3 times from the start of the year to the end.

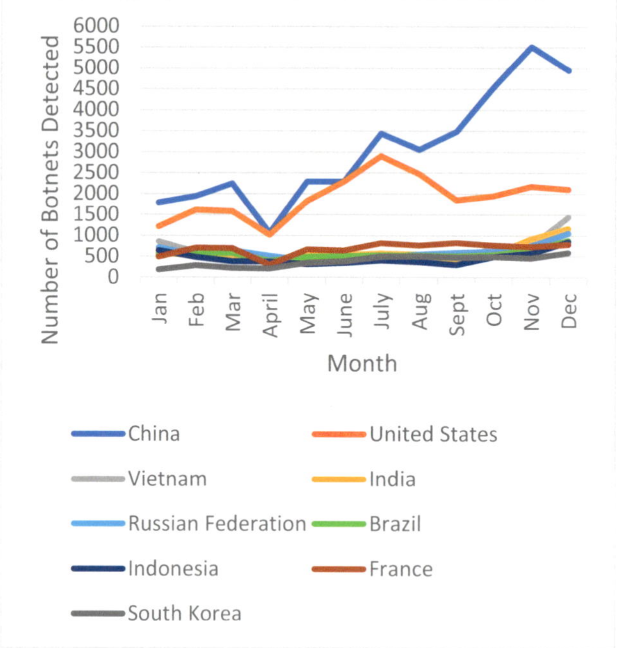

Fig. (3). Suspected botnet IP's by countries for the year 2019.

CONCLUSION

Blockchain provides us with unique solutions to combat a vast amount of security issues. The technology envisions and revolutionizes data management in such a manner that the user can be more in control of the data with the added benefit of the data being protected. We can conclude from the results that threats like botnets, ransomware, and other security threats are still affecting the current status quo of interconnected devices and networks.

In this paper, some of the major security flaws that exist with the current implementation of IoT and Big data are being discussed. Thereafter, some proposed frameworks and architecture were presented as a solution to the aforementioned security issues. However, there are still some challenges in the implementation of blockchain itself like a proper consensus algorithm that does not use too many computational resources or a proper storage facility for ledgers. Thus, a blockchain should only be integrated with the current technologies if it is economically feasible and provides better security.

FUTURE WORK

In the near future, the majority of the field pertaining to verification and authentication via the internet will look toward blockchain as a solution. It will come with a better implementation of the blockchain to their respective fields. It is worth noting that none of the examples given are based on blockchain proposals for IoT security systems which offers complete defense against all future risks and attacks to health. In fact, the realistic application of such defense technologies is also a matter of the future. Some challenges remain, such as consensus models, mining block computational costs, and transaction validation. Blockchain applications often offer solutions, which require significant modifications or complete replacement of existing systems. Therefore, the transfer is not going to be easy and quick. However, we are still in the early stages of blockchain development, and eventually, these obstacles will be overcome, paving the way for many exciting possibilities.

CONSENT FOR PUBLICATION

Not Applicable.

CONFLICT OF INTEREST

The author declares no conflict of interest, financial or otherwise.

ACKNOWLEDGEMENT

Declared none.

REFERENCES

[1] G. Pulkkis, J. Karlsson, and M. Westerlund, *Blockchain-Based Security Solutions for IoT Systems.,* pp. 255-273, 2018.

[2] E. Karafiloski, *Blockchain Solutions for Big Data Challenges A Literature Review*, 2017, pp. 6-8. [http://dx.doi.org/10.1109/EUROCON.2017.8011213]

[3] X. Liang, J. Zhao, S. Shetty, and D. Li, *Towards Data Assurance and Resilience in IoT Using Blockchain*, 2017, pp. 261-266. [http://dx.doi.org/10.1109/MILCOM.2017.8170858]

[4] A.A. Ouaddah, *FairAccess : a new Blockchainbased access control framework for the Internet of Things*, 2017, pp. 5943-596.

[5] N.M. Kumar, and P.K. Mallick, "Blockchain technology for security issues and challenges in IoT", *Procedia Comput. Sci.,* vol. 132, pp. 1815-1823, 2018. [http://dx.doi.org/10.1016/j.procs.2018.05.140]

[6] Z. Zheng, S. Xie, H. Dai, X. Chen, and H. Wang, "An overview of blockchain technology: Architecture, consensus, and future trends", In: *2017 IEEE international congress on big data (BigData congress)*. IEEE, 2017, pp. 557-564. [http://dx.doi.org/10.1109/BigDataCongress.2017.85]

[7] E. Karafiloski, and A. Mishev, "Blockchain solutions for big data challenges: A literature review", In: *In IEEE EUROCON 2017-17th International Conference on Smart Technologies*. IEEE, 2017, pp. 763-768. [http://dx.doi.org/10.1109/EUROCON.2017.8011213]

[8] R. Thakore, R. Vaghashiya, C. Patel, and N. Doshi, "Blockchain-based IoT: A Survey", *Procedia Comput. Sci.,* vol. 155, pp. 704-709, 2019. [http://dx.doi.org/10.1016/j.procs.2019.08.101]

[9] C. Xu, K. Wang, P. Li, S. Guo, J. Luo, B. Ye, and M. Guo, "Making big data open in edges: A resource-efficient blockchain-based approach", *IEEE Trans. Parallel Distrib. Syst.,* vol. 30, no. 4, pp. 870-882, 2018. [http://dx.doi.org/10.1109/TPDS.2018.2871449]

[10] A. Reyna, C. Martín, J. Chen, E. Soler, and M. Díaz, "On blockchain and its integration with IoT. Challenges and opportunities", *Future Gener. Comput. Syst.,* vol. 88, pp. 173-190, 2018. [http://dx.doi.org/10.1016/j.future.2018.05.046]

[11] X. Li, P. Jiang, T. Chen, X. Luo, and Q. Wen, "A survey on the security of blockchain systems", *Future Gener. Comput. Syst.,* 2017.

[12] A. Dorri, M. Steger, S.S. Kanhere, and R. Jurdak, "Blockchain: A distributed solution to automotive security and privacy", *IEEE Commun. Mag.,* vol. 55, no. 12, pp. 119-125, 2017. [http://dx.doi.org/10.1109/MCOM.2017.1700879]

[13] O. Alphand, M. Amoretti, T. Claeys, S. Dall'Asta, A. Duda, and G. Ferrari, "IoTChain: A blockchain security architecture for the Internet of Things", *In 2018 IEEE Wireless Communications and Networking Conference (WCNC),* 2018pp. 1-6 [http://dx.doi.org/10.1109/WCNC.2018.8377385]

[14] D. Puthal, N. Malik, S.P. Mohanty, E. Kougianos, and C. Yang, "The blockchain as a decentralized security framework", *IEEE Consumer Electronics Magazine,* vol. 7, no. 2, pp. 18-21, 2018. [future directions].

[http://dx.doi.org/10.1109/MCE.2017.2776459]

[15] M. Banerjee, J. Lee, and K.K.R. Choo, "A blockchain future for internet of things security: a position paper", *Digital Communications and Networks,* vol. 4, no. 3, pp. 149-160, 2018. [http://dx.doi.org/10.1016/j.dcan.2017.10.006]

[16] N. Kshetri, "Can blockchain strengthen the internet of things?", *IT Prof.,* vol. 19, no. 4, pp. 68-72, 2017. [http://dx.doi.org/10.1109/MITP.2017.3051335]

[17] G. Pulkkis, J. Karlsson, M. Westerlund, and Q. F. Hassan, "Blockchain-based security solutions for IoT systems", *Internet of Things A to Z: Technologies and Applications,* p. 20180501, 2018.

[18] Z. Zheng, S. Xie, H.N. Dai, X. Chen, and H. Wang, "Blockchain challenges and opportunities: A survey", *Int. J. Web Grid Serv.,* vol. 14, no. 4, pp. 352-375, 2018. [http://dx.doi.org/10.1504/IJWGS.2018.095647]

[19] A. Dorri, S.S. Kanhere, and R. Jurdak, "Towards an optimized blockchain for IoT", In: *2017 IEEE/ACM Second International Conference on Internet-of-Things Design and Implementation (IoTDI).* IEEE, 2017, pp. 173-178.

[20] M.A. Khan, and K. Salah, "IoT security: Review, blockchain solutions, and open challenges", *Future Gener. Comput. Syst.,* vol. 82, pp. 395-411, 2018. [http://dx.doi.org/10.1016/j.future.2017.11.022]

[21] D. Minoli, and B. Occhiogrosso, "Blockchain mechanisms for IoT security", *Internet of Things,* vol. 1, pp. 1-13, 2018. [http://dx.doi.org/10.1016/j.iot.2018.05.002]

[22] H.F. Atlam, A. Alenezi, M.O. Alassafi, and G. Wills, "Blockchain with Internet of Things: Benefits, challenges, and future directions", *International Journal of Intelligent Systems and Applications,* vol. 10, no. 6, pp. 40-48, 2018. [http://dx.doi.org/10.5815/ijisa.2018.06.05]

[23] A. Ouaddah, and A. AbouElkalam, "FairAccess: a new Blockchain□based access control framework for the Internet of Things", *Secur. Commun. Netw.,* vol. 9, no. 18, pp. 5943-5964, 2016. [http://dx.doi.org/10.1002/sec.1748]

[24] F. Casino, T.K. Dasaklis, and C. Patsakis, "A systematic literature review of blockchain-based applications: current status, classification and open issues", *Telemat. Inform.,* vol. 36, pp. 55-81, 2019. [http://dx.doi.org/10.1016/j.tele.2018.11.006]

[25] K. Rabah, "Convergence of AI, IoT, big data and blockchain: a review", *Law Inst. J.,* vol. 1, no. 1, pp. 1-18, 2018.

[26] X. Liang, J. Zhao, S. Shetty, and D. Li, "Towards data assurance and resilience in IoT using blockchain", In: *In MILCOM 2017-2017 IEEE Military Communications Conference (MILCOM).* IEEE, 2017, pp. 261-266. [http://dx.doi.org/10.1109/MILCOM.2017.8170858]

[27] X. Liang, S. Shetty, D. Tosh, C. Kamhoua, K. Kwiat, and L. Njilla, "Provchain: A blockchain-based data provenance architecture in cloud environment with enhanced privacy and availability", In: *In 2017 17th IEEE/ACM International Symposium on Cluster, Cloud and Grid Computing (CCGRID).* IEEE, 2017, pp. 468-477. [http://dx.doi.org/10.1109/CCGRID.2017.8]

[28] L. Yue, H. Junqin, Q. Shengzhi, and W. Ruijin, "Big data model of security sharing based on blockchain", In: *In 2017 3rd International Conference on Big Data Computing and Communications (BIGCOM).* IEEE, 2017, pp. 117-121. [http://dx.doi.org/10.1109/BIGCOM.2017.31]

[29] W. Zamora, *2019 State of Malware report: Trojans and cryptominers dominate threat landscape,* 2019. https://blog.malwarebytes.com/malwarebytes-news/ctnt-report/2019/01/2019-state-malware -

report-trojans-cryptominers-dominate-threat-landscape/

[30] C-C. Chin, *Daily Botnet Statistics,* 2008. http://botnet-tracker.blogspot.com/

[31] G. Sagirlar, B. Carminati, and E. Ferrari, "AutoBotCatcher: blockchain-based P2P botnet detection for the Internet of things", In: *In 2018 IEEE 4th International Conference on Collaboration and Internet Computing (CIC).* IEEE, 2018, pp. 1 8. [http://dx.doi.org/10.1109/CIC.2018.00-46]

[32] "Thingbots: The Future of Botnets in the Internet of Things", *Security Intelligence,* 2016.

[33] C. Kolias, G. Kambourakis, A. Stavrou, and J. Voas, "DDoS in the IoT: Mirai and other botnets", *Computer,* vol. 50, no. 7, pp. 80-84, 2017. [http://dx.doi.org/10.1109/MC.2017.201]

[34] M. Antonakakis, T. April, M. Bailey, M. Bernhard, E. Bursztein, and J. Cochran, "Understanding the mirai botnet", In: *In 26th {USENIX} Security Symposium ({USENIX} Security 17)*, 2017, pp. 1093-1110.

[35] J. Fruhlinger, "The Mirai botnet explained: How IoT devices almost brought down the internet", https://www.csoonline.com/article/3258748/the-mirai-botnet-explained-how-teen-scammers--nd-cctv-cameras-almost-brought-down-the-internet.html

[36] A. Young, and M. Yung, "Cryptovirology: extortion-based security threats and countermeasures", In: *IEEE Symposium on Security and Privacy*, 1996, pp. 129-140.

[37] I. Yaqoob, and E. Ahmed, "The rise of ransomware and emerging security challenges in the Internet of Things", *Comput. Netw.,* vol. 129, pp. 444-458, 2017. [http://dx.doi.org/10.1016/j.comnet.2017.09.003]

[38] S. Symanovich, "The Future of IoT: 10 Predictions about the Internet of Things", *Norton.* us.norton.com/internetsecurity-iot-5-predictions-for-the-future-of-iot.html

[39] T. Xu, J.B. Wendt, and M. Potkonjak, "Security of IoT systems: Design challenges and opportunities", In: *2014 IEEE/ACM International Conference on Computer-Aided Design (ICCAD).* IEEE, 2014, pp. 417-423. [http://dx.doi.org/10.1109/ICCAD.2014.7001385]

[40] O'Dwyer Michael, "Internet of Things 101 – IoT Device Authentication Explained", *Defrag This,* 2018. blog.ipswitch.com/internet-of-things-101-iot-device-authentication-explained

[41] C. Harvey, Big Data Challenges, www.datamation.com/big-data/big-data-challenges.html

[42] "77 Big Data Stats for the Big Future Ahead: Updated 2020", *HostingTribunal,* 2020. hostingtribunal.com/blog/big-data-stats/

[43] C. Tankard, "Big data security", *Netw. Secur.,* vol. 2012, no. 7, pp. 5-8, 2012. [http://dx.doi.org/10.1016/S1353-4858(12)70063-6]

[44] J. Kaur, "A Secure and Smart Framework for Preventing Ransomware Attack", *arXiv preprint arXiv,* 2020.

[45] L. Hang, and D.H. Kim, "Design and implementation of an integrated IoT blockchain platform for sensing data integrity", *Sensors (Basel),* vol. 19, no. 10, p. 2228, 2019. [http://dx.doi.org/10.3390/s19102228] [PMID: 31091799]

[46] M.T. Hammi, B. Hammi, P. Bellot, and A. Serhrouchni, "Bubbles of Trust: A decentralized blockchain-based authentication system for IoT", *Comput. Secur.,* vol. 78, pp. 126-142, 2018. [http://dx.doi.org/10.1016/j.cose.2018.06.004]

[47] T. McConaghy, R. Marques, A. Müller, D. De Jonghe, T. McConaghy, and G. McMullen, "Bigchaindb: a scalable blockchain database. white paper, BigChainDB", *McConaghy,* 2016.

[48] O. Protocol, *Ocean Protocol Blockchain-Based Platform Launches Beta to Kick-Start a New Data Economy with Safe, Privacy-Preserving and Borderless Data Sharing.,* 2019. https://prn.to/2TwTsM1

[49] N. Abdullah, A. Hakansson, and E. Moradian, "Blockchain based approach to enhance big data authentication in distributed environment", In: *2017 9th International Conference on Ubiquitous and Future Networks (ICUFN)*. IEEE, 2017, pp. 887-892. [http://dx.doi.org/10.1109/ICUFN.2017.7993927]

SUBJECT INDEX

Sudhir K. Sharma, Bharat Bhushan, Parma N. Astya and Narayan C. Debnath (Eds.)

E

F

K

L

M

N

O

P

Q

R

S

T

W

Z

Made in the USA
Las Vegas, NV
04 November 2026

57436779R00176